Working with Parents and Families in Early Childhood Education

This book reports initiatives to listen to parents and families, to ascertain what families believe and do as they seek to engage collaboratively with their children's educators, and what educators and educational systems might do to facilitate and/or establish barriers to such engagement.

Parental engagement in children's learning and development has many positive benefits. However, in the current environments of accountability and performativity which are pervading early childhood education in many countries, the opportunities for parents and other family members to be part of the development of respectful, collaborative relationships with their children's early childhood educators are becoming more and more restricted. Many educators feel forced to choose between curriculum outcomes and parental engagement, as both involve their time. There is a danger that the voices of parents and families in their children's early learning and development will not always be heard, seen, or fully understood. This volume addresses this important issue.

Researchers, educators, and families will all benefit from this book, to the ultimate benefit of the young children who are the future. This book was originally published as a special issue of the *European Early Childhood Education Research Journal*.

Ute Ward worked in a pre-school, Sure Start local programme, and children's centre before becoming a Senior Lecturer at the University of Hertfordshire, UK. She leads the BA (Hons) Early Childhood Education and teaches on the MA Education. Her research interests focus on parent–practitioner relationships which is reflected in her doctoral research exploring parents' views and expectations of their children's early childhood practitioners.

Bob Perry is recently retired after 45 years in higher education. He is Emeritus Professor in the School of Education at Charles Sturt University, Australia, and Director of Peridot Education Pty Ltd. He has been awarded an Honorary Doctorate from Mälardalen University, Sweden, in recognition of his body of research.

EECERA Collection of Research in Early Childhood Education

Written in association with the European Early Childhood Education Research Association (EECERA), titles in this series will reflect the latest developments and most current research in early childhood education on a global level. Feeding into and supporting the further development of the discipline as an exciting and urgent field of research and high academic endeavour, the series carries a particular focus on knowledge creation and reflection, which has huge relevance and topicality for those at the front line of decision making and professional practice in early years services.

Titles in this series:

Early Childhood Education and Change in Diverse Cultural Contexts
Edited by Chris Pascal, Tony Bertram and Marika Veisson

Early Childhood Care and Education at the Margins
African Perspectives on Birth to Three
Edited by Hasina Banu Ebrahim, Auma Okwany and Oumar Barry

Perspectives from Young Children on the Margins
Edited by Jane Murray and Colette Gray

Working with Parents and Families in Early Childhood Education
Edited by Ute Ward and Bob Perry

For more information about this series, please visit:
https://www.routledge.com/EECERA-Collection-of-Research-in-Early-Childhood-Education/book-series/EECERARES

Working with Parents and Families in Early Childhood Education

Edited by
Ute Ward and Bob Perry

LONDON AND NEW YORK

First published 2019
by Routledge
2 Park Square, Milton Park, Abingdon, Oxon, OX14 4RN

and by Routledge
605 Third Avenue, New York, NY 10017

First issued in paperback 2020

Routledge is an imprint of the Taylor & Francis Group, an informa business

Introduction, Chapters 1–3, 5–10 © 2019 European Early Childhood Education Research Association
Chapter 4 © 2018 Tuula Vuorinen. Originally published as Open Access.

With the exception of Chapter 4, no part of this book may be reprinted or reproduced or utilised in any form or by any electronic, mechanical, or other means, now known or hereafter invented, including photocopying and recording, or in any information storage or retrieval system, without permission in writing from the publishers.
For details on the rights for Chapter 4, please see the chapter's Open Access footnote.

Trademark notice: Product or corporate names may be trademarks or registered trademarks, and are used only for identification and explanation without intent to infringe.

British Library Cataloguing in Publication Data
A catalogue record for this book is available from the British Library

ISBN 13: 978-0-367-72894-6 (pbk)
ISBN 13: 978-0-367-25653-1 (hbk)

Typeset in Minion Pro
by Newgen Publishing UK

Publisher's Note
The publisher accepts responsibility for any inconsistencies that may have arisen during the conversion of this book from journal articles to book chapters, namely the inclusion of journal terminology.

Disclaimer
Every effort has been made to contact copyright holders for their permission to reprint material in this book. The publishers would be grateful to hear from any copyright holder who is not here acknowledged and will undertake to rectify any errors or omissions in future editions of this book.

Contents

Citation Information	vii
Notes on Contributors	ix
Introduction Ute Ward and Bob Perry	1
1 Parents' play beliefs and engagement in young children's play at home Xunyi Lin and Hui Li	5
2 'She thinks her toys don't understand Romanian': family engagement with children's learning during the transition to school Susanne Rogers	21
3 Would it really matter? The democratic and caring deficit in 'parental involvement' Katrien Van Laere, Mieke Van Houtte and Michel Vandenbroeck	31
4 'Remote parenting': parents' perspectives on, and experiences of, home and preschool collaboration Tuula Vuorinen	45
5 An observational assessment of parent–teacher cocaring relationships in infant–toddler classrooms Elly Q. Maras, Sarah N. Lang and Sarah J. Schoppe-Sullivan	56
6 Chinese and German teachers' and parents' conceptions of learning at play – similarities, differences, and (in)consistencies Shu-Chen Wu, Stefan Faas and Steffen Geiger	73
7 How educators define their role: building 'professional' relationships with children and parents during transition to childcare: a case study Janine Hostettler Schärer	90

8 Parental involvement in Finnish day care – what do early childhood
   educators say?   102
   Sevcan Hakyemez-Paul, Paivi Pihlaja and Heikki Silvennoinen

9 How do early childhood practitioners define professionalism in their
   interactions with parents?   118
   Ute Ward

10 Written communication with families during the transition from
   childcare to school: how documents construct and position children,
   professionals, and parents   129
   Joanne S. Lehrer

   Index   153

Citation Information

The chapters in this book were originally published in the *European Early Childhood Education Research Journal*, volume 26, issue 2 (April 2018). When citing this material, please use the original page numbering for each article, as follows:

Introduction
Editorial
Ute Ward and Bob Perry
European Early Childhood Education Research Journal, volume 26, issue 2 (April 2018) pp. 157–160

Chapter 1
Parents' play beliefs and engagement in young children's play at home
Xunyi Lin and Hui Li
European Early Childhood Education Research Journal, volume 26, issue 2 (April 2018) pp. 161–176

Chapter 2
'She thinks her toys don't understand Romanian': family engagement with children's learning during the transition to school
Susanne Rogers
European Early Childhood Education Research Journal, volume 26, issue 2 (April 2018) pp. 177–186

Chapter 3
Would it really matter? The democratic and caring deficit in 'parental involvement'
Katrien Van Laere, Mieke Van Houtte and Michel Vandenbroeck
European Early Childhood Education Research Journal, volume 26, issue 2 (April 2018) pp. 187–200

Chapter 4
'Remote parenting': parents' perspectives on, and experiences of, home and preschool collaboration
Tuula Vuorinen

European Early Childhood Education Research Journal, volume 26, issue 2 (April 2018) pp. 201–211

Chapter 5
An observational assessment of parent–teacher cocaring relationships in infant–toddler classrooms
Elly Q. Maras, Sarah N. Lang and Sarah J. Schoppe-Sullivan
European Early Childhood Education Research Journal, volume 26, issue 2 (April 2018) pp. 212–228

Chapter 6
Chinese and German teachers' and parents' conceptions of learning at play – similarities, differences, and (in)consistencies
Shu-Chen Wu, Stefan Faas and Steffen Geiger
European Early Childhood Education Research Journal, volume 26, issue 2 (April 2018) pp. 229–245

Chapter 7
How educators define their role: building 'professional' relationships with children and parents during transition to childcare: a case study
Janine Hostettler Schärer
European Early Childhood Education Research Journal, volume 26, issue 2 (April 2018) pp. 246–257

Chapter 8
Parental involvement in Finnish day care – what do early childhood educators say?
Sevcan Hakyemez-Paul, Paivi Pihlaja and Heikki Silvennoinen
European Early Childhood Education Research Journal, volume 26, issue 2 (April 2018) pp. 258–273

Chapter 9
How do early childhood practitioners define professionalism in their interactions with parents?
Ute Ward
European Early Childhood Education Research Journal, volume 26, issue 2 (April 2018) pp. 274–284

Chapter 10
Written communication with families during the transition from childcare to school: how documents construct and position children, professionals, and parents
Joanne S. Lehrer
European Early Childhood Education Research Journal, volume 26, issue 2 (April 2018) pp. 285–308

For any permission-related enquiries please visit:
http://www.tandfonline.com/page/help/permissions

Notes on Contributors

Stefan Faas is a professor in, and Head of, the Department of Social Pedagogy and Early Childhood Education at the University of Education, Schwäbisch Gmünd, Germany.

Steffen Geiger is a research assistant in the Department of Social Pedagogy and Early Childhood Education at the University of Education, Schwäbisch Gmünd, Germany.

Sevcan Hakyemez-Paul is a research assistant in the Department of Education at the University of Turku, Finland.

Janine Hostettler Schärer is a postdoctoral researcher at the University of Teacher Education St. Gallen (PHSG), Switzerland.

Sarah N. Lang is a senior research associate in the Department of Human Sciences at the Ohio State University, USA.

Joanne S. Lehrer is an assistant professor in the Department of Education at the Université du Québec en Outaouais, Canada.

Hui Li is a professor in the faculty of Human Sciences at Macquarie University, Australia.

Xunyi Lin is an Assistant Professor in the Department of Preschool Education at Fujian Preschool Education College, People's Republic of China.

Elly Q. Maras is a PhD student at University of Denver in Child, Family, and School Psychology in Colorado, USA.

Bob Perry is recently retired after 45 years in higher education. He is Emeritus Professor in the School of Education at Charles Sturt University, Australia, and Director of Peridot Education Pty Ltd.

Paivi Pihlaja is a senior researcher in the Department of Education at the University of Turku, Finland.

Susanne Rogers is a doctoral researcher in the School of Education at Charles Sturt University, Australia.

Sarah J. Schoppe-Sullivan is a professor in the Department of Psychology at the Ohio State University, USA.

Heikki Silvennoinen is a professor in the Department of Education at the University of Turku, Finland.

Michel Vandenbroeck is an associate professor and Head of the Department of Social Work and Social Pedagogy at Ghent University, Belgium.

Mieke Van Houtte is a full professor and Head of the Research Team 'Cultural Diversity: Opportunities and Socialisation' in the Department of Sociology at Ghent University, Belgium.

Katrien Van Laere is a social pedagogue and works in VBJK, the Centre for Innovations in the Early Years, connected to the Department of Social Work and Social Pedagogy of Ghent University, Belgium.

Tuula Vuorinen is a PhD student and lecturer in the School of Education, Culture and Communication at Mälardalen University, Sweden.

Ute Ward is a senior lecturer at the University of Hertfordshire, UK, and leads the BA (Hons) Early Childhood Education.

Shu-Chen Wu is an assistant professor in the Department of Early Childhood Education at the Education University of Hong Kong.

Introduction

Ute Ward and Bob Perry

Dear Colleagues,

It gives us great pleasure to present to you this special issue of the *European Early Childhood Education Research Journal*. It has arisen from the EECERA Special Interest Group Working with Parents, Families and Communities, and its members' cooperation over several years and several EECERA conferences. EECERA reaches well beyond Europe, and this geographical diversity is reflected in the membership of the special interest group. As a result, the contributions in this special issue come from around the world: Australia, Belgium, Canada, China, Finland, Hong Kong, Sweden, the United Kingdom and the United States of America. Together, we share an interest in the relationships between educators, children, their families and the wider community. This is not a new field for research, and many valuable theories and insights first published decades ago still inform our thinking (e.g. Epstein and Sanders 2002). Equally, we frequently draw on widely used concepts from sociology, psychology, philosophy and other disciplines (e.g. Bourdieu and Passeron 1990; Bronfenbrenner and Morris 1998; Foucault 1977; Rogers 2004). However, the world does not stand still, and society, cultural expectations and educational guidelines are constantly shifting and changing. In many countries, governments are increasingly concerned about low levels of school results, especially in international comparisons like the PISA study (OECD 2016). These concerns are impacting on the provision of early childhood education in many different ways. For example, a plethora of early testing is being introduced in many countries and even internationally (see, for example, Moss et al. 2016; Pence 2016) with explicit links between early and later assessments so that 'countries can have an earlier and more specific indication of how to lift the skills and other capabilities of its young people' (OECD 2016; cited in Pence 2016, p. 54). Curriculum and pedagogical changes in early childhood education which have been designated as further examples of 'schoolification' have begun to appear. For example, in the UK, such moves have led to the introduction of a curriculum for children in preschool and nursery settings, assessments and tests for 5-year-olds, and a tick box approach to recording young children's development and learning. Much of this runs counter to well-established and well-considered early childhood education research and practice and seems to be reducing the professionalisation of the early childhood workforce (Moss 2014).

In such an accountability environment where the easily measured gains prominence, the human relationships around the child, in particular the relationship between the educator and the parent and family, can be pushed to the background. Research has shown how influential the engagement of parents and families can be, both directly in their child's current and future learning and development, and in their child's early childhood setting. However, in constantly changing national and social contexts, these relationships need to be re-examined, re-thought and re-visualised on an ongoing basis. For example, in the last few years, migration has been a particular feature affecting many countries. Because of unrest, civil war and famine, a great number of families are leaving their homes to seek a place of safety. At the same time, harsh economic conditions and austerity measures force many families to move to find work in unfamiliar countries, towns and cities. This means that early childhood settings are becoming more diverse with a greater mix of children and families from different cultural backgrounds and with, at times, difficult experiences. These societal shifts, along with the more political changes highlighted earlier, may necessitate new approaches to working with parents and families and the engagement of these parents and families in their children's education and care.

Against the backdrop of societal and economic change as well as increased performativity pressures, there is a danger that the voices of parents and families in their children's early learning and development will not always be seen, heard or fully understood. The papers in this special issue investigate and report on initiatives to listen to the voices of parents and families, to ascertain what families believe and do as they seek to engage collaboratively with educators in the learning and development of their children, and what educators and educational systems might do to facilitate and/or to establish barriers to such collaborative engagement.

The first three articles in this special issue specifically explore parents' views and contributions to their children's learning. Xunyi Lin's and Hui Li's research into the ways in which Chinese parents support their children's play at home introduces a new Play Beliefs Scale for Parents which could have wide applicability in countries beyond China where it was developed and validated. The study highlights two factors – play for learning and play for fun – parents may hold in regards to their involvement in their children's play. In essence, parents appear to see themselves either as a teacher or as a playmate, using quite different perceptions of the benefits and usefulness of play. Susanne Rogers also considers parents' interactions with their children at home and reveals the many ways in which parents support their children's learning. Through analysis of interview data, Rogers investigates differences in the perceptions of parents and educators concerning parental roles and abilities to support children's learning in the first year of school. She highlights the importance of the development of respectful relationships among parents and educators and the need for time to be given to the building of these relationships. While Rogers sees this relationship building needing to be a collaborative venture, she notes that because of power differentials, much of the initiative needs to emanate from educators. Both Lin and Li and Rogers emphasise that parents are their children's first and most enduring educators, something that may be forgotten in more education-focused early childhood settings. Katrien Van Laere, Mieke Van Houtte and Michel Vandenbroeck's article exploring the views of immigrant parents in Belgium indicates that parents' expectations and priorities do not appear to be heard in early childhood settings and concludes that there is a discrepancy between parents' emphasis on care and educators' focus on education. The study shows some of the difficulties parents can have in even expressing their eagerness to be involved in their children's care and education and advocates for more democratic approaches to parental engagement with stronger support from early childhood settings.

Following the contribution from Belgium with its consideration of children and their parents in the context of early childhood settings, the next two papers develop the themes of *remote parenting* and *cocaring*. Tuula Vuorinen explores how parents understand their collaboration with educators. In such collaborations, parents wish to retain their overall responsibility for their children and are keen to influence and shape their children's experiences while they are in the care of others. The Swedish parents interviewed for this research saw their parenting role as involving *remote parenting* – parenting that continues even when they were not with their child. The paper from Elly Maras, Sarah Lang and Sarah Schoppe-Sullivan builds on previous work in *cocaring* through an observational study of mother/educator interactions in the specific scenarios of drop-off and pick-up times in the USA. An observational tool is developed that shows strong validity and reliability characteristics and allows discussion of both supporting and undermining features of cocaring interactions. The contributions from Sweden and the USA are followed by a cross-cultural study of educators' and parents' understanding of learning at play. Shu-Chen Wu, Stefan Faas and Steffen Geiger's multivocal ethnography uses video material and focus group discussions to compare perspectives, professional practice and curricular policy in Germany and Hong Kong. The authors note the different views formed by individualist and collectivist approaches to pedagogy and education while also highlighting some dissonance in the views of educators and parents in the same cultural context. In the light of the societal shifts and changes mentioned above, this cross-cultural study seems particularly salient and may support educators to understand differences among their own perspectives and those of parents.

The next three papers in the special issue – those from Janine Hostettler Schärer in Canada, Sevcan Hakyemez-Paul, Paivi Pihlaja and Heikki Silvennoinen in Finland, and Ute Ward in the UK – consider what early childhood educators see as their roles in developing parental involvement with them. Schärer reports on case studies of four childcare educators about their professional roles, with specific data on building relationships with parents as their children move into the educators' care. The findings provide more examples of educators seeing themselves 'as experts and not partners of parents', a perception which seems to impact on the closeness of relationships that are developed with parents. The questionnaire-based methods used in the study by Hakyemez-Paul and colleagues provide similar results to those of Schärer. While the Finnish early childhood educators are positively disposed towards parents' involvement, they see that the parents are often barriers to such involvement, as is the 'lack of time' for both educators and parents. Ward presents interview-based research exploring English early childhood educators' conceptualisations of professionalism in the work with parents. This paper points to the broad range of views different educators hold on their roles and responsibilities in relation to parents. One of the relational dimensions discussed focuses on the degrees of educators' closeness to the parent or the child, which echoes the earlier discussion about care and caring in early childhood settings. Some of the English educators see themselves as experts and explain that too much emotional closeness to the child or her parents is unprofessional, which seems to echo Schärer's findings in Canada.

The final paper uses positioning analysis to explore written communication with families as their children start school in Quebec, Canada. The impact of written communication is sometimes overlooked even though its prevalence seems to be increasing. Joanne Lehrer illustrates the importance of written communication in constructing images of all stakeholders in the transition to school. The images constructed may vary across early childhood and school settings. For example, while parents are constructed as 'consumers of information about children' in childcare, they are encouraged to take a more active, collaborative role when their children start school. As has been shown in other papers in this special issue, however, teachers' expertise is seen to be superior to that of parents.

It is well known that parental engagement in their children's learning and development has positive benefits (Ahtola et al. 2011; Sylva et al. 2010). However, in the current environments of accountability and performativity which are pervading early childhood education in many countries, the opportunities for parents and other family members to be part of the development of respectful, collaborative engagement with their children's early childhood educators are becoming more and more restricted. Many educators, under a great deal of pressure to 'perform', seem to be forced to choose between curriculum outcomes and parental engagement as both involve the educators' time. Placed in this position, educators do not really have a choice, and this will impact on collaboration with parents and, we would suggest, be detrimental to the ongoing education and development of the children.

References

Ahtola, A., G. Silinkas, P.-L. Poikoken, M. Kontoniemi, P. Niemi, and J.-E. Nurmi. 2011. "Transition to Formal Schooling: Do Transition Practices Matter for Academic Performance?" *Early Childhood Research Quarterly* 26: 295–302.

Bourdieu, P., and J. Passeron. 1990. *Reproduction in Education, Society and Culture*. London: SAGE Publications.

Bronfenbrenner, U., and Morris, P. A. 1998. "The Ecology of Developmental Processes." In *Handbook of Child Psychology: Vol. 1. Theoretical Models of Human Development*. 5th ed., edited by W. Damon and R. M. Lerner, 993–1028. New York: John Wiley & Sons.

Epstein, J. and Sanders, M. 2002. "Family, School and Community Partnerships." In *Handbook of Parenting, Volume 5: Practical Issues in Parenting*. 2nd ed., edited by M. Bornstein, 407–439. Mahwah, NJ: Lawrence Erlbaum Associates.

Foucault, M. 1977. *Discipline and Punish*. London: Penguin.

Moss, P. 2014. *Transformative Change and Real Utopias in Early Childhood Education*. London: Routledge.

Moss, P., G. Dahlberg, S. Grieshaber, S. Mantovani, H. May, A. Pence, S. Rayna, B. B. Swadener, and M. Vandenbroeck. 2016. "The Organisation for Economic Co-Operation and Development's International Early Learning Study: Opening for Debate and Contestation." *Contemporary Issues in Early Childhood* 17 (3): 343–351. doi:10.1177/1463949116661126.

Organisation for Economic Co-operation and Development. 2016. PISA 2015 Results. Accessed February 4, 2018. http://www.oecd.org/education/pisa-2015-results-volume-i-9789264266490-en.htm.

Pence, A. 2016. "Baby PISA: Dangers That Can Arise When Foundations Shift." *Journal of Childhood Studies* 41 (3): 54–58.

Rogers, C. 2004. *On Becoming a Person*. London: Constable & Robinson Ltd.

Sylva, K., E. Melhuish, P. Sammons, I. Siraj-Blatchford, and B. Taggart, eds. 2010. *Early Childhood Matters: Evidence from the Effective Preschool and Primary Education Project*. London: Routledge.

1 Parents' play beliefs and engagement in young children's play at home

Xunyi Lin and Hui Li

ABSTRACT

Play is a fundamental concept in early childhood development and education. As partners in the child's learning, parents play a crucial role in how play is defined, valued, and practised. The present study explores the constructs of parents' beliefs about and engagement in young children's play in two coastal cities in China. A sample of 483 parents of children aged two to four years (M = 36.48 months, SD = 4.86) completed a newly developed instrument, the Chinese Parent Play Beliefs Scale (CPPBS), to assess their beliefs on play, and two other scales to report on the parents' and children's play engagement at home. Factor analyses confirmed two factors in the CPPBS – *Play for Learning* (PL) and *Play for Fun* (PF). Mediation models found two patterns of parental engagement in children's play: parent involvement mediated the relationship between their PL beliefs and children's engagement with (pre)academic-related play, but did not mediate the relationship between their PF beliefs and children's engagement with entertainment and fantasy play. This finding indicates Chinese parents might support young children's play as teachers, rather than as playmates.

Introduction

Play is critical to early childhood development, and has been declared the right of every child by the United Nations High Commissioner for Human Rights (OHCHR 2006). However, the meaning and value of play vary across cultures and contexts (Roopnarine 2011, 2015). For instance, Confucian heritage culture (CHC), which has dominated Chinese society for 2000 years, tends to view play as frivolous or even harmful because it diverts children from (pre)academic learning (Luo, Tamis-LeMonda, and Song 2013). In contemporary China, however, a series of recently instituted Early Childhood Education (ECE) reforms advocate a child-centred approach and promote play in early educational settings. This paradigm shift has forced Chinese teachers and parents to transform their traditional beliefs, and to 'reconceptualize' their ideas about children's play (Che and Yan 2008; Liu, Pan, and Sun 2005). These changing beliefs may have an indirect but far-reaching influence on child outcomes through parent–child interactions and home–school cooperation within the 'developmental niche' (Harkness and Super 1992; Super and Harkness 1986). However, the limited existing research has relied heavily on either qualitative studies (e.g. Rao and Li 2009), or on quantitative surveys using a translated questionnaire of unproven validity (e.g. Jiang and Han 2016; Lin and Yawkey 2013). This has made the unique constructs underlying contemporary Chinese parents' play beliefs still unknown. Without a reliable instrument for assessing Chinese parents' play beliefs, studies of the beliefs-practices interface have been lacking. To address the limitation, this study first developed, revised, and validated the CPPBS, in collaboration with indigenous parents and ECE experts, and then explored the relationships of parents' play beliefs to their play engagement in the everyday home context.

Conceptualizing early childhood play

Play is a fundamental concept in early childhood development and education. It takes many different forms in the ECE context, including imaginative play, free-flow play, rough-and-tumble play, socio-dramatic play, constructive play, heuristic play, guided play, and games, all of which involve a wide range of behaviours and activities, resulting in varied developmental and learning outcomes (Wood and Attfield 2013). However, most play-related research has heavily relied on researchers' observations of children involved in an activity that is presumed to be play, based on scholarly definitions. There has been, to date, limited research directly investigating how parents define children's play, although a few studies have used parents' beliefs about the value of play as a focal variable (e.g. Fogle and Mendez 2006; Manz and Bracaliello 2016). As parents perceive play in different ways than do play experts (Fisher et al. 2008), it is imperative to obtain a more accurate understanding of what activities and behaviours constitute play, from a parental perspective (Singh and Gupta 2012).

Moreover, research into play has long been framed in ways that privilege Western cultural practices, rather than seeing play as socio-culturally specific (Rogoff 2003; Vygotsky 1978). A wider lens is, therefore, needed to describe the play experiences of young children in multiple non-Western cultural contexts overlooked in contemporary play research (Gaskins, Haight, and Lancy 2007). Previous studies using Chinese parents' self-reports to measure the value of play have relied upon modified questionnaires; however, the absence of a psychometrically sound measurement tool is a methodological problem in these studies. As parental beliefs are unique and specific to a certain time and context (Sigel and McGillicuddy-De Lisi 2002), Chinese parents themselves should participate as fully as possible in identifying, portraying, and valuing their child's play in authentic contexts (Jiang and Han 2016).

Chinese parents' changing beliefs on early childhood play

Chinese culture features a rich tradition of highly valuing academic achievement, behavioural control, conformity, and discipline (Rao, Ng, and Pearson 2010); in words of the Three-Character Classic, 'diligence yields rewards, while play goes nowhere'. This emphasis on diligence and the acquisition of academic knowledge has led Chinese people to view learning as a serious, rather than playful, activity (Luo, Tamis-LeMonda, and Song 2013). However, since the end of the twentieth century, as more exposure to Western ECE practices, an ECE paradigm shift away from didactic, adult-directed, and academically oriented education, towards child-centred and play-based teaching has been occurring in China (Tobin, Hsueh, and Karasawa 2009). Given the tension between traditional Chinese values and imported ones (Li and Chen 2017; Rao, Ng, and Pearson 2010), beliefs regarding more structured early academic training may take precedence over play, or at the very least present a cultural paradox to parents, who are the ECE consumers and the significant adults in children's early years.

A review of the literature on how Chinese parents perceive and value children's play suggests a typical dichotomy – play is important for children's development, but not for their academic preparation. For example, Lin and Yawkey's (2013) study revealed that, while recognizing the contributions of play to their children's development, Taiwanese parents preferred to involve them in academic learning (numbers or letters), rather than in play. This dichotomous belief about the play and (pre-)academic learning was also found among upper-middle-class Chinese parents in mainland China, and Chinese immigrant parents in the United States (Jiang and Han 2016). However, due to the lack of reliable instruments in these large-scale studies, the key constructs underlying parents' play beliefs are still unknown.

On the other hand, Rao and Li (2009) found that Chinese parents in Shenzhen (a mainland city neighbouring Hong Kong) tended to accept the concept of 'eduplay', a fusion of play and pre-academic learning, rather than see them as dichotomous activities. The parents in their case study (Rao and Li 2009) accorded much attention to the form of play-based education in early childhood, and believed early literacy and arithmetic concepts could be embedded in play. Again, case studies in other coastal cities in China, such as Shanghai and Fuzhou (Lin 2013; Lin and Li 2014) revealed the notion of 'eduplay' had been well-embraced by parents of young children. The parents in the studies (Lin 2013; Lin and Li 2014) differentiated between the concepts of *youxi* (structured play) and *wanshua* (unstructured play), believing early learning occurred in *youxi*, rather than in *wanshua*, as *youxi* could be directed by or engaged with the adult, whereas *wanshua* was neither structured nor directed. This study will examine this dichotomy with large-scale data from other Chinese cities.

Parental play beliefs and play engagement in daily home context

Previous studies have shown that, if parents believe in the functions of some types or elements of play, they integrate such play into culturally appropriate everyday activities (Roopnarine 2011). For example, Parmar, Harkness, and Super (2004, 2008) compared Asian (Chinese, Korean, Indian and Pakistani) and Euro-American parents in terms of their beliefs about play and involvement in their children's play, with specific attention to two contrasting roles: playmate and teacher. It was found that parents from the two cultural groups encouraged different kinds of children's daily activities, both through their actual participation and their organization of children's daily living contexts, from the types and number of objects in the home (i.e. toys and books), to loosely or formally arranged daily routines and social interactions (Parmar, Harkness, and Super 2004, 2008). Accordingly, Euro-American children in that study were reported to have more opportunities for free play than their Asian counterparts, who spent a lot of time engaging in early academic preparation at home.

Based on the above understanding and the central role of parental beliefs in determining parental engagement and routines that are part of children's daily lives (Harkness et al. 2011; Harkness and Super 1992; Roopnarine 2015), it is critical to link parental beliefs about the value of play with children's actual play engagement in everyday contexts, to observe both direct and indirect parental influences on children's play experiences.

Research questions

The primary objective of this research was to develop and initially validate a scale for measuring Chinese parental beliefs about children's play, to address above-mentioned knowledge gap. Its second objective was to understand the relationship between parents' beliefs and practices, to test whether parental involvement mediates the relationship between parents' play beliefs and their children's play occurrence at home. Accordingly, the following two questions guided this study:

(1) What are the major constructs in parents' beliefs about children's play?
(2) What patterns exist in parents' engagement with play at home?

Methods

Participants

The study was conducted in Fuzhou and Shenzhen, both of which are in south-eastern China, adjacent to Taiwan and Hong Kong, respectively. We restricted our investigation to parents of pre-kindergarten children aged two to four-years-old. This age group precedes kindergarten education, and is the time in which parents' values and beliefs carry the most weight in arranging and initiating play in a child's life. Participants were recruited through centres and kindergartens mainly serving middle-class families, as determined by community characteristics and moderate tuition rates. In the first wave of data collection, participants were solicited from playgroups in one public kindergarten and two ECE centres in Fuzhou (neighbouring Taiwan). Of 155 questionnaires delivered, 128 were completed, yielding an 83% response rate. A second wave of data collection, conducted two months later, involved recruitment of parents from playgroups in two kindergartens and five ECE centres in Shenzhen (neighbouring Hong Kong). Of 401 questionnaires delivered, 355 were completed, yielding an 89% response rate. Overall, 5%, 10%, and 72% of questionnaires were completed by fathers, mothers, and both fathers and mothers, respectively, with the remaining 13% failing to respond, resulting in a total sample of 483 in the two waves of recruitment.

Demographic information about the participants was collected in two waves (see Table 1). The mean age of the participants' children was 36.48 months (SD = 4.86). The sample included more boys (55.1%) than girls (44.9%), and, in most cases (76%), there was only one child in the family. More than half of the responding parents were university graduates or postgraduates (43.5% and 17.7%, respectively); 24.4% had completed high school or higher technological college, and 14.3% had less than a middle school education. The majority (69%) of the sample population had medium household incomes, based on local levels.

Table 1. Demographic characteristics of the sample used for the CPPBS development.

Characteristic	EFA n (%)	CFA n (%)
Child age (M ± SD)	35.6 ± 4.13	36.8 ± 4.89
Single child		
Yes	59 (84.2)	141 (73.4)
No	11 (15.8)	51 (26.6)
Child sex		
Male	37 (52.9)	109 (56.8)
Female	33 (47.1)	83 (43.2)
Parental education		
Postgraduate	28 (21.9)	65 (18.3)
University undergraduate	56 (43.8)	153 (43.1)
Higher technological college	29 (22.6)	89 (25.1)
High school and below	15 (11.7)	48 (13.5)
Household income[a]		
High	26 (37.1)	61 (31.8)
Medium	30 (42.9)	89 (46.3)
Low	14 (20.0)	42 (21.9)

Note: The EFA subsample had 128 participants (68 mothers and 60 fathers), and the CFA subsample had 355 participants (180 mothers and 175 fathers). There were 70 children in the EFA, and 192 in the CFA. Both the child's parents were given the CPPBS. Participants who provided data for the EFA were not included in the CFA.
[a]High-, medium-, and low-income households in the two cities are based on census data from the *Fuzhou 2013 Statistics Yearbook* and *Shenzhen 2014 Statistics Yearbook*.

Measures

Chinese Parent Play Beliefs Scale

In collaboration with parents and ECE experts in China, we developed, revised, and piloted the Chinese Parent Play Beliefs Scale (CPPBS) to create a measure of Chinese parental beliefs about play. First, individual interviews were conducted with 24 parents (14 mothers and 10 fathers) of pre-kindergarten children, who were asked to describe children's play they observed at home. Each interview lasted approximately 20 min. Parents reported a broad range of child behaviour and parent–child activities as play. All interview responses were transcribed verbatim and then analysed, categorized, and discussed by the two authors, to generate an initial inventory of play activities in the home context. Second, a group of experts in the child development and ECE fields reviewed the items to ensure the list was comprehensive and inclusive, and satisfied a range of theoretical definitions for early childhood play. Third, the scale was piloted with a convenient sample of 42 parents to refine the scale items; parents were asked to comment on the inventory's wording, suitability, and content. This scale development process facilitated eliciting sensitive information from the target population, and prevented the misapplication of relevant concepts due to an over-reliance on expert-driven procedures (Fogle and Mendez 2006). Finally, 26 play activities were subjected to later data analysis. Parents used a five-point scale, ranging from 'not at all important' to 'extremely important', to assess the developmental salience of the 26 play activities.

Parental Play Involvement Questionnaire (PPIQ)

Parents were presented with a list of play activities in PPIQ (identical to those in the CPPBS) and asked, 'How often do you initiate each of these play activities/join playing with the child in each of these play activities?' Parents used a five-point response scale, ranging from 'never' to 'always', to indicate the extent to which they were directly involved in each of their child's play activities. The measure in this study demonstrated high internal consistency, with a Cronbach's alpha of .84.

Home Play Activities Questionnaire (HPAQ)

The principal informant was the primary caregiver most familiar with the focal child's daily activity. The questionnaire was used to rate the frequency of the child's engagement in each of the play activities in the home, as reported in the CPPBS. Primary caregivers were asked to rate the frequency of specific play activities in the home, using a seven-point response scale ranging from 'less often/never' to 'three times or more every day'. The measure in this study had satisfactory internal consistency, with a Cronbach's alpha of 0.71.

Procedures

The participating ECE centres and kindergartens in the two cities served as participant access points. Permission was sought from the principals of the centres and kindergartens. Parents were recruited through a letter explaining the purpose of the study and requesting their consent. Survey packets were hand-delivered to the selected educators, who forwarded them to the parents who had agreed to participate. The survey packets included the demographics questionnaire, the CPPBS, the PPIQ, and the HPAQ. Parents returned the completed questionnaires in person or via their child's school bag, after which the educators contacted the principal investigator to arrange pick-up. Small gifts were distributed to all the families who participated.

Results

Exploratory factor analysis

Exploratory factor analysis (EFA) was conducted to discover the factor structure of CPPBS, using IBM SPSS21.0 software. The factor structure was explored with a sample of 128 parents from Fuzhou, through principal component analyses employing both orthogonal (varimax) and oblique (promax) rotation methods. The principal criteria used to determine factor solutions (Cattell 1966; Cudeck 2000; Gorsuch 1988) were that solutions should: (1) consist of factors with an eigenvalue larger than one; (2) explain a substantial proportion (i.e. more than 10% of the total variance; (3) have an item communality value of .40 or greater; (4) demonstrate adequate internal consistency (i.e. Cronbach's alpha coefficients are .60 or higher); and, (5) have meaningful and interpretable item content. A two-factor solution was selected for retention for its best meeting the criteria described above. Five items were removed because of unacceptably low communalities; two items were removed due to their lack of significant loadings on either of the two factors; finally, one was excluded due to cross-loadings among factors.

As shown in Table 2, the first factor consisted of nine items describing play or play-like activities related to (pre-)academic skills enhancement, such as parent–child reading, letter naming, and numeracy games (so-called academic play). Given the nature of the items, the factor was labelled *Play for Learning* (PL), and indicated the value parents assigned to play with a (pre-)academic goal. The second factor included nine items depicting play activities

Table 2. Structure and loadings for exploratory principal component analysis with varimax and promax rotation of the CPPBS.

Scale item	Factor 1	Factor 2
PL (alpha = .85)		
Playing games of matching words with pictures	**.83**	−.09
Playing flash cards with Chinese characters, alphabets or arithmetic concepts	**.78**	.01
Singing and listening to Three-Character Classic or other Chinese classics	**.74**	−.03
Recognizing Chinese characters in children's story books	**.71**	.10
Playing arithmetic and alphabet games in children's picture books	**.68**	.09
Using electronic products that say words, letters, or numbers when touching buttons	**.65**	.05
Giving performances (e.g. reciting classics, singing, and dancing) to family or friend	**.65**	.00
Playing with puzzles or construction toys	**.64**	.17
Watching educational programmes on TV or DVD	**.56**	.00
Having a book read at bedtime or other time	.39	.33
PF (alpha = .78)		
Jumping and tumbling on bed or sofa	−.01	**.77**
Playing with funny toys or everyday objects as toys (e.g. keys, containers, and tissues)	−.01	**.69**
Playing with sand and water	.06	**.65**
Running and chasing around for no particular reason	−.06	**.63**
Pretending with kitchen sets, doctor's kits, or child-size tools	.14	**.63**
Doodling or painting	.12	**.60**
Riding a tricycle or child's car in the neighbourhood	−.12	**.59**
Going out for a walk	.09	**.48**
Playing with playground equipment (e.g. slide, swing, and seesaw)	−.11	**.40**
Going to visit friends	−.18	.31
Playing games with iPad or iPhone	.12	.19

Note: Salient factor loadings >.40 are in bold. Scale items are presented in abbreviated and/or paraphrased forms.

that primarily focused on fun and sometimes involved imagination/creativity, such as make-believe, physical and motor play, and home and out-of-home entertainment (so-called entertainment and fantasy play). This factor indicated the value parents assigned to play with imagination/creativity and physical movement, and was named *Play for Fun* (PF). These two factors accounted for 47% of the total variance (28% and 19%, respectively). Cronbach's alpha coefficients were .85 and .78, respectively. PL and PF had a negative but non-significant correlation of −.02.

Confirmatory factor analysis

Confirmatory factor analysis (CFA) was carried out (using AMOS 18.0 software) on a sample of 355 parents to test the factor structure explored by the EFA. The model specification constrained items to load only a single factor, and allowed for inter-factor correlation (Albright and Park 2009). One item was deleted due to non-significant loadings on either of the two factors. The model fit indices of the CPPBS and two subscales, and the range of item loadings are presented in Table 3. The results indicate a model-to-data good fit: $\chi^2_{(116)} = 227.67, p < .001$; GFI = .93 AGFI = .90; CFI = .94; NFI = .91; and RMSEA = .053.

Table 3. Model fit statistics for CFA of CPPBS and two subscales.

Scale	No. of items	Item loadings	Chi-square	RMSEA	CFI	GFI	NFI
PL	9	.60–.78	$\chi^2_{(26)} = 61.13$	.062	.970	.962	.950
PF	8	.48–.79	$\chi^2_{(19)} = 59.26$	.077	.945	.960	.922
CPPBS	17	.48–.79	$\chi^2_{(116)} = 227.67$	.052	.943	.930	.907

Although fit indices with higher values are desirable, the levels obtained here are regarded as more than satisfactory (Brown 2015). The internal consistency statistics ranged from .83 to .87. The results of the CFA support the coherence of our conceptual model for the two constructs underlying Chinese parents' beliefs of the value of play.

Raw scores on the PL factor ranged from 18 to 45, with a mean of 35.50 (SD = 5.09). Raw scores on the PF factor ranged from 20 to 40, with a mean 30.61 (SD = 4.14). The mean item scores for PL and PF were 3.95 (SD = 0.46) and 3.82 (SD = 0.51), respectively. Given that item rating ranged from 1 to 5, mean item scores for both of PL and PF were fairly high in the overall sample. Additionally, parents had a higher value on PL than did on PF, but the differences did not reach the level of significance, $t(354) = 1.93$, $p = .06$.

Mediation models

The HPAQ and PPIQ were utilized to report frequencies of children's and parents' engagement with the play activities identified in the CPPBS. The correlations indicated statistically significant relationships between the factor scores in the CPPBS (i.e. PL and PF) and the equivalent composite scores of the other two scales (see Table 4). Correlations between parental beliefs of PL and both children's and parents' engagement in academic-related play were moderately positive and statistically significant ($r = .35$, $p < .01$; and $r = .58$, $p < .001$). Correlations between parental beliefs of PF and both children's and parents' engagement in entertainment and fantasy play were also moderately positive and statistically significant ($r = .40$, $p < .001$; and $r = .41$, $p < .001$, respectively).

The mediating effects of parental play beliefs (i.e. PL and PF) on children's play engagement through parent participation were further tested, using SPSS PROCESS (Hayes 2013), with participants' demographic variables (i.e. child age, sex, household income, and parent education) set as covariates. The results of the mediation model analyses are reported in Table 5.

The total effect coefficient c of each of the two parental play beliefs (i.e. PL and PF) on child play was statistically significant. Next, in each of the two models, the effect coefficient a of parental play beliefs to the hypothesized mediator – parent play involvement, was significant. Finally, the coefficient b and c' were estimated for each of the model PL and the model PF. Once the mediator was included in the model PL, the direct effect coefficient c' of parental beliefs fell substantially to below significance, whereas the coefficient b (relating parent involvement to child play) maintained a significant association. However, when the mediator was introduced in the model PF, the direct effect coefficient c' of parental beliefs on child play was still significant, in light of parental involvement. The mediation effect ab of parental play beliefs (i.e. PL and PF) on child play through parent involvement were further tested, using bootstrapped confidence approach. The results show that significant mediation effect was found in the PL model, but not in the PF model.

Overall, as presented in Figures 1 and 2, parental involvement completely mediated the effect of parental beliefs about PL on children's academic-related play, but no mediating role of parental involvement was found for the effect of parental beliefs about PF on children's entertainment and fantasy play. The findings suggest the two constructs of parents' play beliefs – PL and PF – relate to children's play engagement in the home through different pathways.

Table 4. Correlations among variables in CPPBS, PPIQ, HPAQ, and demographics.

	1.	2.	3.	4.	5.	6.	7.	8.	9.	10.
1. Child sex	1.000									
2. Child age	.009	1.000								
3. Household income	.079	.120	1.000							
4. Parent education	.046	.054	.201*	1.000						
5. Parent beliefs PL	.009	−.048	.255**	.021	1.000					
6. Parent beliefs PF	.058	.136*	−.008	.166*	−.017	1.000				
7. Parent play involvement I	.096	−.029	.175*	.083	.584***	.067	1.000			
8. Parent play involvement II	.053	.115	−.025	.053	.017	.414***	.378***	1.000		
9. Child academic play	.083	−.151*	.111	.154*	.354***	.112	.570***	.250**	1.000	
10. Child entertainment play	.165*	.049	−.043	.103	−.026	.395***	.149	.390***	.317***	1.000

Note: Correlations were computed with two-factor scores of the CPPBS (PL and PF) and the equivalent composite scores of the PPIQ and HPAQ.
*$p < .05$; **$p < .01$; and ***$p < .001$.

Table 5. Mediation model analyses of PL/PF on child play via parent involvement.

	a	b	c'	c	ab+	se	95% CI
Model 'PL'	.630***	.294**	.018	.203**	.185**	.034	**.124, .255**
Model 'PF'	.512***	.027	.301***	.311***	.013	.023	−.039, .054

Note: The mediation effect was tested controlled for demographics in the models. a = the direct effect of IV on M; b = the effect of M on DV; ab = the indirect effect of IV on DV though M; c' = c-ab (c = the total effect of IV on DV). IV = independent variable; DV = dependent variable; and M = mediator.
+Bootstrapped confidence approach was used for statistically testing the mediation effect.
**$p < .01$; ***$p < .001$.

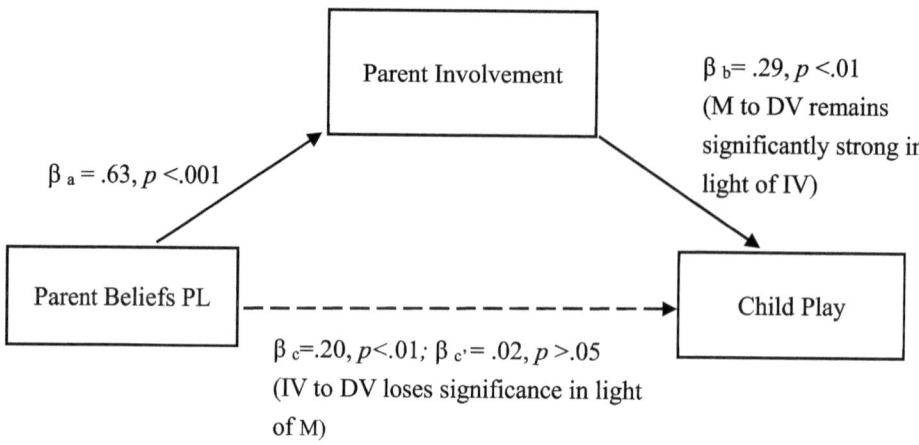

Figure 1. #Direct/indirect effects of PL on child play.
Note: The mediating role of parent involvement was tested controlled for demographics in this model. IV = independent variable; DV = dependent variable; and M = mediator.

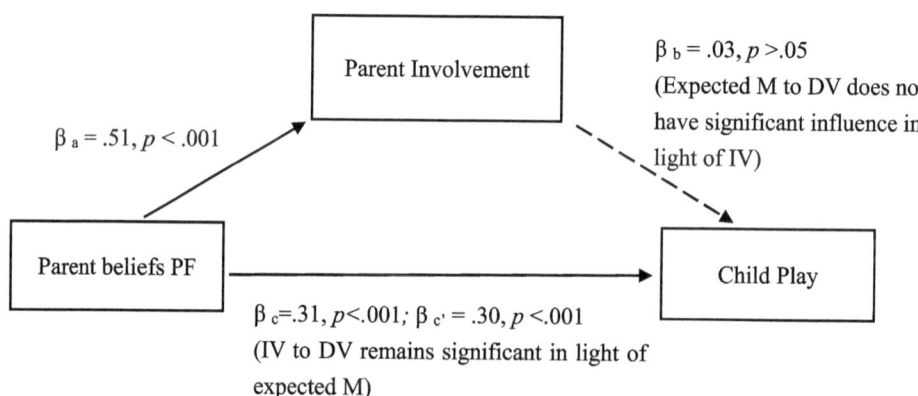

Figure 2. Direct/indirect effects of PF on child play.
Note: The mediating role of parent involvement was tested controlled for demographics in this model. IV = independent variable; DV = dependent variable; and M = mediator.

Discussion

The present study developed the CPPBS in collaboration with indigenous parents and ECE experts in China. The survey data resulted in two reliable constructs of parents' beliefs about the value of play – PL, and PF. In addition, two different patterns of family-based practices (types of play activity) were identified, with a focus on two parental roles in child play: playmate and teacher.

Two constructs of Chinese parents' beliefs on early childhood play

The first factor (PL) includes items of play or play-like activities with early academic enhancement goals, such as learning Chinese characters and classics, numbers, letters, and basic arithmetic concepts. A PL high score indicates the parent assigned a high value to this kind of play activity, and emphasized play that enhanced children's (pre-) academic skills. Chinese parents have high expectations of their children's academic performance, even in very early childhood (Luo, Tamis-LeMonda, and Song 2013). The emergence of this factor suggests parents' views on play might be transforming from traditional (e.g. academic knowledge achieved through diligence, repetition, and drill practices) to more contemporary (e.g. play-based learning, or play as a powerful instrument in early learning). This finding is consistent with Rao and Li (2009), who found that four Chinese parents in Shenzhen tended to believe in the concept of 'eduplay', a fusion of play and early academic acquisition. Although very few cases were considered in that study, the authors were able to triangulate data sources, including responses from interviews, field notes, and videotaped observations in pre-kindergarten settings (Rao and Li 2009). The findings of Rao and Li (2009) and the present study jointly suggest that the academic value of play is a unique and important construct underlying contemporary Chinese parents' play beliefs.

The second construct (PF) is derived from the CPPBS items describing children's behaviour in the pursuit of fun, including imaginary play, fantasy play, physical or rough-and-tumble play, and home/outing entertainment. Fairley PF high scores in the overall sample indicate most parents ascribed great significance to these kinds of play activities in early childhood. This may reflect contemporary notions of 'free' play, 'child-centeredness', and early childhood-appropriate practices introduced by the ECE experts and authorities in China for over two decades. The lack of significant differences in the CPPBS scores of the two factors suggests Chinese parents not only favour structuring their child's play to enhance their (pre-) academic knowledge and skills – as emphasized in PL – but also value free playtime during which children can pursue their own interests, fun, and amusement.

Two patterns of Chinese parents' engagement in children's play

It is widely believed parental beliefs guide parents' decisions on childrearing (Sigel and McGillicuddy-De Lisi 2002). Therefore, two more scales, the HPAQ and PPIQ, which included the same items as the CPPBS, were used to examine the correspondence between parents' play beliefs and their child's daily play in this study. As expected, a significant relationship was found between parental beliefs about the importance of play, and the actual occurrence of such play at home. This is consistent with the existing literature exploring such a link (Harkness et al. 2011; Tudge et al. 1999, 2006) – some of which demonstrated a positive correlation with parents' involving themselves in children's relevant activities (Blevins-Knabe and Musun-Miller 1996; Musun-Miller and Blevins-

Knabe 1998), while others suggested parents structure a home environment that potentially contributes to children's play (Parmar, Harkness, and Super 2004, 2008). This study, therefore, examined whether parents' direct involvement mediated the relationship between parental beliefs about the importance of specific types of play, and the opportunities for such play they provided at home.

The results partly support this hypothesis. When parental involvement was introduced, a new pathway between parents' beliefs about PL and the occurrence of children's play was created, serving to offset the effects on children's play. However, parents' beliefs about PF remained strongly related to play occurrence, even when the variable of parental involvement was introduced. In other words, the pathways through which parental beliefs about play value influenced the occurrence of such children's play were different for the two kinds of play activities identified via the CPPBS. This suggests parents who emphasized play's importance for academic learning involved themselves to enhance their children's play engagement, while parents who emphasized play just for fun increased their children's play engagement in various ways – e.g. planning their child's play space, providing toys and play materials, or organizing play dates with other children – rather than directly engaging themselves in their children's play.

This two-pathway model of parent's involvement is sensible, perhaps because parents would choose a mode of interaction based on children's ongoing play interests, styles, and activities (Johnson, Christie, and Yawkey 1999). Another possibility might involve the traditional emphasis on parental authority in Chinese culture. This is supported by the findings of Parmar, Harkness, and Super's (2008) research, which revealed that European-American parents emphasized parents' role as children's play partners, whereas Asian-American parents emphasized parents' role as academic coaches or teachers. Influenced by Confucianism, which has long dominated Chinese society, parents might view their engagement in children's play as inappropriate; moreover, even if parents played with their children, they might not know how to disengage from teaching and tutoring mode. Therefore, the parents in this study tended to be their children's teacher rather than playmate.

Implications

The present study has both theoretical and practical significance. Theoretically, it provides a culturally relevant measurement through the inclusion of parents themselves in the scale development process. Further, the interaction between parental beliefs and different types of family-based play practices (i.e. educational play versus entertainment play; parent-structured versus child-chosen) was revealed, yielding valuable insights into the mechanisms that contribute to children's play experiences in multiple cultural contexts, an area overlooked in contemporary academic research.

Practically, the CPPBS could be used as a basic tool to implement preventive interventions that aim to promote children's play and outcomes at home. By referring to different pathways for the constructs in the CPPBS, two patterns of parent play engagement were identified – involving themselves in their child's play, and planning settings for it. According Hirsh-Pasek et al. (2009), children learning through play involves two elements: first, a planned play environment that provides enriched objects and toys for experiential learning; and second, adults' intentionally participating in play by co-playing, asking questions, and suggesting, to help children explore materials they might not have thought of by themselves. Parents can provide different materials and toy functions, as well as arrange a play environment that encourages children to explore new experiences (Scarlett 2005). Meanwhile, it is important that parents use the most suitable strategies and roles for involving themselves in different types of play activities – as both playmates and teachers – based on the context, and accounting for the child's own abilities and dispositions (Johnson, Christie, and Yawkey 1999).

Transferable lessons

The findings of the present study, although Chinese focused, are valuable for understanding the place of play in the ever-changing early years context. Over the past few decades, China has launched a series of ECE reforms to import a child-centred approach for replacing the teacher-directed pedagogy prevalent in Chinese preschools. ECE experts and authorities have proclaimed the value of play by primarily focusing on children's choices, exploration, freedom, and autonomy, which obviously conflict with China's deeply rooted Confucian cultural heritage (Li, Rao, and Tse 2012). The findings of the present study, however, show the participating Chinese parents were flexible, in that they tended to modify, rather than completely surrender, their values and beliefs. They were found to have a balanced view of the play, in terms of its academic purposes and the child's interests, fun, and freedom, and integrated Western ideas on child-centred play with Chinese traditions of adult-direct learning into their practices at home. The data suggest parents might have their own views and agendas regarding play and its value in their children's learning and lives. These agendas are complex and sometimes contradict the advice of ECE policymakers and practitioners – who may, therefore, wish to incorporate more extensive discussions of play into their parent education efforts. It is important that education authorities reflect on how to preserve the meaningful aspects of children's 'developmental niches' (Harkness and Super 1992; Super and Harkness 1986), while still incorporating necessary changes, which are likely to become even more pronounced in this global era.

Future research directions

This study has several limitations that should be noted, and that could be addressed in future studies. First, it used a sample of urban Chinese parents who were generally of middle and upper-middle socioeconomic status (SES). The findings, therefore, cannot be generalized to other subpopulations or socioeconomic backgrounds. Additional studies should be conducted with parents from other subpopulations, especially those with lower SES in less-developed regions in China. Second, in this study, parents self-reported their beliefs and practices about their child's play; stronger evidence of the scale's construct validity could be found by examining the CPPBS in relation to observations of children's play and parents' behaviour during their children's play at home. Third, the present study explored Chinese parents' play beliefs, based on their CPPBS ratings. While the emergent factors in the CPPBS might have been evidenced in other cultural groups, the two constructs in the CPPBS were descriptive in nature, and of limited generalizability for comparing Chinese parental play beliefs and those found in other cultures. Therefore, a cross-cultural comparison of play beliefs between Chinese parents and those in other cultures is highly desirable. Finally, Chinese parents who adhered more to traditional values believed that connecting with their children as a playmate might reduce their position as authority figures. Is this specified in Chinese culture or universal in CHC? Future studies examining the relationship of CPPBS to other cultural beliefs, especially those surrounding parents' cultural values and culturally appropriate roles, are really needed to address this question.

Disclosure statement

No potential conflict of interest was reported by the authors.

ORCID

Xunyi Lin http://orcid.org/0000-0002-9954-0618

References

Albright, J. J., and H. M. Park. 2009. "Confirmatory Factor Analysis Using Amos, LISREL, Mplus, and SAS/STAT CALIS." *The Trustees of Indiana University* 1: 1–85.
Blevins-Knabe, B., and L. Musun-Miller. 1996. "Number use at Home by Children and their Parents and its Relationship to Early Mathematical Performance." *Infant and Child Development* 5 (1): 35–45.
Brown, T. A. 2015. *Confirmatory Factor Analysis for Applied Research*. 2nd ed. New York: Guilford Press.
Cattell, R. B. 1966. "The Scree Test for the Number of Factors." *Multivariate Behavioral Research* 1 (2): 245–276.
Che, Y., and C. Y. Yan. 2008. "On Teacher's View of Play and Children's Freedom: Inspirations from Comparison between Preschool Education in Urban and Rural Areas [In Chinese]." *Early Childhood Education (Educational Sciences)* 10 (1): 19–24.
Cudeck, R. 2000. "Exploratory Factor Analysis." In *Handbook of Applied Multivariate Statistics and Mathematical Modeling*, edited by H. E. Tinsley, and S. D. Brown, 265–296. San Diego, CA: Academic Press.
Fisher, K. R., K. Hirsh-Pasek, R. M. Golinkoff, and S. G. Gryfe. 2008. "Conceptual Split? Parents' and Experts' Perceptions of Play in the 21st Century." *Journal of Applied Developmental Psychology* 29 (4): 305–316.
Fogle, L. M., and J. L. Mendez. 2006. "Assessing the Play Beliefs of African American Mothers with Preschool Children." *Early Childhood Research Quarterly* 21 (4): 507–518.
Gaskins, S., W. Haight, and D. F. Lancy. 2007. "The Cultural Construction of Play." In *Play and Development: Evolutionary, Sociocultural, and Functional Perspectives*, edited by A. Göncü, and S. Gaskins, 179–202. Mahwah, NJ: Lawrence Erlbaum Associates.
Gorsuch, R. L. 1988. "Exploratory Factor Analysis." In *Handbook of Multivariate Experimental Psychology*, edited by J. R. Nesselroade and R. B. Cattell, 231–258. New York: Plenum Press.
Harkness, S., and C. Super. 1992. "Parental Ethnotheories in Action." In *Parental Belief Systems: The Psychological Consequences for Children*, edited by I. E. Sigel, A. V. McGillicuddy-DeLisi, and J. Goodnow, 373–392. Hillsdale, NJ: Lawrence Erlbaum.
Harkness, S., P. O. Zylicz, C. M. Super, B. Welles-Nyström, M. R. Bermúdez, S. Bonichini, U. Moscardino, and C. J. Mavridis. 2011. "Children's Activities and their Meanings for Parents: A Mixed-Methods Study in six Western Cultures." *Journal of Family Psychology* 25 (6): 799–813. doi:10.1037/a0026204.

Hayes, A. F. 2013. *Introduction to Mediation, Moderation, and Conditional Process Analysis: A Regression-Based Approach*. New York: Guilford Press.

Hirsh-Pasek, K., R. Golinkoff, L. Berk, and D. Singer. 2009. *A mandate for playful learning in preschool: Presenting the evidence*, Hirsh–Pasek. New York: Oxford University Press.

Jiang, S., and M. Han. 2016. "Parental Beliefs on Children's Play: Comparison among Mainland Chinese, Chinese Immigrants in the USA, and European-Americans." *Early Child Development and Care* 186 (3): 341–352.

Johnson, J. E., J. F. Christie, and T. D. Yawkey. 1999. "Play and Development"." In *Play and Early Childhood Development*, edited by J. E. Johnson, J. F. Christie, and T. D. Yawkey, 25–52. New York: Longman.

Li, H., and J. J. Chen. 2017. "Evolution of the Early Childhood Curriculum in China: The Impact of Social and Cultural Factors on Revolution and Innovation." *Early Child Development and Care* 187 (10): 1471–13. doi:10.1080/03004430.2016.1220373.

Li, H., N. Rao, and S. K. Tse. 2012. "Adapting Western Pedagogies for Chinese Literacy Instruction: Case Studies of Hong Kong, Shenzhen, and Singapore Preschools." *Early Education & Development* 23 (4): 603–621.

Lin, X. Y. 2013. "An Interview Study of Chinese Parents' Beliefs about Play and Learning in Younger Children." *Hong Kong Journal of Early Childhood* 12 (2): 35–42.

Lin, X. Y., and H. Li. 2014. "Eduplay: A Pilot Study of Chinese Parental Beliefs and Practices about Young Children's Play and Learning in Shanghai." Paper presented at the 2014 OMPE Conference, Ireland.

Lin, Y. C., and T. Yawkey. 2013. "Does Play Matter to Parents? Taiwanese Parents' Perceptions of Child's Play." *Education* 134 (2): 244–254.

Liu, Y., Y. Pan, and H. F. Sun. 2005. "Comparative Research on Young Children's Perceptions of Play: An Approach to Observing the Effects of Kindergarten Educational Reform." *International Journal of Early Years Education* 13 (2): 101–112.

Luo, R., C. S. Tamis-LeMonda, and L. Song. 2013. "Chinese Parents' Goals and Practices in Early Childhood." *Early Childhood Research Quarterly* 28 (4): 843–857. doi:10.1016/j.ecresq.2013.08.001.

Manz, P. H., and C. B. Bracaliello. 2016. "Expanding Home Visiting Outcomes: Collaborative Measurement of Parental Play Beliefs and Examination of their Association with Parents' Involvement in Toddler's Learning." *Early Childhood Research Quarterly* 36: 157–167.

Musun-Miller, L., and B. Blevins-Knabe. 1998. "Adults' Beliefs About Children and Mathematics: How Important is it and how do Children Learn About it?" *Early Development and Parenting* 7 (4): 191–202.

Office of the High Commissioner for Human Rights (OHCHR). 2006. General Comment No. 7 (2005): 01/11/2006. *Implementing child rights in early childhood*. http://www2.ohchr.org/english/bodies/crc/docs/AdvanceVersions/GeneralComment7Rev1.pdf.

Parmar, P., S. Harkness, and C. M. Super. 2004. "Asian and Euro-American Parents' Ethnotheories of Play and Learning: Effects on Preschool Children's Home Routines and School Behaviour." *International Journal of Behavioral Development* 28 (2): 97–104.

Parmar, P., S. Harkness, and C. M. Super. 2008. "Teacher or Playmate? Asian Immigrant and Euro-American Parents' Participation in their Young Children's Daily Activities." *Social Behavior and Personality: An International Journal* 36 (2): 163–176.

Rao, N., and H. Li. 2009. "Eduplay: Beliefs and Practices Related to Play and Learning in Chinese Kindergarten." In *Play and Learning in Early Childhood Settings: International Perspectives*, edited by I. Pramling-Samuelsson, and M. Fleer, 97–116. Dordrecht: Springer Academic Publishers.

Rao, N., S. S. Ng, and E. Pearson. 2010. "Preschool Pedagogy: A Fusion of Traditional Chinese Beliefs and Contemporary Notions of Appropriate Practice." In *Revisiting the Chinese Learner*, edited by K. K. Chan and N. Rao, 255–279. Hong Kong: Springer.

Rogoff, B. 2003. *The Cultural Nature of Human Development*. Oxford: Oxford University Press.

Roopnarine, J. L. 2011. "Cultural Variations in Beliefs about Play, Parent–Child Play, and Children's Play: Meaning for Childhood Development." In *The Oxford Handbook of the Development of Play*, edited by A. D. Pellegrini, 19–37. Oxford: Oxford University Press.

Roopnarine, J. L. 2015. "Play as Culturally Situated: Diverse Perspectives on its Meaning and Significance." In *International Perspectives on Children's Play*, edited by J. L. Roopnarine, M. M. Patte, J. E. Johnson and D. Kuschner, 10–17. Maidenhead: Open University Press.

Scarlett, W. G. 2005. *Children's Play*. Thousand Oaks, CA: Sage Publications.

Sigel, I. E., and A. V. McGillicuddy-De Lisi. 2002. "Parent Beliefs are Cognitions: The Dynamic Belief Systems Model." In *Handbook of Parenting: Being and Becoming a Parent*. 2nd ed., edited by M. H. Bornstein, 485–508. Mahwah, NJ: Lawrence Erlbaum Associates.

Singh, A., and D. Gupta. 2012. "Contexts of Childhood and Play: Exploring Parental Perceptions." *Childhood (Copenhagen, Denmark)* 19 (2): 235–250. doi:10.1177/0907568211413941.

Super, C. M., and S. Harkness. 1986. "The Developmental Niche: A Conceptualization at the Interface of Child and Culture." *International Journal of Behavioral Development* 9 (4): 545–569.

Tobin, J., Y. Hsueh, and M. Karasawa. 2009. *Preschool in Three Cultures Revisited: China, Japan, and the United States*. Chicago: University of Chicago Press.

Tudge, Jonathan RH, Fabienne Doucet, Dolphine Odero, Tania M. Sperb, Cesar A. Piccinini, and Rita S. Lopes. 2006. "A Window into Different Cultural Worlds: Young Children's Everyday Activities in the United States, Brazil, and Kenya." *Child Development* 77 (5): 1446–1469.

Tudge, J., D. Hogan, S. Lee, P. Tammeveski, M. Meltsas, N. Kulakova, I. Snezhkova, and S. Putnam. 1999. "Cultural Heterogeneity: Parental Values and Beliefs and their Preschoolers' Activities in the United States, South Korea, Russia, and Estonia." In *Children's Engagement in the World*, edited by A. Göncü, 62–96. New York: Cambridge University Press.

Vygotsky, L. S. 1978. *Mind in Society: The Development of Higher Mental Process*. Cambridge, MA: Harvard University Press.

Wood, E., and J. Attfield. 2013. *Play, Learning and the Early Childhood Curriculum*. 3rd ed. London: Sage.

2 'She thinks her toys don't understand Romanian'
Family engagement with children's learning during the transition to school

Susanne Rogers

ABSTRACT
This article reports on the perspectives of mothers and educators in relation to the engagement of mothers in their children's learning as children living in complex circumstances made the transition to school. For the purposes of this study, family engagement related to engaging with children's learning, which may not necessarily equate to engagement with the school. The study investigated ways in which mothers engaged with their children's learning as they made the transition to school and the perspective of educators in relation to this engagement. It was conducted in four communities characterised by complexity and diversity, in the metropolitan area of the capital city in a southern Australian state. Participating mothers and educators were interviewed individually. Data were analysed using a constructivist grounded theory approach to enable a focus on the lived experiences of individuals in the contexts of their circumstances. The resultant analysis, in relation to the engagement of mothers with their children's learning, identified differences in the perspectives of mothers and educators. Mothers reported a range of ways in which they engaged with their children's learning, the types of learning they valued and their role in that learning. Educators, generally, viewed family members as being deficient in the knowledge and skills to support their children's learning, requiring specific instruction from educators.

Introduction

The importance of family engagement in their child's learning has been researched and documented over time (Bakker, Denessen, and Brus-Laeven 2007; Berthelsen and Walker 2008; Hanafin and Lynch 2002; Siraj-Blatchford 2010). The unique social and cultural contexts of individual families mean that some family practices and values will be more aligned to those of the school setting than others (Bourdieu 1987; Lareau 2011; Moll et al. 1992; Perry 2014). This stronger alignment may result in some families having greater confidence in supporting the school-planned learning of their children at home which is subsequently viewed by educators as engaging with children's learning. In this study, a clear distinction was made between family engagement in their children's learning and family involvement in the school. The notion of family engagement used relates to engaging with children's learning and may not necessarily equate to involvement with the school (Goodall and Montgomery 2014). The transition to school has been identified as having the potential to provide opportunities for adult family members to establish relationships of collaboration with educators to support the learning and well-being of the children. Viewing transition as a set of processes and relationships, as individuals move from one context to another or change their role in educational communities (Dockett and Perry 2007; Fabian 2007), has led to a growing understanding of the opportunities and challenges involved. Contributing factors to both the opportunities and the challenges include the characteristics of the child; family perspectives and circumstances; connections between home, prior-to-school and school settings; educator attitudes; and current political agendas (Griebel and Niesel 2007). Families living in complex circumstances often face challenges in establishing relationships with their children's schools (Auerbach 2011; Dockett et al. 2011; Lareau 2011). The resultant lack of connection and communication means that educators are unaware of family circumstances, their values and the ways in which they engage with their children's learning.

Purpose of the study

The experiences, expectations, aspirations and challenges relating to mothers engaging with their children's learning were considered from the perspectives of mothers and educators. Previous schooling experiences of mothers, be it their own, their siblings or their older children, inform and influence the expectations and aspirations they have as their child makes the transition to school. Mothers aspire to positive educational outcomes for their children, expecting that their knowledge of their children will be respected and that trusting, respectful and reciprocal relationships will be established with educators (Educational Transitions and Change (ETC) Research Group 2011). The study was undertaken in communities where families often experienced circumstances which I described as 'complex'. Such circumstances can impact on the transition experiences of children and their families. Many factors contributed to the complex circumstances experienced by families living in these communities, including poverty, chronic unemployment, substance abuse, social isolation, violence or trauma, ill health and/or related issues (Dockett et al. 2011; Katz, Spooner, and Valentine 2007).

In diverse societies, such as Australia, mainstream values often dictate the behaviour and habits that are considered appropriate within the school setting (Doucet and Tudge 2007). Hence, for some children and families living in complex circumstances, there may well be significant discontinuities as children make the transition to school. Malsch, Green, and Kothari (2011) report their investigation of the perspectives of families living in complex circumstances in relation to the transition to school, and the practices and supports required to achieve a successful transition. Significant elements identified were communication, viewing transition as a long-term process, collaboration across prior-to-school and school settings and opportunities to talk with and learn from other families.

These practices could lead to 'a high degree of continuity between the home and family and community environment, where the child's early experiences are formed, and the new environment of the school creates the best opportunity for a child's success in school'

(Langford 2010, 185). Families provide the social, cultural and emotional support that children need to function successfully at school (Langford 2010). It is therefore imperative that family points of view about transition to school and the establishment of family–educator partnerships – their experiences, insights, expectations and aspirations – are recognised as being critical to designing and implementing effective strategies for ways of working that will benefit children, families, schools and communities.

The use of bioecological theory (Bronfenbrenner and Morris 1998, 2006), as the Person-Process-Context-Time (PPCT) model, in this study highlighted the diversity of the experiences of children and their families, and the nature of the connections between the contexts of home and school. The PPCT model emphasises the importance of contexts – microsystems – in children's lives and the impact of the connections between them – the mesosystems – along with the proximal processes experienced in the different contexts, over time.

Theoretical framework

The PPCT model (Bronfenbrenner and Morris 2006) informed both the data collection and analysis, emphasising the processes of engaging with learning and the related expectations, experiences and aspirations of mothers and educators and the relationships between those in the home and school contexts over time. As children make the transition to school, connections between the microsystems of the family, prior-to-school setting and the new school setting impact on their experiences, as well as those of their families and educators. At the same time, the connections, settings and contexts were influenced by all the stakeholders involved in the transition to school.

The objective of the study was the lived experiences of real people in real settings – understanding how individuals make sense of their everyday lives – to explore human behaviours within the contexts of natural occurrence (Hatch 2002) and to investigate the people and contexts involved with the children and their families at the time of transition to school. Using Bronfenbrenner's (1995) exposition of the elements of person, processes, contexts and time, the nature and extent of interactions between families and educators during the transition to school, the ways in which the contexts of home and school intersect, as well as the relationships generated and the processes utilised to support these, were examined over time. Participants were recruited from settings in areas of identified social and/or economic disadvantage within the metropolitan area of Adelaide, South Australia. All of the participating settings serve communities which are characterised by elements of poverty or marginal income, unemployment and/or social isolation.

A subjectivist epistemology was used, with the researcher and the respondent co-creating understandings, through a methodology of semi-structured interviews and the development of case studies. Through this research paradigm, the PPCT model (Bronfenbrenner and Morris 2006) was used as the framework to investigate the expectations, experiences and aspirations of family members and educators during the process of transition to school and the establishment of family–educator partnerships. The study used a constructivist grounded theory approach to examine the engagement of mothers with their children's learning from the perspectives of both mothers and educators. This approach enabled me, as the researcher, to learn about the views and experiences of the participants through an emergent method, rather than the data being applied to pre-conceived rules or categories (Charmaz 2013).

Method

Participants

Participants were recruited from settings in areas of identified social and/or economic disadvantage within the metropolitan area of Adelaide, South Australia. All of the participating settings serve communities which are characterised by elements of poverty or marginal income, unemployment and/or social isolation. The first group of participants were adult family members, all mothers, of children who had recently made the transition to school or would be making the transition to school the following year. During the recruitment process, approaches were made to mothers, fathers and grandmothers. Only mothers agreed to participate. The second group of participants were classroom-based teachers, principals and allied staff who worked with the children and their families during the transition period and the first year of school. The multistage process of recruitment and interviewing occurred over time, ensuring that each potential participant was provided with information both orally and in writing, had time to consider their participation and provided written consent prior to interviews being conducted. All participants were also reminded of the purpose of the research at the time of the interviews. It was also reiterated that they could withdraw from the study at any time. At all times, it was imperative that I ensured that participants were not left with painful experiences (Liamputtong 2007). This was achieved through careful monitoring of people's reactions and by ensuring that the interview was concluded in a positive frame.

In total, 21 mothers were interviewed. Seven mothers were interviewed twice – prior to their children starting school and again after their children had been at school for several months. Not all participants who were approached for a second interview responded or agreed to the request. Thirteen educators were interviewed. The term educator is used generically to include leaders, classroom educators and those working in specific roles liaising with both educators and families within a community context.

Data collection

Data collection and analysis reflected the use of the PPCT framework by gathering information about the processes of interaction between mothers and educators in different contexts over time. Mothers and educators were asked to reflect on their experiences, expectations and aspirations of both transition and partnerships. These perspectives had formed over varying time frames depending on individual circumstances. The investigation involved five phases of data collection. Initially, individual interviews of participants were conducted 'with the assumption that the perspective of others is meaningful, knowable and able to be made explicit' (Patton 2002, 341). Prior to the interviews, face-to-face meetings were held with leaders in each setting to discuss and plan ways of meeting with and recruiting adult family members.

In the interviews, detailed narratives of participants' experiences, expectations and aspirations relating to the transition to school, for both them and their child, were gathered. Questions were also asked in relation to establishing a partnership with their child's teacher. Initially, it was a challenge to create a balance between asking significant questions and forcing responses (Charmaz 2006). The purpose of the intensive interviewing was to go beneath the surface of the described experiences and provide opportunities to explore a statement or topic. The process enabled participants to tell their stories in a coherent frame, choose what to tell and how to tell it, and describe and reflect on their experiences (Charmaz 2006). The use of the PPCT model as a framework enabled the experiences of the mothers who were interviewed to be understood in terms of the influence of proximal processes experienced in changing contexts and relationships, at any given time and across time (Pianta, Rimm-Kaufman, and Cox 1999).

Data were also collected through direct observation, informal conversations and document examination. The documents for each setting, which were accessed via the schools' websites included site improvement plans, annual reports and various policy statements. The documents were all situated in the particular school context and reflected a particular period of time (Owen 2014). As such, they were used as tools to compare public statements and the experiences and perceptions of the interviewees in each setting.

Data analysis

Data analysis was ongoing through the course of the study based on a constructivist grounded theory approach. Data collected through interviews provided insights into the expectations, experiences and aspirations of both mothers and educators regarding ways that they might work together as children made the transition to school. The participants who were interviewed twice provided their perspectives over time with *looking forward* and *looking back* orientations. Examination of documents in the public domain, produced by the schools, added to the perspective of the educators and provided evidence of the positioning of families in particular settings.

A key component of data analysis in a grounded theory approach is coding, which enables both the interpretation of the data and the planning of future data collection. It is the coding process that begins the theory development. Coding involves categorising segments of data with a short name that both summarises and accounts for each piece of data, giving direction for the selecting, separating and sorting of the data (Charmaz 2006). Two phases of coding were used. Namely, initial coding involving the study of words, lines, sections or incidents looking for significance and focused coding which entailed selecting what presented as the most significant initial codes. These initial codes were then tested against extensive data. The codes identified elements that both stood out in the data and consistently spoke to the data.

A case study method was chosen to report the analyses undertaken using a constructivist grounded theory approach. The use of case studies was congruent with a constructivist grounded theory approach where data collection and data analysis also occur simultaneously, enabling the following of emergent leads and responsive thinking. A case study method reflects the emphasis on the lived experiences in the identified settings, or natural settings as Yin (2006) describes them. 'A case study provides a unique example of real people in real situations' (Cohen, Manion, and Morrison 2011, 289). Each case study was set within its own unique context. At the same time, each context was dynamic. The use of case studies enabled the investigation and reporting of unfolding and changing events and relationships. The case studies combined a description of events with the related analysis, highlighting particular events that are relevant to each case and also focusing on individuals' interpretations and reactions to these events. In this sense, they are interpretive, collective case studies. Using Yin's (2009) classification of case study designs, the study presents each setting as a case within a multiple-case design.

Results

Mothers engaged with their children's learning in a range of ways depending on context, the experiences, expectations and aspirations of the individuals and their current circumstances. In one setting, several mothers talked about the ways they engaged with their children's learning at home. One talked about supporting her son with his reading by using modelling strategies and gradually encouraging him to read independently. Another spoke about gaining insight into her daughter's day and recognising her learning by observing her play at home: 'She's using what she learns at school at home. At home we talk half English, rest Romanian but when she plays she talks only English like she's at school. She thinks her toys don't understand Romanian'. The mother engaged with her daughter's learning through these play scenarios, gaining an understanding of her school experiences … and her perception of the use of Romanian! Although the educators at this setting recognised that families wanted to engage with their children's learning and were keen to affirm the practices within the home that were supportive of the children's learning and development, these mothers had not shared their ways of engaging with the educators. This was despite the provision of regular opportunities for families to meet with educators to exchange information about the children's learning, including experiences undertaken at home.

By contrast, an educator in another setting indicated that adult family members sought direction in engaging with and supporting their child's learning. She reported that parents appreciated the directions and activities she provided in relation to reading and phonics:

> I think that having something formal gives them confidence – something concrete for them to talk about and to do with the children so they're often giving me positive feedback about the learning side of things that they do at home.

None of the mothers interviewed in this setting referred to this direction provided by the school. Indeed, one mother made a strong declaration that school work belonged in the schooling context and that home activities reflected her children's interests of active physical play and outdoor pursuits.

The mothers interviewed at a third setting regularly attended a weekly transition programme offered to families in the year prior to their child starting school. Over time and through the establishment of relationships between the mothers and educators, informal dialogue provided opportunities for the exchange of the children's learning at home.

The processes and interactions used in the fourth setting during the transition to school were perceived differently by the educators and the mothers interviewed. All of the mothers interviewed spoke about the lack of information and support they were given to enable them to engage with their children's learning in the ways they were seeking. One of the mothers who was keen to engage with and support her son's learning recalled that her requests for information about learning activities were dismissed, with the educator saying, 'Oh he can't do that work at home'.

Seeking regular information about their child's achievement, participation and behaviour was a recurring theme from the mothers interviewed, across all four settings (Table 1). The mothers were not seeking occasional or point-in-time events to have a dialogue about their child's progress, nor did they want information sessions about school programmes or practices. The mothers interviewed sought opportunities for regular dialogue with their child's educator to talk about their child, in which they could share insights and concerns and develop relationships of trust, over time. They were seeking opportunities for two-way dialogue to share information with educators about the family circumstances, their perspectives, aspiration and areas of concern or challenge. All the mothers interviewed aspired to positive outcomes for their children, both academically and socially (Arndt and McGuire-Schwartz 2008; ETC Research Group 2011; Perry 2014), as they made the transition to school and beyond.

Discussion

The extent to which families feel a sense of efficacy within the school and their role in their child's education is influenced by a range of factors. Dockett et al. (2011) report that families have a willingness to engage with their child's education and the school particularly at the time of their child's transition, but often feel that their efforts are limited by lack of information and a sense that their participation is not valued. These perceptions and situations rest largely with the attitudes and behaviours of educators (Melton, Limber, and Teague 1999; Perry 2014).

Transition to school is an important time for children, their families and educators. Effective transitions involve cooperative and collaborative relationships between these stakeholders. These collaborative relationships are only successful when it is recognised that family members and educators share the responsibility for children's effective transition to school. While family members and educators have different roles in children's education and the transition process, it is important that both perspectives are recognised and

Table 1. Collated responses of mothers and educators regarding ways of working together.

Mothers	Educators
Regular information about child's achievement, participation and behaviour	Active engagement with children's learning
Ready access to child's educator for two-way communication	Communication regarding children's activities at home
Frequent communication	Regular communication
Relationships of trust and respect with child's educator	Trusting relationship with families
Recognising importance of transition for establishing relationships	Importance of transition for establishing relationships
Greater participation in transition processes	Increasing families' participation in transition processes
Information about classroom practices and environments	**Family members attending workshops and information sessions**
	Family presence and involvement in school
	Attendance at school events
	Utilising family members' skills and expertise
	Welcoming environments

Notes: **Bold type** – theme was evident in at least three of the four settings; Plain type – representation in one or two of the locations.

respected (Wesley and Buysse 2003). The points of difference between family members and educators in relation to the proximal processes, including relationships, established and utilised during the transition to school leads to the hypothesis that family members and educators have varied expectations of the connections and ways of working that might be established during this period and extend beyond.

In this study, the educators' general emphasis was for families to attend information sessions and workshops as scheduled by the school. In some settings, these sessions were part of the transition process and were designed to provide families with information about school programmes, expectations and routines. Perspectives of the mothers varied. Some sought information regarding ways in which they could engage with and support their child's learning. Others engaged with their child's learning through observing their play, reading with them or recognising their interest in a sport or outdoor activity. Generally, educators were unaware of these perspectives or practices.

A number of studies have reported that families from diverse cultural and language backgrounds have been unfamiliar with the Australian schooling system (Gillanders, McKinney, and Ritchie 2012; Kim 2009; Mapp 2003). This was also the case for mothers interviewed in this study. In addition to this unfamiliarity, mothers from diverse cultural and language backgrounds interviewed in one setting were uncertain about the innovative pedagogy being used. They were appreciative of the educators' willingness to talk with them regularly and welcome them into the classrooms, but indicated that questions remained about the achievement and well-being of their children. They were particularly concerned that the pedagogy lacked the formality and rigour they expected for academic success.

This lack of consultation and collaboration, in each of the settings, indicates that the positioning of families in relation to ways of engaging with their children's learning and/or reporting on the ways in which they engage with their children's learning is at the behest of the school.

Implications

Integral to the study was the consideration of the perspectives of both mothers and educators regarding the purpose and nature of an effective transition to school, along with the ways in which families and educators might work together. The transition to school experiences of children and their families may be effectively supported and strengthened by educators acknowledging the processes families employ to engage with their children's learning. It needs to be recognised, however, that families can be involved in their children's learning in a range of ways, dependent on their perspectives and circumstances.

While both mothers and educators identified the importance of relationships based on trust and respect, effective communication and the regular sharing of information, there were differing points of emphasis and understandings of purpose. For the mothers interviewed, the purpose was to maximise their support for their child's learning, development and well-being. For the educators interviewed, the purpose was also about children's learning and development, but this was framed in a 'whole of school' context, with focus on families and children as a group or as identified cohorts within the setting.

Relationships with family members and effective, respectful ways of working with families will be achieved when educators and educational leaders commit time to learn about their communities and acknowledge the strengths and capabilities of the children and their families, regardless of their circumstances. Such understandings and relationships can only be achieved over time. It is therefore imperative that educators and educational leaders dedicate time to these endeavours and recognise their importance.

Disclosure statement

No potential conflict of interest was reported by the authors.

References

Arndt, J. S., and M. E. McGuire-Schwartz. 2008. "Early Childhood School Success: Recognizing Families as Integral Partners." *Childhood Education* 84 (5): 281–285.
Auerbach, S. 2011. "Learning from Latino Families." *Educational Leadership* 68 (8): 16–21.
Bakker, J., E. Denessen, and M. Brus-Laeven. 2007. "Socio-economic Background, Parental Involvement and Teacher Perceptions of These in Relation to Pupil Achievement." *Educational Studies* 33 (2): 177–192.
Berthelsen, D., and S. Walker. 2008. "Parents' Involvement in Their Children's Education." *Family Matters* 79: 34–41.
Bourdieu, P. 1987. "What Makes a Class?" *Berkeley Journal of Sociology* 32: 1–18.
Bronfenbrenner, U. 1995. "Developmental Ecology Through Space and Time: A Future Perspective." In *Examining Lives in Contexts: Perspectives on the Ecology of Human Development*, edited by P. Moen, G. H. Elder Jr., and K. Luscher, 619–647. Washington, DC: American Psychological Association.
Bronfenbrenner, U., and P. A. Morris. 1998. "The Ecology of Developmental Processes." In *Handbook of Child Psychology: Theoretical Models of Human Development*, edited by W. Damon, and R. M. Lerner, Vol. 1, 5th ed., 993–1029. New York: John Wiley & Sons.
Bronfenbrenner, U., and P. A. Morris. 2006. "The Bioecological Model of Human Development." In *Handbook of Child Psychology, Vol.1: Theoretical Models of Human Development*, edited by W. Damon, and R. M. Lerner, 6th ed. 993–1023. New York: Wiley.
Charmaz, K. 2006. *Constructing Grounded Theory: A Practical Guide Through Qualitative Analysis*. London: Sage.
Charmaz, K. 2013. "Grounded Theory Methods in Social Justice Research." In *Strategies of Qualitative Inquiry*, edited by N. K. Denzin, and Y. S. Lincoln, 291–336. Los Angeles, CA: Sage.
Cohen, L., L. Manion, and K. Morrison. 2011. *Research Methods in Education*. 7th ed. New York: Routledge.
Dockett, S., and B. Perry. 2007. *Transitions to School: Perceptions, Expectations, Experiences*. Sydney: UNSW Press.
Dockett, S., B. Perry, E. Kearney, A. Hampshire, J. Mason, and V. Schmied. 2011. *Facilitating Children's Transition to School from Families with Complex Support Needs*. Albury–Wodonga: Research Institute for Professional Practice, Learning and Education, Charles Sturt University.
Doucet, F., and J. Tudge. 2007. "Co-constructing the Transition to School: Reframing the Novice Versus Expert Roles of Children, Parents and Teachers from a Cultural Perspective." In *School Readiness and the Transition to Kindergarten in the Era of Accountability*, edited by R. C. Pianta, M. J. Cox, and K. L. Snow, 307–328. Baltimore, MD: Paul H. Brookes.
Educational Transitions and Change (ETC) Research Group. 2011. *Transition to School: Position Statement*. Albury–Wodonga: Research Institute for Professional Practice, Learning and Education, Charles Sturt University.
Fabian, H. 2007. "Informing Transitions." In *Informing Transitions in the Early Years: Research, Policy and Practice*, edited by A.-W. Dunlop, and H. Fabian, 3–20. Maidenhead: Open University Press.

Gillanders, C., M. McKinney, and S. Ritchie. 2012. "What Kind of School Would You Like for Your Children? Exploring Minority Mothers' Beliefs to Promote Home–School Partnerships." *Early Childhood Education Journal* 40 (5): 285–294.

Goodall, J., and C. Montgomery. 2014. "Parental Involvement to Parental Engagement: A Continuum." *Educational Review* 66 (4): 399–410.

Griebel, W., and R. Niesel. 2007. "Enhancing the Competence of Transition Systems Through Co-construction." In *Informing Transitions in the Early Years: Research, Policy and Practice*, edited by A.-W. Dunlop, and H. Fabian, 21–32. Berkshire: Open University Press.

Hanafin, J., and A. Lynch. 2002. "Peripheral Voices: Parental Involvement, Social Class and Educational Disadvantage." *British Journal of Sociology of Education* 23 (1): 59–68.

Hatch, J. A. 2002. *Doing Qualitative Research in Education Settings*. Albany, NY: State University of New York Press.

Katz, I., C. Spooner, and K. Valentine. 2007. *What Interventions Are Effective in Improving Outcomes for Children of Families with Multiple and Complex Problems?* Perth: Australian Research Alliance for Children and Youth. http://www.sprc.unsw.edu.au/media/File/Report_ARACY_Complex Problems.pdf.

Kim, Y. 2009. "Minority Parental Involvement and School Barriers: Moving the Focus Away from Deficiencies of Parents." *Educational Research Review* 4: 80–102.

Langford, J. 2010. "Families and Transitions." In *Transitions for Young Children: Creating Connections Across Early Childhood Systems*, edited by S. L. Kagan, and K. Tarrant, 185–209. Baltimore: Paul H. Brookes.

Lareau, A. 2011. *Unequal Childhoods. Class, Race and Family Life*. 2nd ed. (with an update a decade later). Berkeley: University of California Press.

Liamputtong, P. 2007. *Researching the Vulnerable: A Guide to Sensitive Research Methods*. London: Sage.

Malsch, A. M., B. L. Green, and B. H. Kothari. 2011. "Understanding Parents' Perspectives on the Transition to Kindergarten: What Early Childhood Settings and Schools Can Do for At-Risk Families." *Best Practices in Mental Health* 7 (1): 47–65.

Mapp, K. L. 2003. "Having Their Say: Parents Describe Why And How They Are Engaged in Their Children's Learning." *The School Community Journal* 13 (1): 35–64.

Melton, G. B., S. P. Limber, and T. L. Teague. 1999. "Changing Schools for Changing Families." In *The Transition to Kindergarten*, edited by R. C. Pianta, and M. J. Cox, 179–216. Baltimore, MD: Paul H. Brookes.

Moll, L. C., C. Amanti, D. Neff, and N. Gonzalez. 1992. "Funds of Knowledge for Teaching: Using a Qualitative Approach to Connect Homes and Classrooms." *Theory Into Practice* 31 (2): 132–140.

Owen, G. T. 2014. "Qualitative Methods in Higher Education Policy Analysis: Using Interviews and Document Analysis." *The Qualitative Report* 19 (52): 1–19.

Patton, M. J. 2002. *Qualitative Evaluation and Research Methods*. 3rd ed. Thousand Oaks, CA: Sage.

Perry, B. 2014. "Social Justice Dimensions of Starting School." In *Transitions to School: International Research, Policy and Practice*, edited by B. Perry, S. Dockett, and A. Petriwskyj, 175–186. Dordrecht: Springer.

Pianta, R. C., S. E. Rimm-Kaufman, and M. J. Cox. 1999. "Introduction: An Ecological Approach to Kindergarten Transition." In *The Transition to Kindergarten*, edited by R. C. Pianta, and M. J. Cox, 3–12. Baltimore, MD: Paul H. Brookes.

Siraj-Blatchford, I. 2010. "Learning in the Home and at School: How Working Class Children 'Succeed Against the Odds'." *British Educational Research Journal* 36 (3): 463–482.

Wesley, P. W., and V. Buysse. 2003. "Making Meaning of School Readiness in Schools and Communities." *Early Childhood Research Quarterly* 18: 351–375.

Yin, R. K. 2006. "Case Study Methods." In *Handbook of Complementary Methods in Education Research*, edited by J. L. Green, G. Camilli, P. B. Elmore, A. Skukauskaite, and E. Grace, 111–122. Washington, DC: American Educational Research Journal.

Yin, R. K. 2009. *Case Study Research Design and Methods*. Thousand Oaks, CA: Sage.

3 Would it really matter? The democratic and caring deficit in 'parental involvement'

Katrien Van Laere, Mieke Van Houtte and Michel Vandenbroeck

ABSTRACT
The discourse on parental involvement as a means to increase the educational attainment of underprivileged children has gained ground in the scholarly and policy field of preschool education. Nevertheless, this discourse is characterised by a 'democratic deficit' in which parents themselves are rarely involved in determining goals and modalities of parental involvement in sociological and educational studies (Tronto, J. C. 2013. *Caring Democracy: Markets, Equality, and Justice*. New York: New York University Press). Ten video-elicited focus groups with migrant parents were organised in the Flemish community of Belgium in order to explore their meaning-making of preschool education and the parent-school relationship. The qualitative data suggest a perceived lack of attention for the care dimension in education. While parents are eager to know more about preschool, they cannot always express this eagerness. Based on these results, we recommend that preschool policies, practices, and research should consider communicative spaces for parents, professionals, and researchers in which multiple, yet opposing, meanings can be discussed.

Introduction

Since the 1960s, the relationship between social inequality and school has been of considerable interest to sociological scholars and policy-makers (Downey and Condron 2016). The mass dissemination of primary education in many countries after WWII and of secondary education in the 1960s was envisioned as an 'equaliser' (Peschar and Wesselingh 1985; Van Houtte 2016). In most affluent countries, the construction of preschool education as an equaliser before compulsory education gained momentum (Zigler and Styfco 2010; Van Laere and Vandenbroeck 2014). This is considered especially important for working class children or children living in poverty, who are believed to need compensation for their 'social-cultural handicaps', enabling them to start 'on an equal foot' with the other children in primary education (Van Laere and Vandenbroeck 2014). The idea of 'preschool as equaliser' gradually permeated policies worldwide, consolidated by various studies that underlined the importance of early learning as a foundation for reaching high educational attainment and employment in later life, especially for children living in poverty and children with migrant backgrounds (Heckman 2006; Matthews and Jang 2007; Unicef Innocenti Research Centre 2008). Despite this gradual shift in focus to the equalising potential of the early years, the educational gap between children with high socioeconomic status and low socioeconomic status (SES) and between children with and without migrant backgrounds, remains persistent in many countries, albeit to a different degree. According to the latest PISA studies, Belgium is one of the countries with the most pronounced educational gap, which is related to the home situation of the children (OECD 2013, 2016).

In order to 'close' the persistent educational gap, international organisations have pleaded for increased parental involvement in preschool (OECD 2006, 2012; European Commission 2015). Similar to studies in primary education (Hoover-Dempsey and Sandler 1995; Carter 2002; Barnard 2004), research suggests that parental involvement in the preschool learning of children is associated with better learning outcomes and later academic success (Marcon 1999; Miedel and Reynolds 2000; Eldridge 2001; Castro et al. 2004; McWayne et al. 2004; Sylva et al. 2004; Arnold et al. 2008; Halgunseth 2009; Galindo and Sheldon 2012). Several of these studies draw upon the Epstein's Overlapping Spheres of Influence model (Epstein 1987, 1995; Epstein and Salinas 2004). In Epstein's model, different types of parental involvement are described in terms of what parents can do at home and in the school environment to help their children perform well at school and in later life (Epstein 1987, 1995; Epstein and Salinas 2004). Scholars in the field of sociology of education have criticised this line of thought for several reasons (Lareau 1987; Lareau and Shumar 1996; Lareau and Horvat 1999). They point out that Epstein promotes a model of consensus by using terms such as 'partnership' and 'reaching common goals'. By assuming consensus, this model fails to acknowledge patterns of unequal power distribution between diverse parents and schools (Lareau and Shumar 1996; Todd and Higgins 1998). When Epstein's theoretical model is translated into educational policies, the focus is on increasing the individual parent's involvement in education, starting from the assumption that all parents are equal. According to Lareau (1987) and other scholars who use concepts of the Bourdieusian social reproduction theory, the equality of parents is a problematic assumption, since parents have to deal with unequal financial, social, and cultural resources. Parents, therefore, have different skills to activate their cultural and social capital in order to create an educational advantage for their child. By ignoring these differences, it is argued that it is hard for parents from working or lower classes to comply with the staff's expectations about parental involvement, as these are permeated by social and cultural experiences of the economic middle class and elites (Lareau 1987; Lareau and Shumar 1996; Lareau and Horvat 1999; Horvat, Weininger, and Lareau 2003). Consequently, scholars point out that schools' efforts to involve parents may paradoxically create greater inequalities in children's learning, resulting in an even larger educational gap (Horvat, Weininger, and Lareau 2003; Lee and Bowen 2006; Gillanders, McKinney, and Ritchie 2012).

A more participatory approach on parental involvement may shed additional light on this debate, by relating this sociological approach to an analysis of daily practice and the lived experiences of parents themselves (Vandenbroeck et al. 2011). It can indeed be noticed that both the work of Epstein and Lareau bear a striking commonality: they do not question the ultimate purpose of parental involvement and the very meaning of preschool as increasing academic performances of especially underprivileged children.

It seems that the goals and modalities of parental involvement are defined without the involvement of parents themselves. Tronto (2013) framed this phenomenon as a 'democratic deficit', 'the incapacities of governmental institutions (such as preschools) to reflect the real values and ideas of citizens' (17). As a result, they risk instrumentalising participation, reducing the parents to spectators of their alleged problems.

This instrumentalisation of parents in the debates on parental involvement has been severely criticised for thinking *for* parents, yet not *with* parents (Hughes and Mac Naughton 2000; Rayna and Rubio 2010). In this instrumentalising discourse, parental involvement has an alleged preventive value in terms of avoiding school failure. One of the side effects of this discourse is that non-participation of parents is considered to be a problem (Brougère 2010; Bouverne-De Bie et al. 2012). All too often, it is assumed that poor and migrant parents therefore need to *learn* to participate. Doucet (2011) and Dahlstedt (2009) pointed out that ways to increase parental involvement are actually codes or implicit strategies to socialise underprivileged parents into the mainstream white middle-class norms, but still within an inequitable educational project. Studies that give voice to these parents, however, are only recently emerging (e.g. Tobin, Arzubiaga, and Adair 2013).

In sum, instead of constructing parental involvement as a 'solution' to the educational gap in preschool, it is important to counter, what Tronto (2013) referred to as, the 'democratic deficit' and gain insight into what is at stake for parents themselves: what meanings do parents attribute to preschool education? How do parents understand the relationship with the preschool staff? In this article we explore multiple perspectives of parents with migrant backgrounds in the Flemish Community of Belgium, as they are objects of concern with regard to parental involvement and potential school failure of their children (Dahlstedt 2009; Doucet 2011). Finally, we discuss what parents' meanings of preschool education signify for conventional approaches to parental involvement.

Research context: the Flemish community of Belgium

The Flemish Community of Belgium is historically characterised by a split system with care services for children from zero to three years old (*kinderopvang*) under the auspices of the Minister for Welfare; and preschool institutions (*kleuterschool*) for children from two and a half to six years old belonging to the educational system (Oberhuemer, Schreyer, and Neuman 2010). Every child is entitled to free preschool from two and a half years onwards. Over 99% of the five-year-old children are enrolled in preschool, and 82.2% of the two-and-a-half-year-olds are enrolled in a preschool in Flanders (Department of Education 2015). Despite almost universal enrolment in preschool education, there is an unequal attendance – children from migrant and/or poor families are more often absent from preschool than their more affluent peers – that causes policy concerns, as it is associated with later school failure (Department of Education 2015).

Methods

We organised 10 focus groups in the autumn of 2014 and spring of 2015 of parents with migrant backgrounds (*n* = 66) in Ghent, Brussels, and Antwerp, the three largest cities of the Belgian Flemish community. All parents in the focus groups had children between two and a half and four years old. They gave permission to participate in this study by oral informed consent and approval was received from the ethical commission of the authors' university. In a period of two weeks prior to the focus group, we met parents several times at the school gates and repeatedly invited them to participate in this study. These focus groups took place at the preschool premises without the presence of the preschool staff. Schools were selected on the basis of their school population that consists out of children with migrant backgrounds. We focused on mainstream schools and did not focus on schools with specific pedagogic profiles such as Freinet, Steiner or Montessori schools. With the aim of including parents who would not feel at ease enough in a school environment, we also invited parents through the staff of five intermediary organisations that work with young children (see Table 1). In order to include fathers, we organised two focus groups solely for fathers. However, the turn-out was low, reaching only one father with migrant backgrounds (FG8) and one focus group was cancelled.

We chose to work with focus groups as they are considered a form of collective research for participants in which the authority of the researcher is decentred (Kamberilis and Dimitriadis 2003; Howitt 2011a). Furthermore, since the method of video-elicited focus groups by Tobin (1992) has proven to be a good way to capture parents' voices with multiple language backgrounds, discussions and reflections among parents were triggered by showing a 20 minute movie of a day in preschool in the focus groups. This self-made movie showed various learning and caring moments and activities in a Flemish reception

Table 1. Participants focus groups.

Parents	#	♂	♀	One of home languages = Dutch	Home languages ≠ Dutch	Language focus group	Invited through	Region
FG1	3	1	2	0	3	Dutch	NGO for undocumented persons	Ghent
FG2[a]	8	0	8	2	6	Dutch, Turkish, Slovak and English[b]	Municipal school	Ghent
FG3	3	0	3	0	3	Turkish and Dutch[b]	Community health centre	Ghent
FG4	11	1	10	1	10	Dutch, Turkish and Arabic	Catholic school	Ghent
FG5	8	0	8	2	6	Turkish[b]	Toy library	Ghent
FG6	2	0	2	2	0	Dutch	Meeting space for young children and parents	Antwerp
FG7	8	1	7	1	7	Dutch, French and English	State school	Brussels
FG8[c]	1	1	0	0	1	French and Dutch	Centre for intercultural community development, out-of-school care and state school	Brussels
FG9	13	1	12	2	11	Dutch, French, Turkish and English	Private NGO school (Catholic)	Brussels
FG10	9	0	9	1	8	Dutch, French, Turkish, Arabic and English[b]	Private NGO school (Catholic)	Brussels
Total	66	5	61	11	55			

[a]Including one grandmother.
[b]With professional translator Turkish–Dutch, Turkish–French.
[c]Three fathers participated in this focus group, one of which has migrant backgrounds.

class starting from the moment the parents and the children arrive at the preschool. Participants were invited to interrupt the movie and discuss it, which gave them the opportunity to discuss meanings of preschool education without necessarily having to criticise the school their children attended. They were also asked whether they found the movie to be 'typical'. While discussing typicality, underlying understandings and meanings of preschool education and the relationship between parents and schools were identified (Tobin 1992). The focus group sessions lasted from between one and a half to three and a half hours. Parents would sometimes translate for each other. In four focus groups, we could foresee professional translators whom we talked to and prepared beforehand concerning the aim of this study and the focus group.

All focus group sessions were audio-taped and transcribed verbatim. In conducting a thematic analysis (Howitt 2011b), we identified several general themes that emerged from the data such as curiosity, inability to speak out loud, care of the body, and belonging. Transcripts were coded along this initial coding scheme. In a next step, we performed secondary coding guided by additional literature on the dimensions of care (Tronto 1993; Hamington 2004, 2015; Wikberg and Eriksson 2008) and scripted practices (Antaki, Ten Have, and Koole 2004; Bernstein 2009; Vuorisalo, Rutanen, and Raittila 2015), which resulted in the identification of three main themes: parents' eagerness to know; the value of caring practices; and parents' subordinate position.

Results

The eagerness to know, experience, and communicate

An eagerness to know more about the daily experiences of their children in preschool ran through the discussions of parents, many of whom expressed the hope that their children would feel well and actively participate in preschool practice. They professed to having little knowledge about what exactly happens at preschool and this was explained as having limited possibilities to communicate with the preschool staff and by an inability to enter the classrooms in many preschools:

> Every day I pass the school at about 10 a.m. You can see the children playing at the playground. And when your child is in one of the classes in front, you can peek inside. But now my child is in one of the classes located on the other side of the playground. I just don't know; I cannot see her. I tried to ask this of the preschool teacher: as I'm not able to see her, are you treating my child well or not? (FG3)

Many parents like this mother wanted to see for themselves and experience how their children were doing in the preschool environment and how they were being approached by the preschool staff. Other parents stated that they did not necessarily need to enter the preschool and talk to the teacher. Still, this did not necessarily mean they were not eager to know what was happening. One father claimed to not have a desire to enter the school; however, it turned out at the end of the focus group that he was very curious to know more. He asked the researcher for a copy of the movie so he could watch and discuss the movie with his children. Generally, most parents expressed the desire to have more contact with the staff and not only as a one-way process of the school giving information to the parents:

Parent 1: It would be a good idea if they could organise times at which the school staff talks to the parents. How is it going for you as a parent?

Parent 2: So they listen to our concerns about what we feel and experience.

Parent 3: It would be good to resolve some frustrations and even fears of parents before the start of preschool. (FG9)

For several parents, the lack of concrete knowledge about what happened in preschool, the perceived lack of reciprocal communication, or the inability to be able to be present in preschool and experience it for themselves, generated feelings of uncertainty, worries, and sometimes even frustration.

Questioning care in preschool practices

The eagerness to know, experience, and communicate about their children's preschool experiences was in many cases associated with questions about physical, emotional, and even political notions of care. A recurrent general remark was that preschool classes were understaffed which was believed to hinder the ability to meet the care needs of all children.

Care as an activity and mental disposition

Many parents had questions about how preschool staff addressed the physiological and emotional needs of the child during various moments of the school day. Parents, for example, problematised toilet events and the perceived lack of follow-up by the staff, some of them having no idea if and when their children were being taken care of after a toilet visit or after a peeing accident or when their diaper was changed. The question of whether children were being well taken care of not only concerned the physiological, but also the socio-emotional, needs of the child.

Parent: I noticed in the movie that the teacher does not want to see the child.

Researcher: What do you mean by that?

Parent: During the whole morning she did not once go to the child that was sitting alone and crying. At the start of the school day the teacher could embrace the child and talk to the child. A teacher for me is a bit like a mother to the children in the class. They have to be able to laugh with the child. Really embrace the child! So the children can feel from the teacher that they are here and they matter. I really was fed up with it last year. My child started in September and everything went well until January. All of a sudden my child did not want to go to school anymore. This lasted until June.

Researcher: So what was happening?

Parent: I don't know! I really don't know. I went to the teacher and asked her what was going on. The teacher just said 'everything is good', nothing more. So I asked my son, he was just crying. Everyday this was happening! I did not know what the problem was. But I don't think it is normal that this took such a long time: six to seven months! The teacher needs to provide warmth if they do this work – taking care of children. The child needs to feel 'my mother is gone, but my teacher is with me'. (FG4)

This mother addressed how care requires actual concrete actions like embracing and talking to the child, which should stem from the preschool teacher being caring and warm to children. Care was viewed as both an activity and a mental disposition that the teacher should embody (Tronto 1993).

Care as a phenomenon

The statements of this mother also reveal several symbolic meanings of care, which – according to Wikberg and Eriksson (2008) – refer to care as a phenomenon. In the last participant quotation, the parent used the words 'the teacher does not want to see the child', which refers indirectly to the importance of attention, a symbolic meaning of care that appeared repeatedly in many stories of the participants. Several parents contested the perceived lack of attentive supervisory staff during recess time: who supports the children, particularly as some children can fall and hurt themselves or can be hurt by other children in the outdoor playground? Although attention as a symbolic meaning of care was highly valued by the majority of parents, the way in which care is acted out was expressed differently depending on the parent's own personality, history, gender, socio-economic, and cultural backgrounds (Tronto 1993; Wikberg and Eriksson 2008). Some parents thought that the supervisory staff should be immediately adjacent to the children and protect them from falling or fighting. Other parents underlined that falling is part of learning life, yet the staff should be attentive and able to comfort and actively listen to children's needs. A few parents – who all happened to be fathers – emphasised that children need to learn to defend themselves as many conflicts can occur in the outdoor playground. They emphasised the importance of an attentive staff that can balance between giving freedom to children and intervening in order to resolve a conflict or in order to physically take care of the child when they are hurt.

Besides the emphasis on attention, we identified other symbolic meanings of care in the focus groups. In her exclamation, 'Really embrace the child!' in the last citation, the mother highlighted the need for bodily contact between the preschool teacher and the child as a way to comfort and interact with the child. At the same time, she symbolically referred to the importance of children 'being there' and 'knowing that they matter'. Care was understood as giving presence to somebody and respecting and acknowledging the child in his/her individual personality. The concern that children may be forgotten in the collective preschool environment was particularly salient, as many children from the participants had not mastered the dominant school language, which according to the parents could jeopardise the full participation of the child in preschool learning activities. From that perspective, parents hoped that children, irrespective of their backgrounds, belonged to the group in preschool and in broader society. The focus on attention, presence, and belonging in the class and in society as symbolic meanings of care, seems to touch upon a more political connotation of care (Tronto 1993; Hamington 2015).

Discontinuity in care

The mother finished her thought by articulating that the child needs to have the feeling that 'my mother is gone, but my teacher is with me'. Attention, giving presence, and being connected are considered important symbolic meanings of the care of a child in every life domain, including preschool and home. As care permeates the human condition (Hamington 2004; Wikberg and Eriksson 2008), several participants drew attention to a discontinuity of care between the home and preschool environment which initiates a desire to keep their children at home. They expressed their wish for a more continuous care across the private-public boundaries between home and preschool.

Adopting a subordinate position

From silent to silenced voices

While parents had questions on how care was provided in preschool, it did not always occur to them that they could raise these questions with the staff:

> Parent 1: But you went to the teacher to ask this. I also have this question but it never occurred to me to ask it, because school is a system and who am I to change this system? Do you think it would really matter if I asked this question?
>
> Parent 2: That is not true. You cannot think like that. I had the same experience: I thought it was too cold for the children to eat their fruit on the outdoor playground. If you have a question, you should raise it. (FG3)

The first mother did not consider addressing questions about care because she identified herself as being powerless in the school system. In response, the second mother urged the first one to raise questions with the staff. But even within the stories of the second mother, a dynamic of being silenced is noticeable when she, for example, tried to ask the teacher why she was not able to see her child in the classroom when she passed the school, as presented earlier in this article.

> I discussed this with the preschool teacher. The teacher told me that when she goes to higher grades, I will not be able to see her either. In the beginning it was difficult for me to accept this, but now I'm used to it. (FG3)

Moreover, this mother found it important to ask questions; yet, she perceived her questions as an indication of being stupid:

> I know that some of my questions are bad or silly questions. It is a personal issue: I experience psychological issues because my mother was never really there for me when I was young.
>
> Researcher: So, according to you, what is another bad or silly question?
>
> Parent: Let me think. For example, is there a toilet connected to the classroom of my child? If not, how does my child has to go to the toilet by herself? I asked this question to the teacher and she responded that children go collectively to the toilets. And then I asked her 'but if they are all together on the toilets which bottom will you wipe first?' (FG3)

It is remarkable that she – by referring to her psychological problems – blamed herself for having 'bad' questions that were actually along the same lines of the concerns of other parents in the focus groups. Another mother implied that staying silent is the best strategy for a parent in order to ensure that your child will receive the best learning opportunities and not fail in preschool. In general, parents tended to be rather compliant and subordinate by adapting their expectations to the implicit and explicit rules, norms, and routines of preschool institutions. Some scholars have called this 'scripted practices' in which material and social space is never a neutral context as it directs human action as scripts (Antaki, Ten Have, and Koole 2004; Bernstein 2009; Vuorisalo, Rutanen, and Raittila 2015). We found that some participants tried to go along with these scripted practices, while others challenged these scripts.

Following scripted practices

Despite some exceptions, most parents wished to have more contact with the preschool staff. Nevertheless, since it was not customary in many preschools to enter the class or have extended talks with the teachers, parents tried to approach the teacher, but restricted themselves to a maximum number of visits per week.

> Parent 2: I don't talk to the teacher every day but I try to do it twice … twice a week is perfect [Other participants nod their heads].
>
> Parent 3: I try to contact the teacher once a week.
>
> Researcher: Why this exact number?
>
> Parent 2: If we talk every day to the teacher, it will be hard for her.
>
> Researcher: Would you like this to be different?
>
> Parent 2: Yes of course. Like, one hour per week so every day we can talk with the teacher for 10 minutes. (FG4)

On the surface, it seems that these participants took a respectful position towards the teachers in order not to bother them too much. Yet, their stance is more likely to be coming from deference, acting according to the assumed wishes or opinions of the teacher. The way parents engaged in activities that the school organised to stimulate parental involvement, can also be interpreted as yet another example of their subordinate position.

> Parent 1: Yesterday it was fruit day at the school. Parents cut the fruits and brought them to all the preschool classes. Although I do not speak Dutch, by showing my presence, the preschool staff, director, and school can feel that I'm an involved parent.
>
> Parent 2: I have noticed that the more a mother is busy with the child, the more the school will be concerned with the child and the mother. A lot of other mothers unfortunately didn't come to the fruit day. I told them they should come since you do not need language to cut fruit … . I would like to ask you what we can do for other mothers so they can become more involved in the school. I don't want the other mothers to feel excluded from the school. How can we make clear to the other mothers 'Please, come to the school and dare to ask questions to the preschool staff!?' (FG3)

By doing these activities and expressing the desire that more mothers do this as well, these mothers confirmed the construction of school-centric approaches of parental involvement (Lawson 2003). Yet, at the same time, by reading the scripts and 'performing' parental involvement accordingly, what they actually hope for themselves and for other mothers is to create a possibility to have more communication with the teachers, even when parents did not speak the school language. Since school-centric parental involvement activities were merely a means to this end, these mothers followed, but simultaneously challenged, scripted practices with regard to parental involvement.

Challenging scripted practices

As parents were often not allowed in the preschool classes, several parents challenged these scripts by using the physical space in unconventional ways in order to gain more information about their child's preschool experience.

> Parent 1: When I am bringing my daughter to preschool, I sometimes try to peek through the windows. One day the teacher caught me doing this! [*Some participants laugh*]. (Grand)Parent 2: You can also watch them from behind the trees! Just try the trees! That is what I do when my grandson is playing on the outdoor playground [*Laughter of other participants increases*] (FG2)

The words 'the teacher caught me' and the laughter in response from the other participants, indicate how the layout of a school is a powerful tool to script human actions according to certain expectations and constructed power relations. The parents told us that the windows in this preschool were recently painted blue so parents would not be able to look inside the classrooms. When parents did manage to have contact with preschool teachers, they stated that it was not easy to discuss matters of caring for children. It is noteworthy that parents who tried to ask questions of the preschool staff wanted to legitimise or excuse their need from a cultural, gender, or personal perspective.

> Parent 1: We, as a group of Turkish mums, we are always concerned. Will my child experience difficulties, will they be sad, will they receive sufficient attention?
>
> Researcher: That is an interesting statement you make. How is this for the others?
>
> Parent 2: No, being concerned for your child is the same for all mothers, not only Turkish mothers. (FG2)

The mothers discussed whether being a caring mother was a typical characteristic of being of Turkish origin. A few mothers explained their urge to discuss questions about care as the result of having only one child or of having a concerned personality ('I'm an extreme case, I know'). This resulted in parents apologising for asking 'stupid' caring questions on issues that seemed to matter less for the preschool staff. These explicit legitimations may also be understood as a form of agency of mothers resisting being submissive to the preschool scripts. By 'blaming themselves' because of their personality, gender, or culture, they actually managed to table their questions in the preschool.

Discussion

We started this article by problematising the democratic deficit in educational and sociological studies on parental involvement (Tronto 2013). Instead of adopting an instrumental role of parental involvement in preschool learning, we explored the meanings parents – in this case with migrant backgrounds – attributed to preschool education and how they position themselves in relation to the preschool staff.

With regard to meaning-making about preschool education, parents in our study concurred with concerns about the academic and economic future of their children and the role played by early learning in preschool in this future; yet, this is not what worried them most. Their primary questions concerned the child and their bodily and socio-emotional care needs in the present and the actual belonging and participation of the child in the classroom, no matter what their backgrounds or language skills are. Reinforced by the alleged importance of early learning as an important foundation for later successful school and work life for children with migrant backgrounds and/or children living in poverty, aspects of care seemed to be undervalued in preschool policies, practices, and research. Parents' requests for more attention, presence, and belonging as symbolic meanings of care activities and attitudes touch upon an even more political connotation of care since parents feared that their children could be excluded from school and society. Tronto (1993) and Hamington (2015) highlighted the political potential of care in public institutions like preschools, claiming that care can 'maintain, contain and repair our 'world', including our bodies, ourselves and our environment, so that we can live in it as well as possible' (Tronto 1993, 101).

With regard to the relationship between parents and preschool, the focus groups revealed an eagerness of parents to know what was happening to their child in preschool, even when they did not show this eagerness by entering the school or communicating with the preschool staff. Our data indicate that parents take a rather subordinate position in relation to the preschool staff and preschool as an institution. Accordingly, Lareau and Shumar (1996), Hughes and Mac Naughton (2000), and Todd and Higgins (1998) drew attention to the fact that relationships between parents and schools are characterised by unequal power dynamics, which are often masked by notions of 'partnerships'. Our results show how subaltern parents find themselves in complex and ambiguous positions in which they adhere to, yet simultaneously challenge, scripted preschool practices.

Despite these attempts, the request to be more connected with the staff and to be able to communicate and share in the care of their children remains somewhat unanswered in the stories of parents. Due to a lack of reciprocal communication and dialogue between parents and preschool staff, aspects of care remain under the radar. Tronto (2013) relates this democratic deficit to a caring deficit; that is, 'the incapacities in advanced countries to meet the caring needs of children' (Tronto 2013, 17). The connection between those two deficits originates from 'the construction of a public/private split that is an outdated inheritance from Western political thought that misses important dimensions of both contemporary caring and democracy' (Tronto 2013, 17). Parents in our study indeed questioned the discontinuity in care between the home and school environment and asked to install a shared caring responsibility, since care permeates the human condition and therefore cannot be compartmentalised (Hamington 2004; Wikberg and Eriksson 2008). In this vein, Tronto (1993, 2013) argued that it is impossible to work on a more socially just and inclusive society when care remains locked up in the private and parochial spheres.

Our study has some important limitations. Despite efforts, the focus groups predominantly consisted of mothers, which could have resulted in gender-biased data. A second limitation is that we predominantly reached parents who felt enough at ease to participate in a focus group in a school environment.

What do these meanings of preschool education and the parent-school relationship signify for policies and practices in parental involvement in preschool education? First, this study demonstrates that when parents' participation is considered an ontological fact rather than an instrument for the sake of 'closing' the educational gap between privileged and underprivileged children, other insights (e.g. the importance of care) appear. Taking into account the position of parents as subalterns, preschool policies and practices should develop conditions in which *voice consciousness* is addressed. This is not a simple endeavour. Rather than claiming an equal partnership, schools may wish to encompass a continuous search for creating moments of reciprocal dialogue within unequal relationships. Instead of the more school-centric approaches of parental involvement (How can the parents help the teacher and the preschool in reaching a higher educational attainment?), more parent and community centred approaches of parental involvement are desirable (Lawson 2003; Doucet 2011). Our results suggest that school-centric approaches risk failing to address what really matters for parents. Parents 'perform' as the good parent in these activities as a means of sharing information and caring responsibilities of the children with preschool staff. Finally, in contrast with the common understanding of parental involvement as an individual responsibility, preschool policies and practices should encompass a systemic view in which the preschool plays a crucial role in initiating connectedness and solidarity with parents and communities.

Our study suggests that parents want to be connected to the preschool and share the care of their children, but face many barriers. Ideas on individual parental involvement as a means to increasing educational attainment of underprivileged children risk perpetuating social inequalities rather than challenging them (Clarke 2006). We therefore advocate that further research take on a more systemic approach towards the parent-school relationship that explores how a democratic and open atmosphere in the context of unequal power dynamics may influence inclusive pedagogical practices for a diversity of children, families, and communities. Quality indicators may be discussed with parents and include well-being and physical health of children or ways in which parents and communities feel supported by the preschool.

Disclosure statement

No potential conflict of interest was reported by the authors.

References

Antaki, C., P. Ten Have, and T. Koole. 2004. "Introduction Special Issue: Scripted Practices." *Discourse Studies* 6 (1): 9–26.
Arnold, D. H., A. Zeljo, G. L. Doctoroff, and C. Ortiz. 2008. "Parent Involvement in Preschool: Predictors and the Relation of Involvement to Preliteracy Development." *School Psychology Review* 37 (1): 74–90.
Barnard, W. M. 2004. "Parent Involvement in Elementary School and Educational Attainment." *Children and Youth Services Review* 26 (1): 39–62.
Bernstein, R. 2009. "Dances with Things Material Culture and the Performance of Race." *Social Text* 27 (4): 67–94.
Bouverne-De Bie, M., R. Roose, T. Maeseele, and M. Vandenbroeck. 2012. "De Tragiek van het Preventiedenken." In *Maatschappelijk engagement: een besef van kwetsbaarheid: Liber Amicorum Nicole Vettenburg*, edited by M. Bouverne-De Bie, R. Roose, and M. Vandenbroeck, 277–294. Gent: Academia Press.
Brougère, G. 2010. "La coéducation en conclusion." In *Parents-professionnels : la coéducation en questions*, edited by S. Rayna, M. N. Rubio, and H. Scheu, 127–138. Toulouse: Erès.
Carter, S. 2002. *The Impact of Parent/Family Involvement on Student Outcomes: An Annotated Bibliography of Research from the Past Decade*. Washington, DC: CADRE.
Castro, D. C., D. M. Bryant, E. S. Peisner-Feinberg, and M. L. Skinner. 2004. "Parent Involvement in Head Start Programs: The Role of Parent, Teacher and Classroom Characteristics." *Early Childhood Research Quarterly* 19 (3): 413–430.
Clarke, K. 2006. "Childhood, Parenting and Early Intervention: A Critical Examination of the Sure Start National Programme." *Critical Social Policy* 26 (4): 699–721.
Dahlstedt, M. 2009. "Parental Governmentality: Involving 'Immigrant Parents' in Swedish Schools." *British Journal of Sociology of Education* 30 (2): 193–205.
Department of Education. 2015. *Kleuterparticipatie: inschrijvingen en aanwezigheden* [Toddler Participation: Subscribed and Present]. Brussels: Flemish Government.

Doucet, F. 2011. "Parent Involvement as Ritualized Practice." *Anthropology & Education Quarterly* 42 (4): 404–421.

Downey, D. B., and D. J. Condron. 2016. "Fifty Years since the Coleman Report: Rethinking the Relationship Between Schools and Inequality." *Sociology of Education* 89 (3): 207–220.

Eldridge, D. 2001. "Parent Involvement: It's Worth the Effort." *Young Children* 56 (4): 65–69.

Epstein, J. L. 1987. "Toward a Theory of Family-School Connections." In *Social Intervention: Potential and Constraints*, edited by K. Hurrelmann, B. Kaufmann, and F. Losel, 121–136. New York: DeGruyter.

Epstein, J. L. 1995. "School/Family/Community Partnerships – Caring for the Children we Share." *Phi Delta Kappan* 76 (9): 701–712.

Epstein, J. L., and K. C. Salinas. 2004. "Partnering with Families and Communities." *Educational Leadership* 61 (8): 12–18.

European Commission. 2015. *Education & Training 2020. Schools Policy. A Whole School Approach to Tackling Early School Leaving*. Brussels: European Commission.

Galindo, C., and S. B. Sheldon. 2012. "School and Home Connections and Children's Kindergarten Achievement Gains: The Mediating Role of Family Involvement." *Early Childhood Research Quarterly* 27 (1): 90–103.

Gillanders, C., M. McKinney, and S. Ritchie. 2012. "What Kind of School Would You Like for Your Children? Exploring Minority Mothers" Beliefs to Promote Home-School Partnerships." *Early Childhood Education Journal* 40 (5): 285–294.

Halgunseth, L. 2009. "Family Engagement, Diverse Families, and Early Childhood Education Programs: An Integrated Review of the Literature." *YC Young Children* 64 (5): 56.

Hamington, M. 2004. *Embodied Care: Jane Addams, Maurice Merleau-Ponty, and Feminist Ethics*. Urbana: University of Illinois Press.

Hamington, M. 2015. "Politics Is Not a Game: The Radical Potential of Care." In *Care Ethics and Political Theory*, edited by D. Engster, and M. Hamington, 272–292. Oxford: Oxford University Press.

Heckman, J. J. 2006. "Skill Formation and the Economics of Investing in Disadvantaged Children." *Science* 312 (5782): 1900–1902.

Hoover-Dempsey, K. V., and H. M. Sandler. 1995. "Parental Involvement in Children's Education: Why Does It Make a Difference?" *Teachers College Record* 97 (2): 310–331.

Horvat, E. M., E. B. Weininger, and A. Lareau. 2003. "From Social Ties to Social Capital: Class Differences in the Relations Between Schools and Parent Networks." *American Educational Research Journal* 40 (2): 319–351.

Howitt, D. 2011a. "Focus Groups." In *Qualitative Research and Educational Sciences: A Reader about Useful Strategies and Tools*, edited by G. Van Hove, and L. Claes, 109–130. Harlow: Pearson Custom.

Howitt, D. 2011b. "Thematic Analysis." In *Qualitative Research and Educational Sciences: A Reader about Useful Strategies and Tools*, edited by G. Van Hove, and L. Claes, 179–202. Harlow: Pearson Custom.

Hughes, P., and G. Mac Naughton. 2000. "Consensus, Dissensus or Community: The Politics of Parental Involvement in Early Childhood Education." *Contemporary Issues in Early Childhood* 1 (3): 241–257.

Kamberilis, G., and G. Dimitriadis. 2003. "Focus Groups. Strategic Articulations of Pedagogy, Politics and Inquiry." In *The Landscape of Qualitative Research. Theories and Issues*, edited by N. K. Denzin, and Y. S. Lincoln, 375–402. Thousand Oaks: Sage.

Lareau, A. 1987. "Social Class Differences in Family-School Relationships: The Importance of Cultural Capital." *Sociology of Education* 60 (2): 73–85.

Lareau, A., and E. M. Horvat. 1999. "Moments of Social Inclusion and Exclusion – Race, Class, and Cultural Capital in Family-School Relationships." *Sociology of Education* 72 (1): 37–53.

Lareau, A., and W. Shumar. 1996. "The Problem of Individualism in Family-School Policies." *Sociology of Education* 69: 24–39.

Lawson, M. A. 2003. "School-Family Relations in Context – Parent and Teacher Perceptions of Parent Involvement." *Urban Education* 38 (1): 77–133.

Lee, J. S., and N. K. Bowen. 2006. "Parent Involvement, Cultural Capital, and the Achievement Gap among Elementary School Children." *American Educational Research Journal* 43 (2): 193–218.

Marcon, Rebecca A. 1999. "Positive Relationships Between Parent School Involvement and Public School Inner-City Preschoolers" Development and Academic Performance." *School Psychology Review* 28 (3): 379–402.

Matthews, H., and D. Jang. 2007. *The Challenges of Change: Learning from the Child Care and Early Education Experiences of Immigrant Families*. Washington, DC: Center for Law and Social Policy.

McWayne, C., V. Hampton, J. Fantuzzo, H. L. Cohen, and Y. Sekino. 2004. "A Multivariate Examination of Parent Involvement and the Social and Academic Competencies of Urban Kindergarten Children." *Psychology in the Schools* 41 (3): 363–377.

Miedel, Wendy T., and Arthur J. Reynolds. 2000. "Parent Involvement in Early Intervention for Disadvantaged Children: Does It Matter?" *Journal of School Psychology* 37 (4): 379–402.

Oberhuemer, P., I. Schreyer, and M. Neuman. 2010. *Professionals in Early Childhood Education and Care Systems. European Profiles and Perspectives*. Farmington Hills: Barbara Budrich.

OECD. 2006. *Starting Strong II. Early Childhood Education and Care*. Paris: OECD.

OECD. 2012. *Starting Strong III. A Quality Toolbox for Early Childhood Education and Care*. Paris: OECD.

OECD. 2013. *PISA 2012 Results: Excellence Through Equity (Volume II)*. Paris: OECD.

OECD. 2016. *PISA 2015 Results (Volume I). Excellence and Equity in Education*. Paris: OECD.

Peschar, J. L., and A. A. Wesselingh. 1985. *Onderwijssociologie: een inleiding* [Sociology of Education: An Introduction]. Groningen: Wolters-Noordhoff.

Rayna, S., and M. N. Rubio. 2010. "Coéduquer, participer, faire alliance." In *Parents-professionels: la coéducation en questions*, edited by S. Rayna, M. N. Rubio, and H. Scheu, 15–25. Toulouse: Erès.

Sylva, K., E. Melhuish, P. Sammons, I. Siraj-Blatchford, and B. Taggart. 2004. *The Effective Provision of Preschool Education (EPPE) Project: Final Report*. Nottingham: Department for Education and Skills.

Tobin, J. 1992. "A Dialogical Approach to Fieldsite Typicality." *City and Society* 6 (1): 46–67.

Tobin, J., A. Arzubiaga, and J. K. Adair. 2013. *Children Crossing Borders. Immigrant Parent and Teacher Perspectives on Preschool*. New York: Russell Sage.

Todd, E. S., and S. Higgins. 1998. "Powerlessness in Professional and Parent Partnerships." *British Journal of Sociology of Education* 19 (2): 227–236.

Tronto, J. C. 1993. *Moral Boundaries: A Political Argument for an Ethic of Care*. London: Routledge.

Tronto, J. C. 2013. *Caring Democracy: Markets, Equality, and Justice*. New York: New York University Press.

UNICEF Innocenti Research Centre. 2008. *Report Card 8. The Child Care Transition*. Florence: UNICEF.

Vandenbroeck, M., F. Coussée, L. Bradt, R. Roose, C. Cameron, and P. Moss. 2011. "Diversity in Early Childhood Education: A Matter of Social Pedagogical Embarrassment." In *Social Pedagogy and Working with Children and Young People. Where Care and Education Meet*, 53–67. London: Jessica Kingsley.

Van Houtte, M. 2016. "Selectie- en allocatiefunctie/differentiatie" [Selection- and Allocation Function/Differentiation]. In *Sociologen over onderwijs: Inzichten, praktijken en kritieken* [Sociologists on Education: Insights, Practices and Criticisms], edited by B. Eidhof, M. Van Houtte, and M. Vermeulen, 197–198. Antwerpen: Garant.

Van Laere, K., and M. Vandenbroeck. 2014. "100 jaar leerplicht in België: en nu de kleuters?" [100 Years of Compulsory Education: and Now Toddlers?] *Pedagogiek* 34 (3): 191 –208.

Vuorisalo, M., N. Rutanen, and R. Raittila. 2015. "Constructing Relational Space in Early Childhood Education." *Early Years* 35 (1): 67–79.

Wikberg, A., and K. Eriksson. 2008. "Intercultural Caring – An Abductive Model." *Scandinavian Journal of Caring Sciences* 22 (3): 485–496.

Zigler, E., and S. J. Styfco. 2010. *The Hidden History of Head Start*. Oxford: Oxford University Press.

4 'Remote parenting'
Parents' perspectives on, and experiences of, home and preschool collaboration

Tuula Vuorinen

ABSTRACT
This article explores parents' perspectives on, and experiences of, home and preschool collaboration. The data consist of in-depth interviews with 10 parents with one or several children attending preschool. The research process of gathering and analyzing data follows the procedures of constructivist grounded theory. The results show how parents seek to practice 'remote parenting' in order to shoulder their parental responsibilities for their child's well-being and care while they are away from their child. Parents approach situations they find difficult at preschool in different ways, including staying in the preschool and appreciating the collaboration with practitioners, working for change, coping with the situation, or changing preschools. Parents' experiences of home and preschool collaboration differ in significant ways, and there is, therefore, a need to visualize and discuss norms and values that shape the conditions for parental collaboration. The results might be useful for stakeholders and policy-makers on different levels.

Introduction

In this article, attention is directed towards parents' perspectives on, and experiences of, home and preschool collaboration in a Swedish context. The field of home and preschool collaboration is in many ways a difficult field to enter because it is characterized by contradictions in research, training, and practice. Parents' experiences and the interaction between parents and staff are, for example, seen as a part of the quality of early childhood education (Urban et al. 2012), but parents are rarely included as participants in research (Larsen et al. 2012, 2013). Further, home and preschool collaboration has been reinforced in Swedish policy documents since the 1990s, but the subject is not significantly supported or focused on in teacher training. In practice, practitioners face demands from different directions when preschool administrators focus on developing and controlling measurable aspects of preschool quality while parents emphasize children's well-being and safety (Tallberg Broman and Holmberg 2007). The contradictions mentioned above may mirror the changing tone regarding the purpose and values of early childhood education when economic, rather than political or ethical, concerns are stressed in education (Moss et al. 2016).

The views on parenting and parents' role in children's upbringing are also diverse, and researchers such as Gopnik (2016) and Gillies (2008) stress that parenting has become less of a relation and more like 'a job requiring certain skills and expertise' (1080). Gillies shows how a political focus might narrow the construct of 'good parenting' as caring aspects are reduced in favor of academic learning. In research, strategies for parents to support children's academic learning at home have been brought forward (Siraj-Blatchford 2010). When strategies such as 'concerted cultivation' are emphasized, other ways for parents to facilitate children's growth, e.g. emotionally or socially, become unrecognized by researchers and early childhood educators. Gillies (2008) stresses the importance for professionals and policy-makers to recognize that 'good parenting' is not only about supporting children's academic learning, but also appreciating the varied and situated roles parents play in children's upbringing. The importance of visualizing norms and values regarding parenting is highlighted by Lightfoot (2004) when arguing that the categorization of parents, e.g. into those who are resourceful and those who are not, makes it difficult for educators to see all parents as equal partners and contributors.

In Sweden, policy documents support a holistic view of the child and stress that preschool activities should be 'designed so that care, socialisation and learning together form a coherent whole' (Swedish National Agency of Education 2016, 4). In practice, however, when external demands on control and a striving for professional status are weighed in, the caring parts might become weakened in favor of the educational (Löfdahl and Péres Prieto 2009), and children's play might be reduced in favor of academic learning (Tobin, Hsueh, and Karasawa 2009; Tobin, Arzubiaga, and Keys Adair 2013). Löfdahl and Péres Prieto (2009) argue that the Swedish model of providing educare, in which education and care are combined, might even be threatened when political ideas are implemented in early childhood education. When the focus is set on academic learning, goal fulfillment, and future academic achievements, activities relating to care tend to end up in the periphery.

Home and preschool collaboration: the Swedish context

In the Swedish national preschool curriculum (Swedish National Agency of Education 2016), parental collaboration is addressed in terms of relationships, influence, responsibilities, and support. The work team, regardless of professional status, should 'show respect for parents and be responsible for developing good relationships' (13) with the children's families. The collaboration between home and preschool should further 'take place in close and confidential co-operation with the home' (13). The importance of 'maintaining an ongoing dialogue with the guardians' (13) and to 'take due account of parents' viewpoints when planning and carrying out activities' (13) is also highlighted in the curriculum. It is made clear that 'the guardian is responsible for the child's upbringing and development' (13), and this coincides with the wording in the Parental Code (1949:381) that states that the custodian not only has the right, but also the obligation, to decide on matters concerning the child (Ch.6, §11). The assignment of preschool workers includes helping families by supporting them 'in their role of bringing up and helping their children to grow and develop' (Swedish National Agency of Education 2016, 4). Preschool should supplement the home, and parents should have the opportunity to influence practice within the framework of the national goals. Information about preschool goals and practice is thus a prerequisite for parental influence.

The above formulations have been unchanged since preschool became a part of the Swedish education system and received its first curriculum in 1998. The context in which collaboration takes place has, however, changed in many respects during the past decades. Preschool, brought forward as 'the foundation for lifelong learning' (Swedish National Agency of Education 2016, 4), became general for 4- to 5-year-olds in 2003 and thus partly free of charge for parents. In 2010, general preschool came to include 3-year-olds as well. Preschool teachers received clarified responsibilities in the curriculum in 2010, and licensing requirements in 2011 reinforced their professional position. Academic subjects (science, math, technology, and language) were added to the curriculum in 2010. In 2008, a voucher system was introduced giving parents the possibility to choose between municipal preschools (80% of all preschools) and independent preschools (20% of all preschools). Today, the preschool system is facing some challenges, including an 'alarming shortage' (Swedish National Agency of Education 2015, 14) of qualified preschool teachers at the same time as the number of children enrolled in preschool activities has increased over the last decade. In 2016, 84% of all children between 1 and 5 years attended preschool (Swedish National Agency of Education 2017). A system of maximum fees and vouchers makes it possible for parents to choose between preschools operated in different ways. In 2012, the Swedish National Agency of Education (2013) conducted a survey among parents and found that preschool activities and care were largely consistent with parents' wishes and needs. Parents were most satisfied with the aspects concerning security, activities being stimulating, opening hours, and the closeness to home.

Aim and research questions

The aim of this article was to explore parents' perspectives on, and experiences of, collaborating with practitioners in their children's preschool. The research questions in this study are how parents express the process of collaborating with preschool practitioners and how parents address their parental responsibilities at preschool.

Methodology

This study is based on the constructivist grounded theory (Charmaz 2014) when the intention is to conceptualize parents' perspectives on, and experiences of, parental collaboration at preschool.

Participants

The results are based on qualitative interviews with 10 parents (9 women and 1 man) who had one or more children attending preschool activities. At the time of the study, the parents were between 29 and 48 years of age and had at least one child attending preschool. One of the participants could be considered a 'professional parent' because she provides foster care for children and also provides an emergency home for infants whose parents, for various reasons, are not able to care for their child. Some of the parents were still relatively new to their parenting role, while others had been parents for more than 20 years. The education level ranged from primary school to university. Four participants were first- or second-generation immigrants, and two of them had been living in Sweden for five years or less. Eight participants were married or lived in long-term relationships, and two were single mothers. All but one had chosen a municipal preschool for their child, but at least three of the participants had experienced independent preschools as well. The one participant who had not chosen a municipal preschool had chosen a preschool that is organized as a family cooperative. The sample included participants from both rural areas and cities.

Data gathering and analysis

In accordance with the constructivist grounded theory (Charmaz 2014), data gathering and analysis were conducted as a simultaneous and iterative process. The method adopted for this study was individual in-depth interviews that lasted between 45 and 60 minutes. All interviews were audio-recorded and transcribed verbatim. The initial approach was inductive when using open-ended questions to explore the participants' main concerns when collaborating with preschool practitioners. As the study progressed, emerging topics were explored in subsequent interviews until saturation was reached. Theoretical sampling was employed to ensure variation and contradicting cases in the sample.

The transcripts were initially analyzed by word-by-word and line-by-line open coding when comparing incidents and by scrutinizing the words used in the interview and identifying processes. Questions and thoughts that the coding process generated were written as memos when striving to elaborate categories, study their relationships, and find gaps. Later in the process, coding became more focused when significant codes from previous codings were used in the analyzing process. The process consisted of constant comparisons, and the aim was to develop abstract analytic categories from the data.

Ethics

All participants gave informed consent before entering the study, and confidentiality has been maintained all through the study (Swedish Research Council 2011). The participants were informed that they were free to interrupt their participation at any time. None of the participants chose to do so.

Findings

In this study, parents sought to practice *remote parenting*, not in order to communicate with or to control or discipline their child, but in order to shoulder their parental responsibility for their child's care and well-being when the child was not with them. Practitioners' ability to indivisualize and individualize practice was reported to be important by the parents. Indivisualization includes practitioners informing parents about the child's doings during the day, and individualization includes practitioners adapting routines or activities to meet the child's individual needs.

The first choice

Parents' first challenge is to find a preschool that suits their ideas about preschool practice and their children's needs. They might receive information about preschools from different sources, including preschool heads, staff, other parents, friends, relatives, and websites. One parent explained that one must use 'all the channels you have access to in order to create an image and get information'. The information received is a way to get a feeling for the preschool's atmosphere and resources. Preschools that are struggling with recruiting and retaining staff are avoided because this is interpreted as a poor social environment that offers no continuity.

The second choice

When the child starts preschool, the parents seem to struggle to decide whether the chosen preschool meets their expectations and requirements. The second choice is, therefore, to decide whether to stay at the current preschool or leave it for another. This choice depends on (1) how content the child and/or the parent feels at the current preschool, (2) how the parent views the possibilities to influence practice in the desired direction, and (3) if there are any other preschools available within a reasonable distance. Depending on the above, parents use the following approaches to address the current situation: (1) stay and appreciate, (2) stay and work for a change, (3) stay and cope with the situation, or (4) change preschools.

The results show how parents might switch between the approaches depending on the current situation and how far in the future the next transition is. Parents might, for example, decide to stay and work for a change, but setbacks might cause them to give up the struggle and become more passive or even change preschools. The efforts might also lead to the desired change, or at least a dialogue that strengthens the parents' trust regardless of the outcome, and parents then come to stay and appreciate the current preschool. Parents who recently changed preschools might decide to work for a change from the very beginning because changing preschools all over again might be their last option. Parents who have decided to cope with the situation might change their minds and start working for a change or might change preschools if possible. The results of the interviews show that the situations that parents need to respond to are fluctuating and so are the parents' approaches.

Stay and appreciate the preschool

In some situations, parents feel very content, and the idea of changing preschools, or even considering another preschool, seems far away. These parents describe the preschool as a warm and safe place for both children and adults. Significant features for a preschool that parents appreciate are continuity, inclusion, equality, knowledge, transparency, and team-building. Continuity is highly valued by all parents in this study, and parents who appreciate their current preschool are no exception. When practitioners choose to remain at a workplace, parents tend to interpret it as a sign of enjoyment and work satisfaction. Parents talk in terms as the work team 'owns the place' or 'they are a close-knit team'. The 'ownership' of the preschool includes a sense of responsibility that is appreciated by the parents. These particular parents express how they are being included in an entity, or a 'we', consisting of both practitioners and families. Continuity promotes the process of deepening the relationship between parents and practitioners, and by that the insecurities that parents might feel regarding preschool and their parental role are reduced. Parents express that they can be authentic in the relationship with the practitioners, meaning that they do not have to hide behind a façade pretending that they are better than they are, for example, that they are more patient or compliant when interacting with the child.

The relationship between parents and practitioners is perceived as equal, reciprocal, and complementary. Teambuilding aspects are brought forward when parents and practitioners share both the concerns and joys of the child's upbringing and the desire to support the child in everyday life. The child is valued and treated as a subject with their own specific challenges, needs, and interests. The opportunity to get a glimpse of the practitioners' views is highly valued by parents. The relationship between parents and practitioners has evolved and deepened over time, and parents have come to trust the practitioners' judgment and knowledge. Practice is characterized by transparency when practitioners not only inform parents about activities, but also share the underlying ideas behind the activities. Parents describe the practitioners as 'professional' when they act in accordance with their role. Parents and practitioners seem to share values, norms, and ideas about practice and children's needs. One parent appreciated that practitioners and parents 'think the same' about boundaries and affirmation. Parents might move away from the area but still choose to let the child stay at the current preschool if the distance is far but still manageable.

Parents working for change

There are situations when parents are dissatisfied with some aspect of the preschool, and therefore decide to approach the situation by working for a change. This is particularly the case when a forthcoming transition is far away in time and no other preschool is available. Parents seem to choose not only what problem to address, but also how to address it, depending on how they value the problem and the possible outcome. Matters relating to the child's individual well-being and need for care and supervision, and matters regarding transparency, are priorities when linked to the child's and parent's feeling of security. A lack of information about the child's doings and about preschool practice is worrisome for parents, and one parent described how a demanding parent is created at preschool when the dialogue between parents and practitioners is poor:

> When you feel you don't get any response, you become a little 'on' [as in activated], almost a little demanding and asking questions about everything.

Parents' concerns about the lack of dialogue and reciprocity become especially visible when the relationship between parents and practitioners is superficial or brief. High staff turnover and a constant flow of substitute teachers are considered to be a major problem for parents, as is a stressful working environment for the practitioners. In some situations, parents join forces with practitioners in order to improve the practitioners' working conditions and thereby create a secure and enjoyable environment for their children.

When parents identify deficiencies in matters concerning the care and supervision of their child, they primarily turn to the practitioners in order to make a change. If the perceived deficiency is not attended to, parents turn to the preschool head. In some situations, parents are reluctant to raise criticism because they do not trust the practitioners to handle criticism in a professional way. Parents who turn to the preschool head interpret the situation as a failure because they are not able to handle the situation on their own. In some situations, parents sense a conflict of loyalty and interest when turning to the preschool head. This is the case when parents seek to build teams with the practitioners and at the same time improve the conditions for their child.

Further, parents' demands on preschool and their way of handling perceived deficiencies might change over time as they become more confident, knowledgeable, and experienced as parents. One parent said, 'I make greater demands on preschool [today] than I dared to when I was younger', thus leading to a more direct way to handle situations she finds worrisome.

Stay and cope with the situation

Parents might decide to cope with the situation without further attempting to address the practitioners or the preschool head about the perceived problem and without changing preschools. Parents might await a forthcoming transition on the grounds that 'it's not worth arguing for three months', or they might decide to treat the perceived problem as a minor one not needing attention when other, more important, aspects are weighed in such as the child's overall care and safety. Parents might also find the current preschool quite good compared to what other parents with children at other preschools are experiencing. Perceived weaknesses are then identified and rationalized in different ways.

Parents might also decide to endure a preschool that they find troublesome when weighing long-term benefits to short-term costs depending on what the family's main concerns are. The lack of communication, dialogue, and reciprocity, which parents seem to handle by coping with the situation, might include deeper differences regarding norms and values related to childrearing and parenting. Parents then perceive themselves as powerless when feeling misunderstood, ignored, or categorized by practitioners in situations where they seek to establish contact and collaboration. They might experience that practitioners are working in the opposite direction or being unsupportive when not understanding the conditions under which the family lives or the choices they feel forced to make. Parents and practitioners might have opposing priorities and views of what the child needs and by whom it needs it. In particular, parents in this situation emphasize communication and dialogue. One parent described how she felt 'invisible' and 'unwelcome' when entering the preschool, and she said, 'I can't stand to go there', but she still went. She valued preschool highly because it promoted her child's future by giving her the opportunity to learn the Swedish language and learning codes, the latter of which differ between cultures. Preschool was then perceived as supplemental education by offering her child support in areas where she could not. Another way for parents to cope with a worrisome situation is to keep the child at home for shorter or longer periods waiting for the situation to change.

Changing preschools

There are situations when parents decide to change preschools, provided that there is an available preschool within a reasonable distance. A change of preschools might be necessary when moving away from the area, but parents might also change preschools when not feeling content with the care and supervision their child is receiving. Parents might also change preschools because they do not experience the environment as being as warm and secure as they wish for themselves and their child. The child might be reluctant to attend preschool, and the parents might feel misunderstood, ignored, or offended by the practitioners. The latter is described as very stressful by parents by making them feel unwelcome or judged.

Changing preschools becomes a solution to a problem that parents cannot solve on their own. For example, one parent struggled to understand, and change, a situation where all other children were welcome to eat breakfast in the kitchen except her two-year-old, who had to eat breakfast by herself in the hall. She could see no reason for that to happen when all of the children, including hers, arrived long before breakfast time. She said:

> I fought for that breakfast [by talking to the practitioners and the preschool head], but it absolutely didn't work / ... / we solved it by changing preschools.

Parents might have worked for a change for a long time and finally given up the struggle by stating 'I can't take this anymore', or they might give up immediately when seeing that the problem is too big to solve within a reasonable amount of time. None of the parents changed preschools for other reasons than strengthening the care and supervision of their child.

Discussion

The aim of this study was to explore parents' perspectives on, and experiences of, collaborating with practitioners in their children's preschool. The core variable in this study is 'remote parenting' in which the parents' main concern is to receive good care and supervision for their children when they are not with them. The term 'remote parenting' usually refers to long-term absence, e.g. parents leaving children behind to find work far away from home (e.g. Locke, Thi Ngan Hoa, and Thi Thanh Tam 2012) or the interaction between a child and an absent parent (e. g. Haunstrup Christensen 2009; Yarosh et al. 2013). However, the results of this study challenge the former understanding by adding a different contextual framing, addressing the relationship between primary and secondary caregivers, and by narrowing the aspect of time and distance. The results show how parents in this study act as customers in a market when making choices and evaluating them in order to find caring practitioners that will overtake their parental responsibilities during their child's stay at preschool. Practitioners might not visualize or discuss caring when documenting or presenting their practice, but parents have found other ways to create an image of how care is manifested at preschool. The aspects of caring that Löfdahl and Péres Prieto (2009) fear have been ignored or taken for granted in preschool are parents' main concerns. Parent relates to children learning as well, but those aspects become secondary if their need for care and safety is not attended to. The well-being and safety of the child, as Tallberg-Broman (2009) identified, are parents' first priority.

The results mirror the difficulties preschools struggle with when it comes to recruiting and retaining staff (Swedish National Agency of Education 2015) when parents, being aware of the situation, opt out of preschools that they perceive as less attractive when not being able to recruit and retain practitioners. In that regard, parents' choices become a reflection of practitioners' choices. The results show that, in their choices and by working for change, parents make an effort to create favorable conditions for collaboration. The possibility to meet the same practitioners on a regular basis is considered a prerequisite when collaboration is portrayed as an ongoing process between team members. Parents' experiences of collaboration differ, however, when perceived as effortless, a struggle, or even degrading, and these are reasons to address matters of equivalency and equality when developing home and preschool collaboration. Preschool practitioners share the responsibility of developing good relationships with the families (Swedish National Agency of Education 2016); and one way to demonstrate that responsibility is to care for the children and their families (Swick 2004). The family is the most valuable resource for the child, and there are, as Gillies (2008) states, varied ways to shoulder parental responsibilities.

Conclusions

The purpose of this article was to explore parents' perspectives on, and experiences of, collaborating with practitioners in their children's preschool. The results show that parents' main concern is to practice remote parenting by ensuring that their child is properly cared for and supervised at preschool. Parents strive for continuity when seeking long-term and deepened relations with practitioners at the preschool. They share a wish to team-up with practitioners in order to facilitate the child's overall well-being and growth.

Implications

The results are useful for stakeholders and policy-makers on different levels by showing how parenting might be embodied in practice and in the early childhood education and care system. There is a need to consider the complexity of parental collaboration at preschool. Parents are not a homogenous group but are individuals striving to attend to their children's needs of care and supervision in very different ways.

Acknowledgements

This research was encompassed within a doctoral thesis by Mälardalens University. Forthcoming articles will provide a more detailed account of 'remote parenting' and the terms 'indivisualizing' and 'individualizing'.

Disclosure statement

No potential conflict of interest was reported by the author.

Funding

This research was financed by Mälardalens University.

References

Charmaz, K. 2014. *Constructing Grounded Theory. A Practical Guide through Qualitative Analysis.* Thousand Oaks: SAGE.

Gillies, V. 2008. "Childrearing, Class and the New Politics of Parenting." *Sociology Compass* 2 (3): 1079–1095. doi:10.1111/j.1751-9021.2008.00114.x.

Gopnik, A. 2016. "The Gardener and the Carpenter." In *What the New Science of Child Development Tells Us about the Relationship Between Parents and Children*. New York: Farrar, Straus & Giroux.

Haunstrup Christensen, T. 2009. "'Connected Presence' in Distributed Family Life." *New Media & Society* 11 (3): 433–451. doi:10.1177/1461444808101620.

Larsen, M. S., J. Kampmann, S. Persson, T. Moser, N. Ploug, and D. Kousholt. 2012. *Forskningskortlægning og forskervurdering af skandinavisk forskning i året 2010 i institutioner for de 0-6årige (førskolen)*. Clearinghouse Forskningsserien. 2012:10. København: Dansk Clearinghouse for Uddannelsesforskning, Aarhus Universitet. http://edu.au.dk/fileadmin/edu/Udgivelser/Sr11finalreport.pdf.

Larsen, M. S., J. Kampmann, S. Persson, T. Moser, N. Ploug, D. Kousholt, H. Bjørnøy Sommersel, and K. Steenberg. 2013. *Forskningskortlægning og forskervurdering af skandinavisk forskning i året 2011 i institutioner for de 0-6 årige*. Clearinghouse – forskningsserien 2013: 14. København: Dansk Clearinghouse for Uddannel-sesforskning, Aarhus Universitet. http://edu.au.dk/fileadmin/edu/Udgivelser/Clearinghouse/Review/Skandinavisk_forskning_i_aaret_2011_i_institutioner_for_de_0-6_aarige.pdf.

Lightfoot, D. 2004. "'Some Parents Just Don't Care'. Decoding the Meanings of Parental Involvement in Urban Schools." *Urban Education* 39 (1): 91–107. doi:10.1177/00420859032559290.

Locke, C., N. Thi Ngan Hoa, and N. Thi Thanh Tam. 2012. "Visiting Marriages and Remote Parenting: Changing Strategies for Rural-Urban Migrants to Hanoi, Vietnam." *The Journal of Development Studies* 48 (1): 10–25. doi:10.1080/00220388.2011.629650.

Löfdahl, A., and Héctor Péres Prieto. 2009. "Between Control and Resistance: Planning and Evaluating Texts in the Swedish Preschool." *Journal of Education Policy* 24 (4): 393–408. doi:10.1080/02680930902759548.

Moss, P., G. Dahlberg, S. Grieshaber, S. Mantovani, H. May, A. Pence, S. Rayna, B. Swadener Blue, and M. Vandenbroeck. 2016. "The Organisation for Economic Co-Operation and Development 's International Early Learning Study: Opening for Debate and Contestation." *Contemporary Issues in Early Childhood* 17 (3): 343–351. doi:10.1177/1463949116661126.

Parental Code. 1949:381. Stockholm: Swedish Code of Statutes.

Siraj-Blatchford, I. 2010. "'Learning in the Home and at School': How Working Class Children Succeed 'Against the Odds'." *British Educational Research Journal* 36 (3): 463–482. doi:10.1080/01411920902989201.

Swedish National Agency of Education. 2013. *Föräldrars val och inställning till förskola och fritidshem. Resultat från föräldraundersökningen 2012* [Parental Choice and Approach to Preschools and Leisure Time Centres. Results from the Parent Survey 2012]. Stockholm: Fritzes.

Swedish National Agency of Education. 2015. *Skolverkets Lägesbedömning* [An Evaluation by the Swedish National Agency for Education]. Rapport 421. Stockholm: Fritzes.

Swedish National Agency of Education. 2016. *Curriculum for the Preschool*. Stockholm: Fritzes.

Swedish National Agency of Education. 2017. *Barn och personal i förskolan hösten 2016* [Children and Staff at Preschool in Autumn 2016]. Stockholm: The Department for Pre-school and Elementary School Statistics.

Swedish Research Council. 2011. *Good Research Practice*. Stockholm. https://publikationer.vr.se/produkt/good-research-practice/.

Swick, K. J. 2004. "What Parents Seek in Relations with Early Childhood Family Helpers." *Early Childhood Education Journal* 31 (3): 217–220.

Tallberg-Broman. 2009. "No Parent Left Behind: Föräldradeltagande för inkludering och effektivitet." [Parental Participation for Inclusion and Efficiency]*Educare* 2-3: 221–249. Malmö University: Malmö.

Tallberg Broman, I., and L. Holmberg. 2007. *Lärare i förskola och grundskola om inflytande, jämställdhet och mångfald* [Teachers at Preschool and Primary School on Influence, Equality and Diversity]. Malmö University: School of Teacher Education.

Tobin, J., A. E. Arzubiaga, and J. Keys Adair. 2013. *Children Crossing Borders*. Immigrant Parent and Teacher Perspectives on Preschool. Thousand Oaks: Russell SAGE Foundation.

Tobin, J., Y. Hsueh, and M. Karasawa. 2009. *Preschool in Three Cultures. Revisited*. Chicago: The University of Chicago Press.

Urban, M., M. Vandenbroeck, Katrien Van Laere, A. Lazzari, and J. Peeters. 2012. "Towards Competent Systems in Early Childhood Education and Care. Implications for Policy and Practice." *European Journal of Education* 47 (4): 508–526. doi:10.1111/ejed.12010.

Yarosh, S., A. Tang, S. Mokashi, and G. D. Abowd. 2013. "'Almost Touching': Parent–Child Remote Communication Using the ShareTable System. *CSCW '13*." Proceedings of the 2013 conference on computer supported cooperative work, San Antonio, Texas, USA. February 23–27: 181–192. doi:10.1145/2441776.2441798.

5 An observational assessment of parent–teacher cocaring relationships in infant–toddler classrooms

Elly Q. Maras, Sarah N. Lang and Sarah J. Schoppe-Sullivan

ABSTRACT

Cocaring encompasses how parents and teachers work together to coordinate caregiving. Two critical components of cocaring have demonstrated importance for child and parent well-being: support and undermining. Although parent–teacher relationships have been studied via qualitative interviews and through self-administered questionnaires, little observational research has been conducted. This study sought to develop an observational approach to measure the quality of cocaring relationships by recording and coding parent–teacher interactions. Eighteen mother–teacher dyads of 6- to 36-month-old children from six childcare centers were video recorded during morning drop-off and evening pick-up times. Fifty-eight videos were coded for eight dimensions of cocaring quality, representing observed support and undermining. Results indicated strong inter-rater reliability and associations amongst the individual dimensions consistent with theory, thus supporting initial construct validity. This study offers a new observational tool to assess cocaring relationships and provides practical information about the kinds of behaviors that convey support and undermining in everyday interactions.

Much of the literature on family–teacher partnerships has focused on communication with families, parental engagement or involvement (Jor'dan, Wolf, and Douglass 2012; Hujala et al. 2009; NAEYC 2009), and parents' or teachers' collective experiences in these partnerships (Bernhard et al. 1998; McGrath 2007; Nzinga-Johnson, Baker, and Aupperlee 2009). Few researchers have attempted to understand family–teacher partnerships at the dyadic level. The cocaring framework (Lang, Tolbert, Schoppe-Sullivan, and Bonomi 2016), influenced by coparenting theory and research (Feinberg 2002, 2003), offers a new lens for researchers and practitioners to understand parent–teacher interactions by defining the key components of parent–teacher relationships. Cocaring encompasses how parents and teachers work together in their caregiving roles to coordinate childrearing and contains two critical components that have demonstrated importance for child and parent well-being: support and undermining (Lang et al. 2016; Lang, Schoppe-Sullivan, and Jeon 2017; Wells, Lang, Jeon and Schoppe-Sullivan 2016). Support represents the level of trust, comfort, endorsement, encouragement and cooperation between cocaring partners, whereas undermining represents the level of distrust, contradiction, or criticism between partners, or subversion of each other's caregiving actions.

Child Care Aware of America (2016) estimates that over 11 million children aged birth to 5 years attend childcare in the United States; thus it is critical to understand the relationships among parents and teachers in early childhood settings to better support children's development. Strong parent–teacher partnerships foster a mutual understanding of the child, and hence, better collaboration in addressing a young child's needs (Lang et al. 2017; Reedy and McGrath 2010). Indeed, Halgunseth et al. (2009) found that strong parent–teacher relationships in children's early developmental years were associated with greater academic motivation, academic success, school readiness and stronger social–emotional skills later in their lives.

Cocaring relationships are especially important to the quality of care and education of infants and toddlers, as these children depend on adult caregivers to communicate their daily experiences and needs at home and school (Bradley 2010). Thus research using the cocaring framework has focused on the relationships between parents and their infant's or toddler's teacher, which, for many families in the United States, is their first cocaring experience (Lang et al. 2016). Although cocaring relationships have been studied via qualitative methods and through self-administered questionnaires (Bernhard et al. 1998; Lang et al. 2016; Lang et al. 2017; McGrath 2007; Nzinga-Johnson et al. 2009; Wells et al. 2016), observational research is necessary to understand the specific behaviors parents and teachers display to communicate support or undermining to one another. In addition, although parents' and teachers' perceptions of their relationships in early care and education settings are undoubtedly important, parent and teacher reports are more subject to known systematic biases than observations (Jeon, Buettner, and Snyder 2014; Mangelsdorf, Schoppe, and Buur 2000). Guided by the rich theory and tools within the coparenting literature, this study sought to develop an observational assessment of the quality of cocaring relationships and deepen our understanding of these relationships by recording and coding daily parent–teacher interactions.

An understanding of cocaring born from coparenting research

The cocaring concept is rooted in a multidimensional model of coparenting developed by Feinberg (2002, 2003), who defined coparenting as how well parents work together in their caregiving or parenting roles. The coparenting literature has relied heavily on observational assessments of support and undermining, and for good reason, as observational methods can provide more detailed information on the actions that constitute each dimension, as well as avoid the biases inherent in asking members of a relationship to report on their behavior within that relationship (Van Ijzendoorn et al. 2004). Indeed, observed support and undermining have consistently predicted child social–emotional outcomes (Teubert and Pinquart 2010). In an effort to better understand how parents and teachers work together, we sought to build on this strong body of coparenting research by developing a similar observational method of assessing cocaring interactions between early childhood teachers and parents.

Beginning in infancy, young children use their parents or other primary caregivers as social references for direction when experiencing new or uncertain situations (Walden

1991). Parents also act as co-regulators of young children's attention, behavior, emotions and physiology until children mature enough to take control of these functions (Hofer 2006). Indeed, coparenting interactions may not only directly impact children (Teubert and Pinquart 2010) but also influence how well each partner parents (Feinberg 2003). Thus strong cocaring relationships likely operate in a similar fashion, helping to strengthen parent–child relationships, which in turn support children's development (Wells et al. 2016).

Cocaring: a systems approach

Previous research in early childhood education has examined children's development through Bronfenbrenner's (1986) ecological systems theory (EST), with a typical focus on EST's microsystem level (e.g. direct interactions in families or schools) rather than a focus on the mesosystem level, or the interactions between microsystems (Bradley 2010; Bronfenbrenner 1986; Wells et al. 2016). Although several studies have examined the importance of parental involvement for child development via the mesosystem (Bradley 2010; Nzinga-Johnson et al. 2009), others contend that the field has not placed enough importance on the teacher's role in cultivating or deterring family engagement or family–teacher partnerships (Hughes and MacNaughton 2000). Lang et al. (2016) recent study sought to expand the research supporting the importance of parent–teacher interactions at the mesosystem level. Their findings, from qualitative interviews and self-report questionnaires, indicate that parent–teacher, or cocaring relationships, are multidimensional (Lang et al. 2017), and that dimensions within the cocaring relationship are indeed associated with child social–emotional functioning (Wells et al. 2016).

In addition to EST, previous cocaring research has drawn insight from family systems theory (FST) (Minuchin 1985). According to FST, families are organized systems of relationships, and coparenting functions as an 'executive subsystem', in which parents co-manage family interactions and the growth and development of individual family members – particularly children (Minuchin 1985; Teubert and Pinquart 2010). In their work on cocaring, Lang et al. (2016) discovered that a similar executive subsystem operates in parent–teacher cocaring relationships. In particular, aspects of the cocaring relationship were associated with parental involvement, parent–child relationship quality and child social–emotional functioning (Lang et al. 2017; Wells et al. 2016).

FST is the main theoretical framework behind coparenting research; it assumes and seeks to understand how parents navigate and coordinate their caregiving roles, and how this coordination, or lack thereof, influences how others in the system function and develop. It is this attention to the interactions among co-managers of caregiving contexts that underlies the current study. Our ultimate goal is to develop tools to further study and thus better understand cocaring relationships between parents and teachers.

Cocaring and its key associations

A growing body of research indicates that the degree of consistency in parenting techniques influences social–emotional development for young children (Landry et al. 2001). Similarly, having the same preschool teacher throughout the year, versus multiple teachers, positively impacts child outcomes (Hale-Jinks, Knopf, and Knopf 2006).

Combining these findings, the strength of a home–school connection becomes essential to the development of young children, especially for infants and toddlers given that effective communication and coordination rest in the hands of their parents and teachers (Reedy and McGrath 2010). In addition, children likely learn from watching and participating in parent–teacher interactions. When a cocaring relationship exhibits empathy, attention and support during interactions, children may learn to mirror these positive social–emotional tendencies with others. On the other hand, when a parent or teacher acts as if the other caregiving partner should not be trusted or that his/her requests are not valid, the child may have trouble adjusting in the childcare context, or meaningfully bonding with their caregivers (Wells et al. 2016).

When a cocaring relationship is characterized by undermining behavior, this may negatively influence teacher–child attachment, consequentially disrupting the development of children's emotional regulation skills, and instead foster or sustain internalizing and externalizing behaviors (Howes et al. 1988; Wells et al. 2016). The quality of cocaring relationships may also affect child social–emotional development via parenting. Lang et al. (2017) reported that parents' perceptions of cocaring support were significantly associated with greater parental involvement at home, within the childcare center and within the child's classroom with his/her main caregiver.

Current study

Given that the quality of relationships between teachers and parents may make a lasting impression on children's social–emotional development (Halgunseth et al. 2009; Nzinga-Johnson et al. 2009; Wells et al. 2016), the current study aimed to develop an additional tool – the Cocaring Behavior Coding Manual – to evaluate the quality of cocaring relationships. Adapted from an observational measure of coparenting, this observational assessment of cocaring will also help to avoid biases associated with reliance on parent- and teacher-report measures and will increase understanding of how cocaring behaviors are enacted in daily exchanges between parents and teachers. In addition, having a valid observational tool will support future research to examine further aspects that influence cocaring functioning and its outcomes.

Methods

Sample and demographics

This study included the mothers and teachers of 18 infants and toddlers between 6 and 36 months of age, who were video recorded during pick-up and/or drop-off times in their childcare center classroom. This sample came from six full-time, licensed childcare centers in a large Midwestern city in the United States. Fifteen of the teachers identified as females and three as males. 72.2% of parents had a graduate/professional degree and 66.7% of teachers had a bachelor's degree. The mean family income was $126,400 (SD = $57,788) in U.S. Dollars. Regarding race, 72.2% of parents identified as White and 16.7% as Black. Similarly, 72.2% of teachers identified as White and 22.2% as Black. To be eligible to participate, parents needed to have a child between 6 and 36 months of age and be able to read and speak English, and their child must have attended childcare at least 25 hours per week and have been with their respective teacher participant for at least 3 months. Teacher participants were all full-time, lead teachers in an infant and/or toddler classroom.

Recruitment and data collection

After obtaining approval from the university's Institutional Review Board, the first author contacted childcare center directors to confirm that they wished to be part of the study. Once the research team received approval from the center directors, the lead author contacted teacher participants. Upon confirming teacher interest and written consent, the team contacted one family from each classroom to participate through paper flyers and face-to-face interactions at the childcare center. During recruitment, a member of the research team explained the nature of the study, i.e. video recording up to four morning drop-off and/or evening pick-up exchanges between the specific family and teacher to further understand parent–teacher relationships. Like teachers, all eligible parents provided written consent prior to participating, and we focused on only one parent–teacher dyad per classroom. To respect the parents' and teacher's interaction, research team members tried to stay out of the way and video recorded from a pre-determined location towards the back of the room with a small handheld camera. Participants were assured that they could stop participation at any time, although none chose to do so. As much as possible, we took care during the video recording to capture only the consenting teacher, parent and their child; in the event another teacher, family or child from the classroom or center entered the scene, this footage was ignored and not coded. To compensate participants, each family received a $5 gift card and each teacher received a $10 gift card.

Observational assessment

To minimize the potential influence of the video camera on these interactions, and to obtain a more complete picture of how individual dyads functioned, we gathered more than one observation of each parent–teacher pair; all dyads included in this study had between two and four coded observations. We coordinated with parents and teachers to observe and record their pick-up and drop-off times, trying, as much as possible, to capture both a pick-up and a drop-off interaction for each dyad. We recorded the entirety of each interaction until the parent left the classroom. The average length of an interaction was 364.4 seconds or 6 minutes (SD = 201.12 seconds, approximately 3.5 minutes).

Coding process

Over the course of the study, the research team recorded 58 interactions from 18 mother–teacher dyads. An undergraduate research assistant and the lead author coded each video recorded interaction using the Coparenting Behavior Coding Scale (Altenburger et al. 2014; Cowan and Cowan 1996) as their guide, adjusting where appropriate to develop the new Cocaring Behavior Coding Manual (CBCM), which allowed for objectivity and consistency between coders. The team selected the Coparenting Behavior Coding Scale[1] as the foundation of their coding process based on its strengths in providing scales that address both individual and collective behaviors of a dyad, and the measure's previous success in displaying significant associations to relevant antecedents and outcomes of observed coparenting functioning (Altenburger et al. 2014; Teubert and Pinquart 2010). The Coparenting Behavior Coding Scale, and the newly developed Cocaring Behavior Coding Manual, both contain eight dimensions including anger, coldness, competition, cooperation, displeasure, interactiveness, pleasure and warmth, each rated on a scale from very low (1) to very high (5). More details on the CBCM are provided in the Results section.

Based on the recordings, and in consultation with the other two authors who have expertise in observational and coparenting coding, the first author altered each of the eight scales to reflect cocaring actions. Because four scales are coded individually (I), i.e. coldness, displeasure, pleasure and warmth, and four scales are coded dyadically (D), i.e. anger, competition, cooperation and interactiveness, the coding team made 12 ratings per interaction. The team coded all 12 scales for each of the 58 episodes.

Scale adaptation

The two members of the coding team individually coded each interaction and used a scoring sheet to record scores as well as note general observations that influenced scoring. The coding team met on several occasions to review and discuss their individual scores. During these meetings, the team worked to distinguish between similar scales and identify behaviors that should represent them in the manual (e.g. what exactly is pleasure, and how is it different from warmth? What are behaviors exclusive to each scale?). In consultation with the other authors, the coding team gradually developed new definitions of each scale; the first author updated each of the eight cocaring scales to reflect their shared definitions regarding the behaviors and conversations observed during coding the 58 interactions. By meeting consistently, the team was able to create the CBCM with clarity and specificity that could not have been achieved without such extensive collaboration.

Conference process

After firmly establishing the criteria for each scale, both coders independently coded each video, and only conferenced when there was a discrepancy in coding. Criteria for the team to conference on an interaction were as follows: being 1 point off on 4 or more of the 12 ratings and/or being 2 points off on 1 or more ratings. If a video met one of these conference criteria, the coding team reviewed the video together and assigned joint final scores. Overall, the team conferenced on 19% (11/58) of the interactions.

Results

Cocaring behavior coding manual

In general, the definitions and defining characteristics of each scale within the CBCM were highly similar to those within the Coparenting Behavior Coding Scale. Below we provide a general overview of what each scale represents and, when appropriate, describe adaptations we made to the Coparenting Behavior Coding Scale to account for differences in cocaring versus coparenting relationships.

Observed support

Observed Support is an overarching construct that is characterized by indications of giving and receiving help and support, engaging in effective communication and enjoying the overall connection within the cocaring relationship. It is composed of four coding scales: cooperation (D), interactiveness (D), pleasure (I) and warmth (I). See Figure 1 and Table 1 for further details.

1. Cooperation (D). Cooperation reflects the degree to which partners work together to help and support one another in caring for the child; support can be instrumental, emotional or both.

Cocaring cooperation was demonstrated both through physical cooperation, e.g. packing up child's things from the day, as well as verbal conversations about home/

Observed Support: indications of giving and receiving help and support, engaging in effective communication, and enjoying the overall connnection within the cocaring realtionship.
- **Cooperation:** help and support between partners (D)
- **Interactiveness:** degree to which partners engage with each other (D)
- **Pleasure:** partner enjoys sharing in cocaring roles (I)
- **Warmth:** connection between partners is visible (I)

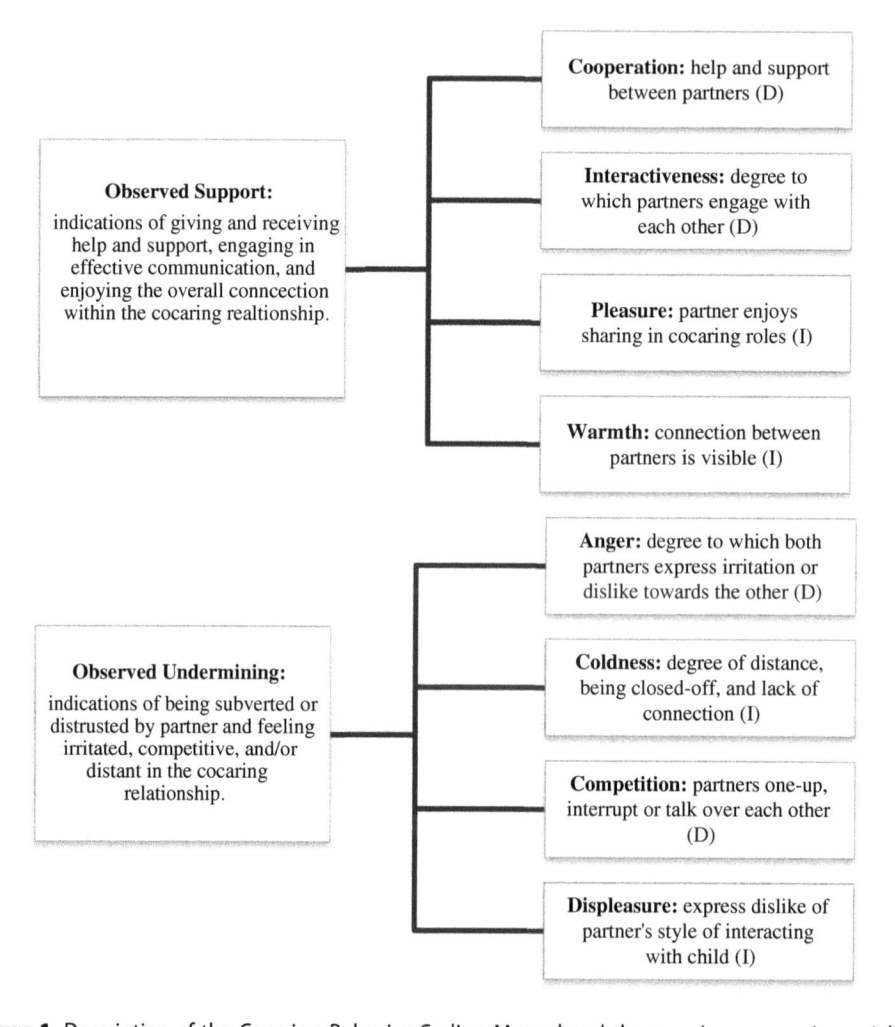

Observed Undermining: indications of being subverted or distrusted by partner and feeling irritated, competitive, and/or distant in the cocaring relationship.
- **Anger:** degree to which both partners express irritation or dislike towards the other (D)
- **Coldness:** degree of distance, being closed-off, and lack of connection (I)
- **Competition:** partners one-up, interrupt or talk over each other (D)
- **Displeasure:** express dislike of partner's style of interacting with child (I)

Figure 1. Description of the Cocaring Behavior Coding Manual and the cocaring composite variables.
Note: These scales were adapted from the Coparenting Behavior Coding Scales (Altenburger et al. 2014; Cowan and Cowan 1996). As each mother–teacher dyad was video recorded two to four times, we averaged each dyad's scores across their recorded interactions. (D) indicates the scale is coded at the dyadic level, whereas (I) indicates it is coded at the individual level.

Table 1. Descriptive Statistics of the cocaring scales that compose observed support and undermining.

Support

Scale	Cooperation	Interactiveness	Teacher pleasure	Parent pleasure	Teacher warmth	Parent warmth
M	2.74	3.08	2.86	2.80	2.83	2.70
SD	.53	.58	.46	.50	.47	.58
ICC	.86	.77	.83	.88	.82	.87
Range	1.75–3.67	1.88–4.5	2.00–4.00	2.00–3.67	1.75–3.50	1.25–3.67

Undermining

Scale	Anger	Teacher coldness	Parent coldness	Competition	Teacher displeasure	Parent displeasure
M	1.46	1.51	1.79	1.69	1.48	1.60
SD	.36	.45	.66	.44	.42	.48
ICC	.77	.86	.87	.80	.84	.86
Range	1.00–2.25	1.00–2.50	1.00–3.63	1.00–2.63	1.00–2.50	1.00–3.00

Note: M = mean; SD = standard deviation; ICC = intraclass correlation coefficient; Range = minimum and maximum scores, averaged across two to four observations per mother–teacher dyad (total number of observations = 58, total sample = 18 dyads). ICCs are calculated based on the 58 observations; the M, SD and range are based on the scores averaged across coders, or when appropriate, the conferenced scores and the average across the two to four observations per mother–teacher dyad.

center practices. We expanded upon the previous definition of coparenting cooperation by including physical and verbal examples of the kinds of cooperation evident in cocaring relationships, e.g. 'Parent feels comfortable transferring child to teacher for the day and the teacher aids in a positive transfer through conversation and/or action.' Examples of partners displaying moderate to high cooperation included having constructive conversation about how long the child napped while at the center and agreeing on ways to improve sleeping through the night at home, or when one partner retrieved the child's belongings from her cubby while the other partner helped to guide the child off the playground.

2. Interactiveness (D). Interactiveness reflects the degree to which partners engage and talk with one another. Either partner can initiate the interaction, and while interactiveness is often verbal, it can also be demonstrated non-verbally in the form of smiles, glances, nods or other expressions. The interactiveness rating is more an assessment of quantity of interaction. Although the emotional tone of the interaction can be positive or negative, this dimension most closely aligned with observed support as higher interactiveness among cocaring partners was typically positive and usually added to the overall quality of the interaction. The defining features of interactiveness for coparenting and cocaring interactions remained essentially the same, except that our team eliminated examples of interaction that exclusively pertain to those in a romantic relationship (i.e. spouses who are also parents), for example removing any mention of the word 'touch'. In addition, we added new examples of interactiveness that reflected the more professional nature of a cocaring relationship: (1) partners carry on a conversation about their personal lives, daily happenings or other related topic and (2) partners pursue discussion of tangents in their conversation, which adds to the length and overall depth of interaction.

3. Pleasure (I). Pleasure reflects that a partner enjoys collaborating and sharing in a caregiving role (e.g. by laughing or smiling), and that he/she appears pleased with and is comfortable watching the other caregiver's relationship with the child. In addition, a partner may display humor or playfulness with the other about his or her respective caregiving practices/styles and his or her relationship with the child. The cocaring definition of pleasure is identical to Altenburger et al. (2014) coparenting definition; it was only edited to remove the term 'couple', replacing it with 'partners'.

4. Warmth (I). Warmth reflects the positive regard one partner displayed for the other (e.g. by smiling at and conveying kind messages). High warmth is characterized by an authentic generosity of affect and self, and the partner provides appropriate and authentic reassurance, encouragement and emotional support – the partner is responsive. Cowan and Cowan (1996) and Altenburger et al. (2014) coparenting definition of *Warmth* gives a significant amount of attention to the couple's level of affection – whether it is physical or inferred. Due to the more professional nature of the cocaring relationship, we restructured this definition of warmth, removing phrases like 'touch' and 'playfulness' that did not appropriately fit the parent–teacher context. Indeed, physical affection was very rare and if seen was rated as '5'. Additionally, the defining features were updated to include greetings/goodbyes as a way to quantify a warm regard toward the other partner; purposeful, genuine greetings/goodbyes conveyed the connectedness that existed between partners.

Observed undermining

Observed undermining is an overarching construct that is characterized by indications of being subverted or distrusted by the partner and feeling irritated, competitive, and/or distant in the cocaring relationship. It is composed of four coding scales: anger (D), coldness (I), competition (D) and displeasure (I). Please see Figure 1 and Table 1 for further details.

1. Anger (D). Anger reflects the degree to which partners express dislike or irritation toward each other or each other's actions. Anger may be expressed more indirectly (e.g. becoming quiet and withdrawn with an annoyed quality) or more directly (e.g. through sarcasm, verbal irritation). There were no changes to the coparenting definition of anger. We expanded the cocaring definition around the concept of partner disapproval to provide a clearer definition of moderate anger: there is obvious disapproval about the child's care from either partner (e.g. frustrated facial expression, verbal sighs), but that partner does not verbally state or more overtly act out their anger.

2. Coldness (I). Coldness reflects a partner's closed-off, and generally uninterested and apathetic approach toward the other. High coldness is evident when a partner keeps distance between him/herself and the other partner, and/or displays disdain for the other caregiver (e.g. by being curt, snubbing or generally aloof when a partner attempts to engage). When editing the coparenting definition of coldness, we replaced phrases like 'affection' with 'emotional connection' to reflect the less intimate nature of the cocaring relationship. One aspect of coldness that was not evident in the coparenting definition is how the partners treat the child during the interaction; we adapted the coldness definition to account for these instances: 'Partner ignores any attempt for interaction with the child'. This expression of coldness may include one partner not reacting to the other's dyadic interaction with the child or one partner withdrawing from the situation so the other can take over the care of or interaction with the child (i.e. transition from home to school).

3. Competition (D). Competition reflects partners trying to outdo each other's efforts to play with, work with or teach the child. Partners may interrupt or talk over one another and vie for the child's attention. Generally, the coparenting and cocaring definitions of competition remain nearly identical. However, we adapted the definition for moderate competition to include more covert displays of how one partner is better at caring for or attending to the child. For example, a conversation about how the child is at home versus at the center where partners display varying opinions or perspectives on the issue, indicating through statements or body language, the other partner may be incorrect.

When discussing and coding the observations, we noted there were interactions which, in general, had a more positive tone (i.e. higher on the dimensions listed under support), as well as interactions with a more negative tone (i.e. lower on the dimensions listed under support and higher on the aspects of undermining), that included conversations with a more subtle competitive nature, specifically focused around child progress at home versus at the center (e.g. taking naps, eating specific foods, learning to crawl). Therefore, we updated the coding manual to account for these instances. Specifically, the definition of moderate cocaring competition states

> Partners are visibly trying to "one up" each other but only on occasion; competition doesn't interfere with child's play, performance, or progress. One clear instance of competition is displayed (or a number of more subtle instances). These instances are not considered intentional (intentional instances get at least a "4"). There may be a conversation about how the child is at home versus at school, and partners have a varying opinion/perspective on it.

As one specific example, in one interaction, a mother and teacher discussed encouraging the child to sit up at the center to support his attempt at turning over onto his stomach. When the mother replied that he always does that (and successfully) at home, the conversation's tone changed from relaxed and positive to competitive and negative. Through identifying the overall shifts in tone and affect during interactions, our team was able to more accurately differentiate between specific scales when it came to assigning scores.

4. Displeasure (I). Displeasure reflects that the partner does not like conversing or working with the other caregiver. The partner may express dislike of the other's relationship with or interaction style with the child either directly or indirectly (e.g. through sarcasm). The definition for cocaring displeasure remained largely the same as that within coparenting interactions, with the exception of updating the terminology where appropriate, i.e. changing 'parent(s)' to 'partner(s)'.

Observational scales

In order to address the reliability of these adapted scales, we first assessed the inter-rater reliability of each scale by calculating the Intraclass Correlation Coefficient (ICC), or the percentage of absolute agreement between the coders, for each of the eight scales. The typical standard for inter-rater reliability in observational research is .7 (Koch 1982). Intraclass correlations for the 12 ratings, across the 58 video recorded observations, indicated high inter-rater reliability, ranging from .77 to .88 (see Table 1).

Scale intercorrelations

Appropriate correlations among the scales offered initial validity for the newly adapted observational cocaring coding system and also promoted theoretical construct validity (Table 2, Figure 1). For example, parent and teacher pleasure positively correlated with cooperation $r = .73$, $p < .01$ and $r = .84$, $p = < .05$, respectively, offering evidence that when both cocaring partners are individually enjoying the interaction, it is reflected in observed behaviors indicative of collaboration that are dyadically coded. This finding is consistent across all combinations of other individual supportive behaviors and their supportive dyadic counterparts (i.e. warmth and interactiveness, warmth and cooperation, and pleasure and interactiveness).

In addition, findings show that cocaring partners may mirror behaviors at an individual level; for example, teacher displeasure was positively correlated with parent displeasure $r = .70$, $p = < .01$. Notice that though high, the correlation was not 1.0, indicating that although there are often similarities across cocaring partners, each partner's behavior is also unique and the individual scales facilitate assessment of these differences.

Significant negative correlations among the eight dimensions were also evident. For example, anger was negatively associated with cooperation $r = -.61$, $p = < .01$, offering further evidence that the cocaring dimensions were related in expected ways.

Composite variables for observed support and undermining

Consistent with research on coparenting (Jia and Schoppe-Sullivan 2011) and in alignment with the intercorrelations among the scales (Table 2), we grouped the eight scales (i.e. 12 ratings) under two overarching dimensions of observed cocaring: support and undermining (see Figure 1, Table 1). To create the composite representations of support and undermining, we summed the scales by averaging each individual and dyadic score together. The Cronbach's alpha for support, comprised of parent pleasure, teacher pleasure, parent warmth, teacher warmth, cooperation and interactiveness, was 0.94. The Cronbach's alpha for undermining, comprised of parent displeasure, teacher displeasure, parent coldness, teacher coldness, competition and anger, was 0.86. The mean score for observed support was 2.84 (SD = 0.46) and the mean score for observed undermining was 1.91 (SD = 0.44), indicating participants' cocaring relationships were generally positive. The mean, standard deviation and range for each individual scale are reported in Table 1.

Discussion

Our study – the first to use an observational assessment of the cocaring relationship – has yielded valuable information regarding the cocaring interactions that may affect parents' and teachers' relationships with children and ultimately children's development. In particular, the adaptation of the Cocaring Behavior Coding Manual furthers a fine-grained

Table 2. Correlations between cocaring scales.

	T. pleasure	P. pleasure	T. warmth	P. warmth	Cooperation	Interactiveness	T. displeasure	P. displeasure	T. coldness	P. coldness	Anger	Competition
T. pleasure	1											
P. pleasure	.82**	1										
T. warmth	.81**	.79**	1									
P. warmth	.76**	.94**	.83**	1								
Cooperation	.73**	.84**	.56*	.82**	1							
Interactiveness	.53*	.69**	.77**	.78**	.41	1						
T. displeasure	-.52*	-.46	-.42	-.37	-.39	-.16	1					
P. displeasure	-.47*	-.66**	-.54*	-.59*	-.48*	-.42	.70**	1				
T. coldness	-.80**	-.77**	-.83**	-.75**	-.60**	-.71**	.67**	.70**	1			
P. coldness	-.66**	-.82**	-.79**	-.90**	-.80**	-.74**	.41	.60**	.80**	1		
Anger	-.38	-.48*	-.35	-.49*	-.61**	-.07	.37	.62**	.43	.61**	1	
Competition	-.05	-.17	-.04	-.11	-.09*	-.08	.21	.49*	.34	.32**	.52*	1

Note: **$p < .01$; *$p < .05$; T = Teacher; P = Parent.

scholarly understanding of the behaviors that characterize more positive or more negative cocaring relationships. The high levels of inter-rater reliability achieved by the coding team, as well as the appropriate intercorrelations among the scales and high alphas for the composite variables, provide initial evidence of the reliability and construct validity of the observational assessment and coding manual, highlighting the CBCM's potential as a strong tool for future cocaring research.

Our study has also provided valuable practical information to the field of early child education, as it helps educators of young children understand how they can better communicate support, and decrease displays of undermining, in their everyday interactions with parents. The CBCM can be used as a guide to analyze parent–teacher relationships in practice. When used as a practical tool, the manual can provide childcare directors and teachers with new insight into specific qualities of supportive and undermining behaviors, exclusive to parent–teacher interactions. Through the extensive observation of parent–teacher interactions, we are closer to educating parents and teachers on how to successfully navigate new cocaring relationships.

The critical actions of support

Unlike in coparenting relationships, support from teachers is expected by families in childcare settings and is often regulated by childcare center policies and rules (Lang et al. 2017). The conceptualization of support born from this observational research with its emphasis on cooperation, interaction and warmth in parent–teacher relationships, is similar to that of family-centered practices, which emphasizes that parents are the key decision makers in their children's lives as well as the need to collaborate with families in caregiving. These family-centered intervention-based techniques focus on individual, flexible and responsive care and have been associated with positive outcomes for families and children (Dunst 2002; Forry et al. 2011). However, our conceptualization of support also extends this work, in that it includes an emphasis on encouragement and enjoyment in parent–teacher interactions.

In this study, teachers and parents who displayed high levels of interactiveness also typically exhibited high pleasure and warmth, which in turn was associated with high cooperation. When parents are able to express themselves openly (e.g. engaging in a positive off-topic conversation or feeding off of positive non-verbal cues of the partner), they may feel validated and encouraged to share more during interactions with teachers. In turn, they become more assured and comfortable in their decision to put their child in the care of this teacher, leading to increased parental involvement in the classroom. From these supportive cocaring interactions, parents may also be able to collect pertinent information that can aid them in being more involved as parents at home, ultimately strengthening their relationship with their child as well.

In Lang et al. (2017) recent self-report study, parents' perceptions of cocaring support demonstrated unique positive associations with three forms of parent-reported parental involvement; in addition, aspects of the cocaring relationship are related to parent–child closeness (Wells et al. 2016). Thus a key factor in cultivating cocaring support may simply be initiating greater interaction in the daily exchanges during drop-off and pick-up (sometimes called welcoming and reunion), which can establish strong relationships between partners and aid in positive child development. However strong these associations are, it is important to note that parents who are highly involved tend to develop more supportive relationships, spend more time at home and at the child care center with their child, and experience more opportunities to receive the teacher's support (Lang et al. 2017). Because connections between support and parental involvement may be bidirectional, future research should focus on examining these pathways with longitudinal or experimental methods, investigating interventions aimed at strengthening cocaring relationships.

The critical actions of undermining

Undermining can adversely impact cocaring relationships and, consequentially, child development as its presence may prevent children from establishing proper self-soothing strategies or taking age-appropriate risks in their exploratory, sensory and social experiences (Wells et al. 2016). In our observations, the high correlations between teacher and parent coldness, and parent and teacher displeasure, suggest that cocaring partners tend to mirror each other's behaviors. For example, multiple parents withdrew from the cocaring interaction by allowing their child's teacher to take over the care of the child during transition from home to school. In response, the teacher would focus solely on the child, closing off potential opportunities to foster deeper engagement or initiate coordinated care with the parent. In this way, undermining can deter partners from sharing important information (e.g. routines and useful ideas about the child's sleeping and eating patterns) and reinforcing habits across home and child care center settings that are beneficial for the child (Lang et al. 2017). Additionally, this type of interaction may demonstrate to the child that his/her parent (or teacher) is incapable of effective care, disturbing the parent–child or teacher–child relationship (Wells et al. 2016).

On the basis of our observations, we believe it is important for teachers to model warmth and pleasure in their interactions with parents with the intention of successfully collaborating as cocaring partners, and to purposely and consciously interact with parents, not only with the child. However, it is also important to consider how children's characteristics, such as temperament or social–emotional challenges, may influence parent–teacher interactions and potentially place greater stress on the cocaring relationship. The presence of child dysregulation and internalizing behaviors may be a cause as well as a consequence of undermining in cocaring relationships (Wells et al. 2016). Future research should examine how observed cocaring interactions are associated with child characteristics, following changes over time to illuminate directional pathways of influence.

Limitations

Because this study introduces the first observational assessment of parent–teacher cocaring relationships in childcare settings, we should consider the results within the parameters of our research design and sample. First, we must address the potential effect that the observer and video recording may have had on participants. Because parents and teachers were aware of our presence, they may have consciously chosen to enhance or suppress the discussion of certain topics or actions towards one another. We attempted to minimize this effect by video recording each dyad more than once, trying to capture each dyad a total of four times. In addition, observing these daily interactions at welcoming and reunion provides one window into parent–teacher relationships; however, the interactions may be very different from those that take place within parent–teacher conferences, which may occasionally be more contentious as parents and teachers discuss children's developmental progression or lack thereof. Future research should examine cocaring interactions across multiple contexts involving parents and teachers.

Second, it is important to consider the constraints on our sample's generalizability in relation to the study's capacity to represent the quality of cocaring relationships across diverse populations. We collected our data in a large city in the Midwestern United States. In general, participants were well educated and although our sample represented a variety of childcare settings (i.e. urban and suburban neighborhoods), our sample was predominantly White, with only 16.7% of parents and 22.2% of teachers identifying as Black. Also, parents who chose to participate in the study may have already been more involved at the childcare center or had a strong interest in their child's development, especially as it relates to their relationships with teachers.

Conclusion

In conclusion, the information provided by this study furthers our theoretical understanding of parent–teacher relationships for very young children and offers a new tool – the adapted Cocaring Behavior Coding Manual – to advance research and practice in the early childhood education field. The manual provides a way to identify and interpret supportive and undermining behaviors as they play out in parent–teacher interactions, and could be used to educate parents and teachers on how to improve the quality of their cocaring relationships. Thus the manual can serve as the foundation for the development and evaluation of intervention strategies aimed at strengthening the cocaring relationship by targeting behaviors of both parents and teachers, in addition to a research tool to further investigate parent–teacher relationships. In light of this study's contributions, we are one step closer towards improving cocaring relationships to support the positive development of the increasing number of children in care settings.

Note

1. The epistemological framework of the CBCM is positivist in nature; it assumes that with carefully defined scales an external observer, given enough time and an appropriate context, can make an objective assessment of the quality of the interactions they observe and assign a number to quantify the level of each dimension displayed.

Disclosure statement

No potential conflict of interest was reported by the authors.

References

Altenburger, L. E., S. J. Schoppe-Sullivan, S. N. Lang, D. J. Bower, and C. M. Kamp Dush. 2014. "Associations between Prenatal Coparenting Behavior and Observed Coparenting Behavior at 9-months Postpartum." *Journal of Family Psychology* 28 (4): 495–504.

Bernhard, J., M. L. Lefebvre, K. M. Kilbride, G. Chud, and R. Lange. 1998. "Troubled Relationships in Early Childhood Education: Parent–Teacher Interactions in Ethnoculturally Diverse Childcare Settings." *Early Education & Development* 9 (1): 5–28. doi:10.1207/s15566935eed0901_1

Bradley, R. H. 2010. "From Home to Day Care: Chaos in the Family/Child-care Mesosystem." In *Chaos and its Influence on Children's Development: An Ecological Perspective*, edited by G. W. Evans, and T. D. Wachs, 135–153. Washington, DC,US: American Psychological Association doi:10.1037/12057-009.

Bronfenbrenner, U. 1986. "Ecology of the Family as A Context for Human Development: Research Perspectives." *Developmental Psychology* 22: 723–742. doi:10.1037/0012-1649.22.6.723

Child Care Aware of America. 2016. *Child Care in America 2016 State Fact Sheets*. Arlington, VA: Child Care Aware of America.

Cowan, C. P., and P. A. Cowan. 1996. "Schoolchildren and Their Families Project: Description of Co-parenting Style Ratings." Unpublished coding scales. Berkeley.

Dunst, C. J. 2002. "Family-centered Practices: Birth through High School." *The Journal of Special Education* 36 (3): 141–149. doi:10.1177/00224669020360030401

Feinberg, M. E. 2002. "Coparenting and the Transition to Parenthood: A Framework for Prevention." *Clinical Child and Family Psychology Review* 5 (3): 173–195.

Feinberg, M. E. 2003. "The Internal Structure and Ecological Context of Coparenting: A Framework for Research and Intervention." *Parenting: Science and Practice* 3 (2): 95–131. doi:10.1207/S15327922PAR0302_01

Forry, N. D., S. Moodie, S. Simkin, and L. Rothenberg. 2011. *Family–Provider Relationships: A Multidisciplinary Review of High Quality Practices and Associations with Family, Child, and Provider Outcomes (Issue Brief OPRE 2011-26a)*. Washington, DC: Office of Planning, Research and Evaluation, Administration for Children and Families, U.S. Department of Health and Human Services.

Hale-Jinks, C., H. Knopf, and H. Knopf. 2006. "Tackling Teacher Turnover in Child Care: Understanding Causes and Consequences, Identifying Solutions." *Childhood Education* 82 (4): 219–226.

Halgunseth, L. C., A. Peterson, D. R. Stark, and S. Moodie. 2009. *Family Engagement, Diverse Families, and Early Childhood Education Programs: An Integrated Review of the Literature*. Washington, DC: NAEYC. Retrieved from: http://www.naeyc.org/files/naeyc/file/ecprofessional/EDFLiterature%20Review.pdf.

Hofer, M. A. 2006. "Psychobiological Roots of Early Attachment." *Current Directions in Psychological Science* 15 (2): 84–88. doi:10.1111/j.0963-7214.2006.00412.x.

Howes, C., C. Rodning, D. C. Galluzzo, and L. Myers. 1988. "Attachment and Childcare: Relationships with Mother and Caregiver." *Early Childhood Research Quarterly* 3 (4): 403–416. doi:10.1016/0885-2006(88)90037-3

Hughes, P., and G. MacNaughton. 2000. "Consensus, Dissensus, or Community: The Politics of Parent Involvement in Early Childhood Education." *Contemporary Issues in Early Childhood* 1 (3): 241–258. doi:10.2304/ciec.2000.1.3.2

Hujala, E., L. Turja, M. F. Gaspar, M. Veisson, and M. Waniganayake. 2009. "Perspectives of Early Childhood Teachers on Parent–Teacher Partnerships in Five European Countries." *European Early Childhood Education Research Journal* 17 (1): 57–76. doi:10.1080/13502930802689046

Jeon, L., C. K. Buettner, and A. R. Snyder. 2014. "Pathways from Teacher Depression and Childcare Quality to Child Behavioral Problems." *Journal of Consulting and Clinical Psychology* 82 (2): 225–235. doi:10.1037/a0035720

Jia, R., and S. J. Schoppe-Sullivan. 2011. "Relations Between Coparenting and Father Involvement in Families with Preschool Aged Children." *Developmental Psychology* 47 (1): 106–118. doi:10.1037/a0020802

Jor'dan, J. R., K. G. Wolf, and A. Douglass. 2012. "Strengthening Families in Illinois: Increasing Family Engagement in Early Childhood Programs." *Young Children* 67 (5): 18–23.

Koch, G. G. 1982. "Intraclass Correlation Coefficient." In *Encyclopedia of Statistical Sciences*, Vol. 4, 213–217. New York: John Wiley & Sons.

Landry, S. H., K. E. Smith, P. R. Swank, M. A. Assel, and S. Vellet. 2001. "Does Early Responsive Parenting have a Special Importance for Children's Development or is Consistency Across Early Childhood Necessary?" *Developmental Psychology* 37 (3): 387–403. doi:10.1037/0012-1649.37.3.387

Lang, S. N., S. J. Schoppe-Sullivan, and L. Jeon. 2017. "Examining A Self-report Measure of Parent–Teacher Cocaring Relationships and Associations with Parental Involvement." *Early Education and Development* 28 (1), doi:10.1080/10409289.2016.1195672.

Lang, S. N., A. R. Tolbert, S. J. Schoppe-Sullivan, and A. Bonomi. 2016. "A Cocaring Framework for Infants and Toddlers: Applying a Model of Coparenting to Parent–Teacher Relationships." *Early Childhood Research Quarterly*, 34 (1): 40–52. doi:10.1016/j.ecresq.2015.08.004

Mangelsdorf, S. C., S. J. Schoppe, and H. Buur. 2000. "The Meaning of Parental Reports: A Contextual Approach to the Study of Temperament and Behavior Problems in Childhood." In *Temperament and personality development across the lifespan*, edited by V. J. Molfese, and D. L. Molfese, 121–140. Mahwah, NJ: Erlbaum.

McGrath, W. H. 2007. "Ambivalent Partners: Power, Trust and the Partnership in Relationships between Mothers and Teachers in a Full-time Child Care Center." *Teachers College Record* 109 (6): 1401–1422.

Minuchin, P. 1985. "Families and Individual Development: Provocations from the Field of Family Therapy." *Child Development* 56 (2): 289–302.

National Association for the Education of Young Children. 2009. Developmentally Appropriate Practice in Early Childhood Programs Serving Children from Birth Through Age 8. *Position Statement*. http://www.naeyc.org/files/naeyc/file/positions/PSDAP.pdf.

Nzinga-Johnson, S., J. A. Baker, and A. Aupperlee. 2009. "Teacher–Parent Relationships and School Involvement among Racially and Educationally Ddiverse Parents of Kindergartners." *The Elementary School Journal* 110 (1): 81–91. doi:10.1086/598844

Reedy, C. K., and W. H. McGrath. 2010. "Can You Hear Me Now? Staff–Parent Communication in Childcare Centers." *Early Child Development and Care* 180 (3): 347–357. doi:10.1080/03004430801908418

Teubert, D., and M. Pinquart. 2010. "The Association Between Coparenting and Child Adjustment: A Meta-Analysis." *Parenting: Science and Practice* 10 (4): 286–307. doi:10.1080/15295192.2010.492040

Van Ijzendoorn, M. H., C. M. Vereijken, M. J. Bakermans-Kranenburg, and J. M. Riksen-Walraven. 2004. "Assessing Attachment Security with the Attachment Q Sort: Meta-analytic Evidence for the Validity of the Observer AQS." *Child Development* 75 (4): 1188–1213.

Walden, T. A. 1991. "Infant Social Referencing." In *The Development of Emotion Regulation and Dysregulation. Cambridge Studies in Social and Emotional Development*, edited by J. Garber, and K. A. Dodge, 69–88. New York, NY: Cambridge University Press. doi:10.1017/CBO9780511663963.005.

Wells, M. B., S. N. Lang, L. Jeon, and S. J. Schoppe-Sullivan. 2016, May. "Children's Social-emotional Adjustment and the Importance of the Parent–Teacher Cocaring Relationship." Presented at the Biennial International Conference on Infant Studies, New Orleans, LA.

6 Chinese and German teachers' and parents' conceptions of learning at play – similarities, differences, and (in)consistencies

Shu-Chen Wu, Stefan Faas and Steffen Geiger

ABSTRACT
This qualitative study investigated Chinese and German teachers' and parents' conceptions and understanding of learning at play. A total of 28 teachers and 12 parents took part in this study. Among the participants, 12 kindergarten teachers (6 German and 6 Chinese) were interviewed to obtain their perspectives on learning at play. These participants assisted the researchers in the selection of exemplary play episodes used in their own classrooms. Four three-minute videos containing the largest amount of learning elements based on the teachers' views were selected from each culture. Applying video-cued multivocal ethnography, the selected video clips were shown to 16 other teachers (8 German and 8 Chinese) and 12 parents (6 German and 6 Chinese) in focus groups to elicit their conceptions and understanding of learning at play. The findings revealed different social and cultural representations of educational activities between Hong Kong and Germany, the contributions of which are important and useful for professional practices and curricular policies in these two countries currently undergoing education reforms.

The importance of play in children's development and learning in early childhood education was already recognized by Friedrich Fröbel (1782–1852) and confirmed by current research in many ways: Play is deemed not only a medium of learning and child development but also a context of learning possibilities (Wood 2009). Moreover, play facilitates children's thinking (Craft, Matthews, and McConnon 2012; Robson and Rowe 2012), cognitive and emotional development (Singer, Golinkoff, and Hirsh-Pasek 2006), creativity (Howard-Jones, Taylor, and Sutton 2002; Russ 2004), language (Galeano 2011), literacy (Roskos and Christie 2007), and development of social competence (Uren and Stagnitti 2009). However, the relationship between play and learning (e.g. play leads to learning) is not viewed as a matter, of course, in different cultures. For example, in the Chinese tradition, play and learning are juxtaposed as two different activities. The Trimetric Classic, an enlightening book for children, introduced the famous saying *qin you gong, xi wu yi* ('hard work makes the master, while play brings no good'), while there was also the traditional Chinese idiom *ye jing yu qin, huang yu xi* ('a career is refined by hard work but ruined by play'). These conventional notions are often quoted when instructing children, which has affected Chinese perceptions of play. In today's Chinese classrooms, play continues to be regarded as unimportant, as it is often used instrumentally by teachers to achieve learning and teaching objectives (Cheng and Wu 2013). However, in certain Western societies, play is considered as a part of learning: 'By that we could conceive of play and learning as being inseparable and also associated to children's life-world and how they experience their surrounding world' (Merleau-Ponty 1962, cited in Pramling Samuelsson and Johansson 2006, 50). Flitner (1972, 41), a German educational scientist, underlines this statement as follows:

> What the child learns, above all, in playing is – play. He acquires the adroitness or adeptness; the ways of behavior; the techniques; the improvisation and the social systems that are required for the appropriate methods of play. The child becomes at home in a life style or aspect of living that is indispensable for humanity, for the assertion of persons as persons within a system of pressure.

This conception of play and learning is typical in the German tradition, where it is often associated with a holistic approach to early childhood education rather than specific subject areas, scientific disciplines, and instructional methods (Standing Conference of the Ministers for Youth Affairs in Germany and Standing Conference of the Ministers of Education and Cultural Affairs in Germany 2004).

According to these orientations, it is reasonable to conclude that teachers in Hong Kong and Germany may have culturally different conceptions and understandings of play and learning, particularly learning at play. This may also be true as far as the interpretation of play theories and the implementation of learning through play are concerned (Cheng and Stimpson 2004). Wu and Rao (2011) were able to show plausibly that Chinese teachers in Hong Kong, in contrast to German kindergarten teachers' very clear concept of free play, regard various activities and games as play. Moreover, Chinese teachers usually do not associate play with learning, and therefore conceive and practice play and learning differently (Wu and Rao 2011; Wu 2014). Chinese teachers also instill academic learning in children's play (Cheng and Stimpson 2004; Fung and Cheng 2012), whereas German teachers seek rules, social learning, and decision-making in free play (Wu and Rao 2011). Such findings instigated the current study to further investigate teachers' and parents' conceptions of learning at play in Hong Kong and Germany.[1]

Reflecting on these aspects is important because teachers and parents are 'human agents' (Dahlberg, Moss, and Pence 1999, 62) of kindergarten education. Teachers integrate their beliefs into their practices (Fang 1996), which influences their teaching practices to some extent, although sometimes their beliefs may not be consistent with their practices (Stipek and Byler 1997). Alternatively, although parents may not directly influence classroom teaching and learning, their beliefs are reflected in how they educate their children, who in turn reflect this in their classroom activities. For example, Parmar, Harkness, and Super (2004) have shown that parents' notions about play may affect how children play in kindergarten, while Göncü, Mistry, and Mosier (2000) have shown that the way children play may be influenced by adults' beliefs. Furthermore, parents may have perspectives that are either consistent (Hegde and Cassidy 2009) or inconsistent

(Bennett, DeLuca, and Bruns 1997; Joshia 2009) with those of teachers, and the (in)consistencies between parents' and teachers' beliefs can have implications for education policies and practices (Piotrkowskia, Botskob, and Matthews 2000).

Background of the study

This study investigated teachers' and parents' conceptions of children's learning at play in two different contexts, namely Germany and Hong Kong. In Germany, where the first kindergarten was founded, 'free play', the spontaneous ability of children to choose the mode of play according to their own enjoyment and psychological needs (Flitner 1972), is pivotal in the early curriculum and is deemed what children should mainly do in kindergarten (Wu 2011). However, this conceptual orientation was questioned with the publication of the first results of the OECD Programme of International Student Assessment (PISA), which placed Germany below the PISA average (Gruber 2006). It was followed by a debate regarding whether Germany's kindergarten curriculum with its heavy emphasis on play was enough to prepare children for school readiness (Oberhuemer 2012). An interesting comparison can, therefore, be made between the German model and the situation in the postcolonial Hong Kong, where hybridizes a pedagogy between traditional Chinese pedagogy and contemporary early childhood education (Rao, Ng, and Pearson 2009). One may question whether Hong Kong is a 'typical' case for studying the influence of Chinese culture in education, given its colonial history and western influence. The fact is though politically Hong Kong was handed over to China in 1997, in cultural terms, Chinese traditional ideas and values had often played a significant role in Hong Kong education practice even before the handover (Biggs 1996). Besides, in Hong Kong, the imported approach of play-based learning has been reiterated and advocated in early curriculum policy since the 1980s. However, a discrepancy has been found between practices and policies (Cheng 2011), as kindergartens in Hong Kong continue to focus on teaching pre-academic skills (Ho 2006; Wu and Rao 2011). Therefore, it is important to compare the conception and practice of play and learning in Hong Kong with Germany. This exploratory qualitative study examined learning at play from teachers' and parents' perspectives in two contexts: one has a long history of play pedagogy, while the other is trying to implement a globalized play-based learning approach in the classroom (Faas, Wu, and Geiger 2017).

Against this background, in the empirical study to be presented below, it was central to explore the following questions:

(1) What are the features of Chinese and German teachers' and parents' conceptions of learning at play?
(2) What are the similarities and differences between Chinese and German teachers' and parents' understanding of learning at play?

Participants

In relation to the cultural comparison established in the research questions, two Hong Kong and two German kindergartens were selected according to the following specified criteria: they (i) are run by non-profit agencies; (ii) are recognized as ordinary kindergartens in their societies; and (iii) comply with curriculum guidelines for mainstream programs. In Hong Kong, 80% of the Hong Kong kindergartens are operated on a non-profit basis (Education Bureau 2017). Two kindergartens located among public housing in Kowloon and New Territories, where 45.6% of Hongkongers live (Hong Kong Housing Authority 2016), were approached. In Germany, 33.1% of children's day-care centers are publicly owned, 63.9% are non-profit organizations (e.g. churches), and 3% are other independent organizations (i.e. for-profit organizations). In the federal state of Baden-Württemberg, where the two publicly owned kindergartens examined in the study are located in an urban area, 41.9% of the kindergartens are publicly owned, 56.3% are non-profit organizations, and 1.8% are private for-profit organizations (www.laendermonitor.de).

A total of 28 teachers and 12 parents participated in this study: six Hong Kong teachers from three class levels (Nursery, Lower-, and Upper-kindergarten classes) and six German teachers were interviewed and observed. The Chinese teachers were trained to receive a Certificate in Early Childhood Education or above, which is consistent with most (92.7%) of the Hong Kong teachers' qualification in 2016–2017 (Education Bureau 2017), while the Chinese parents' education level was secondary school. In Germany, 70% of the employees in children's day-care centers have a degree as an *Erzieherin* (a graduate of a vocational training school for social pedagogy), 13% have a qualification as a *Kinderpflegerin* (from a lower level vocational training school), and 5% have an academic degree. The remaining employees have no specific degree or early childhood education degree (Autorengruppe Fachkräftebarometer 2014). All the interviewed kindergarten teachers in Germany had a degree as an *Erzieherin*. In addition, eight teachers and six parents of children from three age groups (3–4, 4–5, and 5–6 years old) from each country watched and discussed filmed episodes of learning at play in a focus group of three to four persons. In Hong Kong, four out of the eight teachers in the focus group discussion were interviewed individually before viewing the videos.

This composition of the sample was a deliberate, non-random selection, in the sense of 'theoretical sampling' (Glaser and Strauss 2017). The focus was on their suitability for the investigation of differences and similarities in the implementation of learning at play in ordinary day-care centers in Hong Kong and Germany.

Methods

The research questions presented above were investigated by observations and interviews with the aim to triangulate the data. Participant observations during the play and learning activities were recorded to capture learning at play episodes, which provided broad in-depth information about the participants and the settings (Gay, Mills, and Airasian 2009). To ensure that the settings were unaltered and to diminish the 'observer effect' (McMillan 2012), the researchers tried to be unobtrusive and remained in the background. Because the children's learning episodes were filmed, ethical issues arising from the involvement of children in research, including informed consent, access, relationships, confidentiality, and protection (Einarsdóttir 2007), were treated seriously.

Semi-structured interviews were conducted to obtain the teachers' thoughts. The teachers were first interviewed individually and then in focus groups. The interviews consisted of the same set of questions for each respondent (Patton 2002) to form a basis for comparing their answers. The main interview questions for individual teacher are: What do you think young children should learn in kindergarten? How do you teach/assist them to learn? How do your children usually play in the kindergarten? Do you think that your children learn at play? How? Can you give us some examples?

The method of video-cued multivocal ethnography (Tobin, Hsueh, and Karasawa 2009) was used to elicit more in-depth discussions on learning at play. The focus group discussions were designed to stimulate dialogue on the focused issue of learning at play and the filmed episodes were used to support the discussion. The process was videotaped to ensure that the participants' voices were heard and to reduce difficulties in transcribing the interviews verbatim (Bogdan and Biklen 2007). In addition, because some group members did not wish to be visually identified, an unobtrusive video camera was set up behind a semi-circle of participants upon their consent (Williams 2003). The main questions asked in the focus groups are: What is particularly thought-provoking in this clip? What do you think about their activity in the classroom? What do you think children can learn from the activity? What do you think is the biggest difference you see between Hong Kong and German activities? Which video presents the theme 'learning at play'? Why? If none of them, what it should be? What would you think if we arranged the German/Chinese activities to take place in your kindergarten?

Data collection

This study was conducted in two phases. In Phase One, three teachers from each kindergarten were interviewed individually to obtain their understanding of learning at play. The semi-structured interview questions were piloted before they were used. During the observations, the researchers followed the teachers' instructions to film what they regarded as learning at play episodes. The researchers confirmed the episodes' content with the teachers afterward and edited the video clips accordingly. Four representative three-minute videos from each culture containing the most learning elements in play were selected. In Phase Two, the selected videos were shown to focus groups of three to four teachers and parents for discussion. Before the videos were shown, some background information and facts about Hong Kong kindergarten such as ages of children, daily schedule, staffing, and teacher–child ratio were introduced to the German participants, and vice versa. Some inquiries about education system were raised by the participants before and in the group discussions. Only factual information were given in the process, without any interpretation or personal understanding involved. As German kindergartens advocate an education partnership (*Erziehungspartnerschaft*), the teachers and parents were grouped together for the discussions. However, the Chinese parents' and teachers' discussion groups were conducted separately because they were used to being interviewed independently. The Hong Kong groups watched and discussed the episodes videotaped in the Hong Kong kindergartens first, then those from the German kindergartens, while their German counterparts viewed and discussed the videos in the reverse order.

The data were categorized based on themes that were identified by referring to previous research (e.g. Cheng and Stimpson 2004; Wu and Rao 2011; Fung and Cheng 2012) and those found during the process of data collection (Bogdan and Biklen 2007). Manifest and latent contexts of similar meanings were classified into different presumed themes for making inferences. Possible conceptual perspectives of play, learning, the teacher's role in play, learning elements in play, and learning at play were elicited from the interviews. The descriptive information was thus coded and reduced via organization. The data were interpreted to identify important meanings. Relevant existing studies were also examined for interpretations that were pertinent to this study. Peer debriefing (Lincoln and Guba 1985) was used to probe the research design and methodology. Overall, the present study did not aim at attaining representative results, but instead focused on its exploratory approach. Central to this study is the description of specific pedagogic practices and the elucidation of the concepts and orientations behind them, with an emphasis on approaching and understanding similarities and differences in two cultural contexts (Stebbins 2001). It also took extraordinary precaution not to generalize within a particular culture, but paid special attention to the possible differences among the education practitioners belonging to the same culture.

The design of the study as a comparative qualitative study in different cultural contexts implied specific challenges and difficulties for the processes of data collection, analysis, and interpretation. The difficulties arose, in particular, from the fact that the study compared 'linguistic material' of two different languages and cultures. But comparison requires equality of meaning. Against this background, attempts were made to offset semantic differences and different cultural interpretive practices in data analysis through intensive discourses of the participating scientists. A mediating role played thereby the first author. Since she is from Taiwan and an outsider of both cultures, she was able to take a 'third', more neutral perspective. In addition, because of her mastery of the German and Chinese languages and her education in Germany and Hong Kong, she was able to question both semantic and cultural meaning-related interpretations. This was important for the scientific discourse and, in particular, served the purpose of improving the validity of the data or results.

Findings

With regard to the selection of practice examples for learning at play by early childhood professionals in Germany and Hong Kong, they revealed very clear differences, which followed the traditional pedagogy of the respective countries. Thus, all of the Hong Kong examples included activities in a group oriented to collective learning objectives. This implies that all children were included and involved in the activity, and each child was guided under a teacher's supervision. These tightly structured activities were rather similar to games, as rules and competition were clearly identified. In summary, the focus of play was on learning in the group, whereas the German examples contained only individual activities or activities in small groups based on the children's aims and psychological needs. To select situations of learning at play in their own pedagogical practices, the German teachers focused on daily activities and specific learning situations were given much less consideration. In addition, the teachers stressed the importance of the environmental setting and the children's self-initiative and self-experience. The professional role of kindergarten teachers in Germany was characterized by their reaction to the children's curiosity and autonomy. In contrast, the Chinese teachers emphasized a systematic learning approach focused on learning objectives, the rules of play/games, and a specific course of play. On the other hand, some similarities are observed in both cultures. For example, teachers' presence in children play plays an important role in either guiding or instructing children's learning at play. In addition, children are engaged in play and enjoyed both the teacher-directed and child-initiated play.

After examining the results of the group discussions, the differences between the German and Chinese learning at play pedagogy described above were no longer as clear as presumed. In the following, this aspect will be elaborated through selected results. In this context, the content of the video sequences shown in the group discussions will be referred to explicitly – e.g. color play, role play (Germany), fireman play, transportation play, and Bauhinia play (all Hong Kong). An Appendix describes each video in more detail for better understanding.

Identifying learning at play

The parents and teachers commented on each video clip and determined which video represents the most scenario of learning at play. The Chinese teachers and parents held various and mostly inconsistent views on each episode, which could be viewed as having more elements of play, learning, or sometimes the combination of both. However, color play (see Appendix), which was selected as the most representative episode of learning at play, elicited some common comments:

> [T]his [color play] has more learning elements. (HK_parent_F02)

> [I]t [color play] looks like 'learning in errors' at play. (HK_teacher_T02)

However, only one Chinese parent regarded the episode of Hong Kong's fireman play (see Appendix) as most representative of learning at play, though she was disputed by others. Her reason was that the activity made the children happy, the teachers guided the play well, and the children could bring the idea home to play.

Moreover, Chinese parents and teachers were concerned about whether children learned anything from the play/game. They also commented on the degree of difficulty of play. For instance, more than half of them thought that fireman play, role play, and Bauhinia play were too easy for the children and that more profound knowledge should be added. Moreover, some parents believed that the play/game should not take place in a chaotic manner, as children should learn discipline, particularly when they are at pre-school age:

> What the teacher wants the children to learn [in fireman play] is too simple, too easy. (HK_teacher_F03)

> I think that transportation play is easy. Children who are three years old may have mastered the basic knowledge about the classification of vehicles at sea, land, and air. There should be more to learn. Teachers should intervene more. For example, add more learning elements like different buses, some trains on rails, and some not so. Children can learn more vocabularies and think more. (HK_parent_T01)

The German participants did not determine explicitly which video most represented the idea of learning at play. However, more than half of the German teachers surveyed singled out color play as well as teacher-guided art work in German kindergartens, which have a stronger sense of learning at play. Although the German teachers thought that color play best represented learning at play, they did not give any reasons for this. However, the German parents found that the element of one's own activities (*Eigentätigkeit*) fulfilled the idea of learning at play, for example, in role play:

> First I found that it [color play] was age-appropriate, child-appropriate, as it was learnt. They [children] have experimented … when one works something out, tries out and also notices okay, so it works, or when I try again and fail, in quotation marks, I try again and then make it, then only the first time I get stuck, a learning setback, and the second time I master it [role play: princess]. It is playful, child-appropriate. I think that it also prepares [the children] for future life. (G_parent_01_E01)

To sum up, Chinese teachers and parents have inconsistent views on each video clip, but most of them identify the German color play as the most representative episode of learning at play. On the other hand, most of the German teachers also think that the color play represents learning at play while the German parents have found the element of one's own activities (*Eigentätigkeit*) as the main idea.

Teachers' and parents' images of learning at play

All of the Chinese parents and teachers, except one parent, thought that the episode of the German color activity most represented learning at play. Some features that constituted learning at play were identified: for the parents, they were teachers' guidance, children's participation, being engaged in play, happiness, as well as hands-on experience; and for the teachers, they were child-directedness, happiness, teachers' intervention, guidance, and involvement in play, as well as not all teacher-directed. Although the terms used, sequence, and priority of the features were not the same, all the participants strongly recognized the importance of children's self-initiative, which was not presented in the Hong Kong episodes. Particularly, the teachers prioritized the children's self-initiative compared with the parents, who emphasized the importance of the teachers' intervention and guidance in play:

> In color play, the children play the leading roles and the teachers support them. Other play/games are teacher-directed … Color play is initiated by the children … More child autonomy. (HK_teacher_T03)

> I think that the children are happiest in color play among all the episodes. They are most sincere. The teacher intervenes appropriately to teach them more, some deeper things … (HK_teacher_T02)

> I saw the teachers' guidance, the children's participation, and happiness. Actually, [fireman] play wants to make children happy. The most important thing is that children get engaged in the activity. Besides, the teachers' guidance is clear and children have learned from it. They can even apply it at home. This is authentic learning. (HK_parent_F01)

The Chinese teachers identified differences in initiative and guidance between their children's and their German counterparts' play and attributed it to their conventional teaching mode, which contains preset learning contents and objectives:

> I think that the big difference is the teacher, [whether the play is] teacher- or child-directed. In Hong Kong, teachers only lead the play/game. Now we play [the game]. All the rules are there. (HK_teacher_F03)

Hong Kong teachers may think that learning at play is group play. Or teachers may think that the play/game should contain learning elements, usually with learning objectives. That is always our Hong Kong teaching mode. (HK_teacher_F01)

On the other hand, the German teachers' understanding differed in three aspects. First, they believed that children at play learn through teachers' support, mainly language support, when they are accompanied by teachers. In other words, children learn when they are encouraged by teachers during play activities:

Through the counting 1, 2, 3, 4, they [the children] eventually learn counting. Also, they learn once again through the accompanying language. (G_teacher_01_F3)

Second, learning at play is related to interactions and contact with other children. Thus, knowledge is passed from older to younger children through role models, social ability, and communication:

I think that one sees the good thing in this example that children learn through imitation. They [the children] have role models when they are in a mixed-age group. Then they see what the older children do and how to get along with older children. Then they also see things for themselves. Thus, they play out the situation for themselves. (G_teacher_01_F1)

Finally, the German teachers believed that learning at play was about one's own conflicts with subjects. Since the children had the opportunity to undertake their own activities, the central aspect of learning at play was in their own undertaking of activities and experiences:

Thus, they [the children] can activate their ideas in the morning, in free play. That happens only in free play without time pressure. Today [role play: princess], I would like to be a queen, what do I need for that? (G_teacher_01_F4)

I think that people learn through their own business and make experiences on their own. I can tell the child five times—front, back, beside, up and down, the water is cold—but [he/she] needs comparisons. (G_teacher_02_F4).

The German parents also believed that the central aspect of learning at play was the children's own activities (*Eigentätigkeit*). The teachers agreed that, on the one hand, learning comes from children and is deemed an individual process, while on the other hand, from the parents' perspectives, children learn through their own experiences in situations:

I think that it really depends on whether the child wants to learn something, whether she/he does not want to learn, what she/he wants to learn. Then we support [it].... (G_parent_01_E2)

In addition, the German parents believed that learning through one's own activities (*Eigentätigkeit*) should reflect the teachers' didactics; they also suggested that a very strong teacher-directed activity was inappropriate, but that teachers should accompany children in their own (*eigentätige*) play situation. The parents considered that children learn less through directness than through self-initiative:

Children should do things as much as possible by themselves, as less influenced as possible in what they do. But teachers then have learning success to uphold and to confirm; when he is there, I now have the colors mixed. What happens then? (G_parent_02_E1)

Remarkably, the German teachers and parents reiterated that the children's own activities (*Eigentätigkeit*) were the most important element of learning at play. Moreover, the teachers' role in play, interactions with peers, and subjects also counted. In sum, both the Chinese and the German teachers and parents believed that children play the most important role in learning at play, but the German teachers and parents stressed this more strongly compared with their Chinese counterparts. On the other hand, the teachers' intervention and guidance were emphasized more by the Chinese teachers and parents than their German counterparts.

Feasibility of play episodes in counterparts' kindergartens

The Chinese teachers and parents agreed that the German color play episode represented learning at play most, but the teachers had some concerns about its feasibility in Hong Kong kindergartens. They thought that it would be difficult to implement because of time and space constraints and parents' concerns. However, the Chinese parents believed that color play was feasible in Hong Kong kindergartens, where the children could learn how to make colors by hands-on experience and learn to communicate and cooperate with other children.

Moreover, the German counterparts believed that the Chinese play activities were very teacher-directed. For the German teachers, the aspect of self-determination was vital. The German parents agreed but their views on this aspect were less detailed. In one group discussion, the parents believed that the Hong Kong activities were difficult to imagine. Both the parents and teachers believed that the Chinese activities were too teacher-directed and would therefore not be transferable or applicable to German kindergartens, especially since doing one's own activities (*Eigenaktivität*) was a central factor in learning.

Discussion

The institutions of early childhood education are socially constructed. Their role, aims, methods, and everyday practices are not self-evident, as '[t]hey are what we, as a community of human agents, make them' (Dahlberg, Moss, and Pence 1999, 62). To that extent, one should expect that the concepts and practices of early childhood education in different societies or different social and cultural contexts, as well as teachers' and parents' conceptions and understanding of learning at play, will vary. In the older academic literature on cultural comparison, the relative emphasis on individualism versus collectivism has been described as the most important dimension of cultural differences in social behavior or social practice (Hofstede 1983; Triandis 1988) – and this distinction still seems to be an important categorization pattern: In collectivist cultures, individuals are often seen as parts of a whole (e.g. a family, a community, or a nation) and their behavior is mainly motivated by the interests of the collective entity. In individualist cultures, the focus lies on the preferences of individuals and their personal interests, needs, and goals (Triandis 1995). Thus, educational practices and objectives are often based on these orientations (Stamm and Edelmann 2013; Hu et al. 2015).

The present results of the study initially seem to confirm such a collectivism–individualism dichotomy:

- All of the Hong Kong videos included activities that involved the whole group, oriented to collective learning objectives. The focus of play in the group was on learning, whereas the German videos showed only individual activities or activities in small groups, based on the children's aims and psychological needs.
- To select situations of learning at play in their own pedagogical practices, the German teachers focused on daily activities, and specific learning situations were given much less consideration. In addition, the teachers stressed the importance of the environmental setting, children's self-initiative, and self-experience. Their professional role was characterized by reacting to the children's curiosity and autonomy. In contrast, the Chinese teachers emphasized a systematic learning approach, focusing on learning objectives, the rules of play/game, and a specific course of play.
- There were also differences in opinions concerning the pedagogical concept of playing. Thus, the participants from Hong Kong emphasized the learning approach and the importance of the teachers' intervention and guidance in play, while the German participants believed that the central aspect of learning at play was children's own activities.

However, a closer look at the findings questioned the distinction between individualism and collectivism. Overall, the statements in the study included Chinese participants in the group discussions were inconsistent: on the one hand, they mostly emphasized the learning approach and the importance of the teachers' intervention and guidance in play; on the other hand, many Chinese teachers and parents also saw the importance of children's self-initiative and self-experience. A central finding was that some Chinese teachers' conceptions of learning at play changed after watching the play episodes from their German counterparts, from focusing on learning objectives and a specific course of play to the players, the teachers' role in play, and the children's self-initiative. Furthermore, almost all teachers and parents from Hong Kong agreed that the German color play episode represented learning at play most, and the majority of the parents thought that it would be feasible in Hong Kong kindergartens. In contrast, the teachers interviewed believed that it may be difficult to implement such activities because of time and space constraints and parents' concerns.

Against this background, it should be noted that in terms of the selected videos, choice differences between Hong Kong and Germany were observed, although they did not fit consistently into the individualism–collectivism dichotomy. Instead, they pointed to the coexistence of individualistic and collectivist orientations (Tamis-LeMonda et al. 2008), especially in Hong Kong, possibly because of a curriculum that was a hybrid of Eastern and Western cultures (Sweeting 2004). For example, almost all of the respondents in Hong Kong preferred a practice that took into account the individuality and self-initiative of children, such as that in the German color play video. Nonetheless, the teachers involved in the study objected to implementing the color play activity based on circumstantial reason, not on educational practices. These findings suggest that a change of culture in Hong Kong may be taking place, which may have an effect on education policies and practices.

With an exclusive view to the conception of learning at play in both cultures, the findings demonstrate one central similarity. Concerning the interviewed German teachers' and parents' conceptions of learning at play, they differed only in the details of their conceptions. For example, the teachers' conceptions were more sophisticated, which can be ascribed to their professional education (Ministry of Culture, Youth and Sports Baden-Württemberg 2010), while the parents focused on the aspect of the children's own activities. The conception of learning at play in Hong Kong was similar to that in Germany. The analysis of data revealed that both the majority of teachers and parents recognized the importance of children's self-initiative as a central factor in learning. Thus, the results suggest that the studied teachers and parents in both Germany and Hong Kong have a similar conception of learning at play that emphasizes the importance of children's self-initiative. Further research should focus on the relationship between teachers' and parents' conceptions of educational terms, such as learning at play, to understand how conceptions emerge and what factors influence them.

Such conceptions and practices interact with each other to some extent. Many studies have revealed that beliefs drive teaching practices (Pajares 1992) and vice versa (i.e. practices influence beliefs [Buehl and Beck 2015]). The gap between the studied Chinese teachers' conceptions of learning at play and practices is noteworthy. In this study, the underlying factors for this gap can be discerned from the interviewed teachers' and parents' concerns about school readiness for primary education. For teachers, the dilemma is having to achieve many preset objectives at the cost of more child-centered activities, resulting in learning that is more teacher-directed (Cheng 2012). This corresponds to some studies that have found that certain teaching approaches can be enacted more appropriately according to teachers' beliefs rather than their practices (Hegde et al. 2014). The inconsistency between conceptions and practices may be attributed to the social context and milieu, as well as the tension between theory and practice. However, as the German case has shown, the nuance between teachers' beliefs and practices may be associated with parents' support of play and their consistent views on play and learning. Moreover, the German teachers involved in the study had more room to implement learning at play compared with their Chinese counterparts.

Teachers are the ultimate implementers of education policies. However, their beliefs have often been ignored by policy-makers, which is the reason for repeated reforms (Cuban 1990). For example, Cheng (2011) has shown that there is inconsistency between curriculum policy and practices in Hong Kong early education. If, as Eisenhart et al. (1988) have suggested, there are discrepancies between education policies and teachers' beliefs, the policies may not be implemented in the way they were intended to. Therefore, this study suggests that teachers' beliefs about the co-constructed features and conceptions of learning at play should be taken into consideration when making top-down centrally determined policies.

Finally, there are some limitations in this study. First, in terms of the research design and the methodological approach, it is necessary to consider the explorative nature of the study. The aim was to elicit similarities and differences in education practices and the teachers' and parents' views on the importance of learning at play. Second, although the sample was not representative of the respective cultures, it was suitable in terms of the subject matter and the research questions; thus, based on the generalization of cultural descriptions, which relate to individual cases (Hansen 2009), the results cannot be generalized. Not least, the respective cultures' influence on language, culture-specific concepts, and different language structures made an equivalent translation difficult (Haas 2009). Therefore, the translation of the interviews and group discussions may have affected the validity of the findings, although attempts have been made to mitigate this problem through the intensive mediated discourse between the scientists involved.

Note

1. In Germany, *Lehrer* (teacher) is used to denote primary school teachers only, while *Erzieher* (educator) is used for kindergarten education. For convenience, 'teacher' will replace 'educator' accordingly in this paper.

Disclosure statement

No potential conflict of interest was reported by the authors.

References

Autorengruppe Fachkräftebarometer. 2014. *Fachkräftebarometer Frühe Bildung 2014*. München: Deutsches Jugendinstitut.
Bennett, T., D. DeLuca, and D. Bruns. 1997. "Putting Inclusion into Practice: Perspectives of Teachers and Parents." *Exceptional Children* 64 (1): 115–131.
Biggs, John. 1996. "Western Misperceptions of the Confucian-Heritage Learning Culture." In *The Chinese Learner: Cultural, Psychological, and Contextual Influences*, edited by David Watkins and John Biggs, 45–67. Hong Kong: CERC & ACER.
Bogdan, Robert C., and Sari K. Biklen. 2007. *Qualitative Research for Education: An Introduction to Theory and Methods*. Boston, MA: Pearson/Allyn and Bacon.
Buehl, Michelle M., and Jori S. Beck. 2015. "The Relationship Between Teachers' Beliefs and Teachers' Practices." In *International Handbook of Research on Teachers' Beliefs*, edited by Helenrose Fives and Michelle G. Gill, 66–84. New York: Routledge.
Cheng, Pui-Wah D. 2011. "Learning Through Play in Hong Kong: Policy or Practice?" In *Rethinking Play and Pedagogy in Early Childhood Education: Concepts, Contexts and Cultures*, edited by Sue Rogers, 100–111. London: Routledge.
Cheng, Pui-Wah D. 2012. "The Relation Between Early Childhood Teachers' Conceptualization of 'Play' and Their Practice: Implication for the Process of Learning to Teach." *Frontiers of Education in China* 7 (1): 65–84.
Cheng, Pui-Wah D., and P. Stimpson. 2004. "Articulating Contrasts in Kindergarten Teachers' Implicit Knowledge on Play-based Learning." *International Journal of Educational Research* 41: 339–352.
Cheng, Pui-Wah D., and S.-C. Wu. 2013. "Serious Learners or Serious Players? Revisiting the Concept of Learning Through Play in Hong Kong and German Classrooms." In *Perspectives on Play and Learning: Theory and Research on Early Years' Education*, edited by Ole F. Lillemyr, Sue Dockett, and Bob Perry, 193–212. Charlotte, NC: Information Age Publishing.
Craft, A., A. Matthews, and L. McConnon. 2012. "Child-initiated Play and Professional Creativity: Enabling Four-Year-Olds' Possibility Thinking." *Thinking Skills and Creativity* 7 (1): 48–61.
Cuban, L. 1990. "Reforming Again, Again, and Again." *Educational Researcher* 19: 3–13.
Dahlberg, G., P. Moss, and A. Pence. 1999. *Beyond Quality in Early Childhood Education and Care: Postmodern Perspectives*. London: RoutledgeFalmer.
Education Bureau. 2017a. "Kindergarten Education." Accessed 2 August, 2017. http://www.edb.gov.hk/en/about-edb/publications-stat/figures/kg.html.
Education Bureau. 2017b. "Profile of Kindergartens and Kindergarten-Cum-Child Care Centres 2016–17 School Year." Accessed 2 August, 2017. http://www.chsc.hk/kindergarten/.
Einarsdóttir, J. 2007. "Research with Children: Methodological and Ethical Challenges." *European Early Childhood Education Research Journal* 15 (2): 197–211.

Eisenhart, M. A., A. M. Cuthbert, J. L. Shrum, and J. R. Harding. 1988. "Teacher Beliefs About Their Work Activities: Policy Implications." *Theory into Practice* 27 (2): 137–144.

Faas, S., S.-C. Wu, and S. Geiger. 2017. "The Importance of Play in Early Childhood Education: A Critical Perspective on Current Policies and Practices in Germany and Hong Kong." *Global Education Review* 4 (2): 75–91.

Fang, Z. 1996. "A Review of Research on Teacher Beliefs and Practices." *Educational Research* 38 (1): 47–65.

Flitner, Andreas. 1972. "Playing – Learning. Interpretation of Children's Play." In *Education. A Biannual Collection of Recent German Contributions to the Field of Educational Research, Vol. 7*, edited by the Institute for Scientific Co-operation, 32–46. Tübingen: Göbel.

Fung, C. K. H., and P. W. D. Cheng. 2012. "Consensus or Dissensus? Stakeholders' Views on the Role of Play in Learning." *Early Years: An International Research Journal* 32 (1): 17–33.

Galeano, R. 2011. "Scaffolding Productive Language Skills Through Sociodramatic Play." *American Journal of Play* 3 (3): 324–355.

Gay, Lorraine R., Geoffrey E. Mills, and Peter W. Airasian. 2009. *Educational Research: Competencies for Analysis and Application*. 9th ed. Upper Saddle River, NJ: Merrill.

Glaser, Barney G., and Anselm Strauss. 2017. *The Discovery of Grounded Theory: Strategies for Qualitative Research*. New York: Routledge.

Göncü, A., J. Mistry, and C. Mosier. 2000. "Cultural Variations in the Play of Toddlers." *International Journal of Behavioral Development* 24 (3): 321–329.

Gruber, Karl H. 2006. "The German PISA-Shock: Some Aspects of the Extraordinary Impact of the OECD's PISA Study on the German Education System." In *Cross-national Attraction in Education: Accounts from England and Germany*, edited by Hubert Ertl, 195–208. Oxford: Symposium Books.

Haas, H. 2009. "Übersetzungsprobleme in der Interkulturellen Befragung[Problems of Translation in Intercultural Surveys]." *Interculture Journal* 10: 61–77.

Hansen, K. P. 2009. "*Die Problematik des Pauschalurteils*[The Problem of Generalization]." *Interculture Journal* 10: 5–17.

Hegde, A. V., and D. J. Cassidy. 2009. "Kindergarten Teachers' Perspectives on Developmentally Appropriate Practices." *Journal of Research in Childhood Education* 23 (3): 367–381.

Hegde, A. V., C. Sugita, L. Crane-Mitchell, and P. Averett. 2014. "Japanese Nursery and Kindergarten Teachers' Beliefs and Practices Regarding Developmentally Appropriate Practices." *International Journal of Early Years Education* 22 (3): 301–314.

Ho, C. W. D. 2006. "Understanding the Complexity of Preschool Teaching in Hong Kong: The Way Forward to Professionalism." *International Journal of Educational Development* 26 (3): 305–314.

Hofstede, G. 1983. "The Cultural Relativity of Organizational Practices and Theories." *Journal of International Business Studies* 14 (2): 75–89.

Hong Kong Housing Authority. 2016. "Housing in Figures 2016." Accessed 2 August, 2017. https://www.housingauthority.gov.hk/en/common/pdf/about-us/publications-and-statistics/HIF.pdf.

Howard-Jones, P. A., J. Taylor, and L. Sutton. 2002. "The Effects of Play on the Creativity of Young Children." *Early Child Development and Care* 172 (4): 323–328.

Hu, B. Y., K.-I. Vong, Y. Chen, and H. K. Li. 2015. "Expert Practitioner's Views About the Chinese Early Childhood Environmental Rating Scale." *European Early Childhood Education Research Journal* 23 (2): 229–249.

Joshia, A. 2009. "What Do Teacher-Child Interactions in Early Childhood Classrooms in India Look Like? Teachers' and Parents' Perspectives." *Early Child Development and Care* 179 (3): 285–301.

Lincoln, Y. S., and E. G. Guba. 1985. *Naturalistic Inquiry*. Beverly Hills, CA: Sage.

McMillan, James H. 2012. *Educational Research: Fundamentals for the Consumer*. 6th ed. Boston, MA: Pearson/Allyn and Bacon.

Ministry of Culture, Youth and Sports Baden-Württemberg. 2010. "Curriculum for Business College." Professional School for Social Pedagogy. Accessed 15 August, 2016. http://www.ls-bw.de/bildungsplaene/berufschulen/bk/bk_entw/fs_sozpaed_BK/fs_sozpaed_BK/BK-FS-Sozpaed_Bildung-Entwicklung-I_09_3693_05.pdf.

Oberhuemer, Pamela. 2012. "Balancing Traditions and Transitions: Early Childhood Policy Initiatives and Issues in Germany." In *Debates on Early Childhood Policies and Practices: Global Snapshots of Pedagogical Thinking and Encounters*, edited by Theodora Papatheodorou, 17–26. London: Routledge.

Pajares, M. F. 1992. "Teachers' Beliefs and Educational Research: Cleaning Up a Messy Construct." *Review of Educational Review* 62 (3): 307–332.

Parmar, P., S. Harkness, and C. M. Super. 2004. "Asian and Euro-American Parents' Ethnotheories of Play and Learning: Effects on Preschool Children's Home Routines and School Behavior." *International Journal of Behavioral Development* 28 (2): 97–104.

Patton, Michael Q. 2002. *Qualitative Research & Evaluation Methods*. 3rd ed. Thousand Oaks, CA: Sage Publications.

Piotrkowskia, C. S., M. Botskob, and E. Matthews. 2000. "Parents' and Teachers' Beliefs About Children's School Readiness in a High-Need Community." *Early Childhood Research Quarterly* 15 (4): 537–558.

Pramling Samuelsson, I., and E. Johansson. 2006. "Play and Learning – Inseparable Dimensions in Preschool Practice." *Early Child Development and Care* 176 (1): 47–65.

Rao, N., S. S. N. Ng, and E. Pearson. 2009. "Preschool Pedagogy: A Fusion of Traditional Chinese Beliefs and Contemporary Notions of Appropriate Practice." In *Revisiting the Chinese Learner: Changing Contexts, Changing Education*, edited by Carol K. K. Chan and Nirmala Rao, 255–280. Hong Kong: The University of Hong Kong, Comparative Education Research Centre/Springer Academic.

Robson, S., and V. Rowe. 2012. "Observing Young Children's Creative Thinking: Engagement, Involvement and Persistence." *International Journal of Early Years Education* 20 (4): 349–364.

Roskos, Kathleen A., and James F. Christie. 2007. *Play and Literacy in Early Childhood: Research from Multiple Perspectives*. New York: Lawrence Erlbaum Associates.

Russ, Sandra W. 2004. *Play in Child Development and Psychotherapy: Toward Empirically Supported Practice*. Mahwah, NJ: Erlbaum Associate Publishers.

Singer, Dorothy, Roberta M. Golinkoff, and Kathy Hirsh-Pasek. 2006. *Play = Learning: How Play Motivates and Enhances Children's Cognitive and Social-Emotional Growth*. New York: Oxford University Press.

Stamm, M., and D. Edelmann. 2013. "Zur Pädagogischen Qualität Frühkindlicher Bildungsprogramme: Eine Kritik an Ihrer Ethnozentrischen Perspektive." In *Handbuch Frühkindliche Bildungsforschung*, edited by M. Stamm and D. Edelmann, 325–341. Wiesbaden: VS Springer.

Standing Conference of the Ministers for Youth Affairs in Germany and Standing Conference of the Ministers of Education and Cultural Affairs in Germany. 2004. "A Common Framework for Early Education." In *Early Childhood Education and Care in Germany*, edited by Pestalozzi-Fröbel Verband, 15–21. Weimar: das netz.

Stebbins, R. A. 2001. *Exploratory Research in the Social Sciences*. Vol. 48Thousand Oaks, CA: Sage.

Stipek, D. J., and P. Byler. 1997. "Early Childhood Education Teachers: Do They Practice What They Preach?" *Early Childhood Research Quarterly* 12 (3): 305–325.

Sweeting, A. 2004. *Education in Hong Kong, 1941 to 2001: Visions and Revisions*. Hong Kong: Hong Kong University Press.

Tamis-LeMonda, C. S., N. Way, D. Hughes, H. Yoshikawa, R. K. Kalman, and E. Y. Niwa. 2008. "Parents' Goals for Children: The Dynamic Coexistence of Individualism and Collectivism in Cultures and Individuals." *Social Development* 17 (1): 183–209.

Tobin, J., Y. Hsueh, and M. Karasawa. 2009. *Preschool in Three Cultures Revisited: China, Japan, and the United States*. Chicago, IL: The University of Chicago Press.

Triandis, H. C. 1988. "Collectivism v. Individualism: A Reconceptualisation of a Basic Concept in Cross-cultural Social Psychology." In *Cross-cultural Studies of Personality, Attitudes and Cognition*, edited by Gajendra Verma and Christopher Bagley, 60–95. London: Palgrave Macmillan.

Triandis, H. C. 1995. *Individualism & Collectivism. New Directions in Social Psychology*. Boulder, CO: Westview Press.

Uren, N., and K. Stagnitti. 2009. "Pretend Play, Social Competence and Involvement in Children Aged 5–7 Years: The Concurrent Validity of the Child-Initiated Pretend Play Assessment." *Australian Occupational Therapy Journal* 56: 33–40.

Williams, M. 2003. *Making Sense of Social Research*. London: Sage.

Wood, E. 2009. "Developing a Pedagogy of Play." In *Early Childhood Education: Society & Culture*, edited by Angela Anning, Joy Cullen, and Marilyn Fleer, 27–38. London: Sage.

Wu, S.-C. 2011. "The Role of Free Play in the German Kindergartens." *The Hong Kong Journal of Early Childhood* 10 (1): 85–90.

Wu, S.-C. 2014. "Practical and Conceptual Aspects of Children's Play in the Hong Kong and German Kindergartens." *Early Years: an International Research Journal* 34 (1): 49–66.

Wu, S.-C., and N. Rao. 2011. "Chinese and German Teachers' Conceptions of Play and Learning and Children's Play Behaviour." *European Early Childhood Education Research Journal* 19 (4): 471–483.

Appendix. Description of the video clips

German 01: One-on-one situation

In free play, a girl plays independently in a children's kitchen. She clears the game plates from the cupboard, covers the table, etc. Next, she carries a basket of toys and plays with a car and the people in the car. Then she experiments with water in the bathroom and bathes her doll. In all three parts of the film, the teacher is close to her, watching and supporting her play. She tells the child where to find plates to cover the table, or asks if the water is hot or cold.

German 02: Role play: Princess

In free play, a boy has chosen a card game. The teacher is with him, looking at the pictures with him and asking him about the objects that can be seen on the cards, for example a pair of glasses or a hat. The child answers the questions. Other children join, watching the scene. Then the teacher helps another group of children to make crowns that they would like to have for their role play. Afterwards, the children put the crowns on their heads and play princess. They also took towels and disguised themselves.

German 03: Cards with vegetables and fruits

In free play, a boy and a teacher sit on the floor and play with cards printed with images of various vegetables and fruits. The teacher talks to the child and asks, for example, which vegetables and fruits he sees on the cards. In the background other children are playing. Sometimes other children come and go again. The boy also interrupts the card game and does something different, but then continues again.

German 04: Color play

In free play, a group of children are experimenting with colors with the support of the teacher. The children have three colors to choose from: blue, yellow, and red. One child has made the color purple and the teacher asks the children how the color purple is made. Another child is experimenting with the three colors with the teacher's support to make the color purple. Then another child asks how to make the color orange. The teacher asks the child who made the color purple how to make the color orange, who continues to experiment and explains to the other child how to make the color orange.

Hong Kong 01: Fireman play

First, the teacher explains to the students how to play fireman. Some children act as firemen to put out the fire, which is represented by other children. When the music starts, all participating children walk around the play area. When the music stops, the children acting as firemen pretend to put out the fire, and the children who represent fire lie down on the ground.

Hong Kong 02: Transportation play

The children are wearing crowns with pictures of different transportation vehicles and they walk around when the music starts. When the music stops, they stand in the hula hoop representing the vehicles shown on their crown. The teacher then checks whether the children are standing in the correct place.

Hong Kong 03: Bauhinia play

The children and teacher make a circle and walk around. The teacher asks how many times the Bauhinia blossoms. The teacher says 'two,' and two children stand together and tell the teacher whether 'two' is an odd or even number.

Hong Kong 04: Play: Which is longer?

The teacher gives the same amount of newspapers to two groups of children. The children use the newspapers to make a line as long as they can. The teacher judges which group made the longest line.

7   How educators define their role
Building 'professional' relationships with children and parents during transition to childcare: a case study

Janine Hostettler Schärer

ABSTRACT
Using case study methodology including weekly focus group meetings and individual interviews, this article reports results of a study in a Canadian childcare centre in which four educators shared their attitudes and experiences on their role as educators and on building relationships with the children transitioning into their care and their parents. Analysis of the data reveals that educators are most concerned with their role as professionals, and that their interpretations of professionalism influences structural and organizational elements in the centre like shifts and schedules of the educators, but also their relationships with children in their care, and with parents.

Introduction

The transition to out-of-home care is a significant time of change for the whole family with a widespread impact. Although the importance of transitions has been acknowledged and transitions from early childhood programmes to elementary school have been well researched (i.e. Margetts and Kienig 2013; Perry, Dockett, and Petriwskyi 2014), transitions from home to centre-based care have received less research emphasis. Canada offers parents 12 months of maternity/parental leave, after which almost 70% of women with children under age 3 rely on some sort of childcare (data from 2011; as quoted in Vanier Institute 2013). Due to the current parental leave policy childcare attendance after age 12 months is assumed to be a common cultural trend in Canada. Children attending licenced childcare centres in Canada encounter educators with basic certificates (e.g. 477 hours course work, 425 hours practicum, and 500 hours supervised workplace experience in British Columbia). In addition, educators of children younger than 3 years old hold Infant/Toddler certifications (250 hours course work and 200 hours practicum) (Early Childhood Educator Registry of British Columbia 2015).

The purpose of my main study is to provide an in-depth understanding of how parents and childcare educators experience infants' transitions to childcare and how relationships are built during the settling-in process and beyond it. The question posed for the sub-study discussed here is how educators view their role in these transitions and what they do to build relationships with parents and children.

Theoretically, my study is based on a cultural-historical perspective (Bodrova and Leong 2007; Vygotsky 1978). From this perspective, to understand the role of dyadic relationships in the child's development, the larger social structures in which those relationships occur must also be considered. When analysing individual relationships in the social context of starting childcare I take the social structure of the childcare (shifts, schedules, policies, staff absences), as well as the cultural level (Canadian parental leave policy) into account. Further, I use attachment theory (Bowlby 1969) as an investigative lens, to deepen my understandings of the transition to childcare.

Relationships in the social context of starting childcare

In infant and toddler care and education relationships are the heart of best practices (McMullen and Dixon 2009). A relationship-based approach is one in which relationship partners respect and value each other within their multiple spheres of interaction. Transitions to childcare are typically about building relationships among children, parents, and childcare educators (Brooker 2008; Goldschmied and Jackson 2004; Lieberman 1993). Attachment theory posits that all children need a stable and secure relationship with at least one caregiver for healthy socioemotional development to occur (Bowlby 1969). Such relationships develop and thrive when a caregiver is perceptive of a child's signals and responds promptly and appropriately to them. Both caregivers as well as children need opportunities and time to understand each other's behaviours and cues so that secure, stable relationships can develop (Barnas and Cummings 1994; Goldschmied and Jackson 2004; Howes and Hamilton 1992a, 1992b).

Attention to children's emotions has been widely emphasized in early care and education research and policy and enabling such attention has been achieved through attachment interactions with staff. However, facilitating such interactions in an optimal way for children depends on educators' critical professional reflection (reasoning to make meaning) about how these interactions are managed with children, families, and between educators; and such reflections need to include attention to emotional experience of educators and children (Elfer 2012), as starting childcare affects children, parents, and educators. During the child's transition the needs, fears, and expectations of all three parties come together. For educators, welcoming a child is a regular although unpredictable occurrence as each child reacts differently to transitions, and has different caretaking needs. My paper examines how educators experience and navigate this very important transition.

Methodology

The intent of my inquiry is to explore children's transitions to a childcare centre (the case) using detailed, in-depth data collection from multiple sources (educators, parents, childcare documents) over a sustained period of time (Creswell 2012). I purposefully selected a typical case to address my research questions through an inductive qualitative approach: collecting data through emerging methods and open-ended questions in interviews, observations, and documents in order to analyse, interpret, and search for themes and patterns

(Creswell 2009). This paper concentrates on educators, and the research question considered is:

(1) What are the educators' perspectives on transitioning children to childcare?

Participants include the four educators on staff at an infant/toddler centre with 12 children, which is part of a childcare society with 7 infant/toddler, and 5 preschool centres. Educators participated in 16 months of first weekly (later bi-weekly) inquiry meetings, as well as an individual interview and a group video-discussion of one child recorded during her transition to childcare. Over this extended time period and through in-depth relationships I was able to verify my findings with participants at critical points in the investigation.

In inquiry meetings I examined teachers' understandings and practices through discussing theory and practice, and I was able to draw out educators' perspectives on attachment models of care. These inquiries helped me to develop a semi-structured interview guide for parents. The interview guide for educators was developed after coding all parental data and entailed detailed inquiries on educators' perspectives and experiences orienting children to care, and on building relationships with children and parents. Interviews were recorded and later transcribed for analysis.

Analysing data I followed Creswell (2014), reading interview transcripts as whole, making margin notes, before forming provisional codes according to questions asked. Radnor (2002) called this *topic ordering* as the questions formed the framework from which my analysis was generated. As first coding cycle I used *in-vivo coding*, where a code refers to a word or short phrase in the transcript, to honour participants' voices (Saldaña 2013). In a second cycle I used *pattern coding* to develop major categories from the data (Saldaña 2013). In a further step, I chose categorical aggregation (Creswell 2012, 2014; Stake 1995) and reduced pattern codes to *themes* (Stake 1995), for a better understanding of the case. I added educator information to themes derived from parents. I further took Stake's (1995) advice that case studies need both categorical aggregation and direct interpretation of individual instances in that I pulled data apart and put them back together in more meaningful ways, in an effort to make sense of things. Through this process, I ended up with nine categories falling under three themes that allowed me to make generalizations about the case as I could compare and contrast them with published literature (Creswell 2014). Transcripts from inquiry meetings were thematically coded at phrase level, as they related to my research questions, and information was mainly used to compare theoretical concepts explained in my study with daily practices of educators.

I am aware that studying people in their work environment can create ethical challenges that might not be present in another kind of investigation. The presence of the childcare manager in inquiry meetings (as educators' boss), for example, might have influenced educators' contributions to the discussions. In order to acknowledge anticipated ethical issues (i.e. confidentiality of children or incidents discussed) arising through this study, I informed participants about the purpose of the investigation. All involved parties signed informed consent forms prior to participation, and were instructed that they are free to withdraw permission to participate at any time without any consequences. Interviews were conducted individually and took place at times and places convenient to the interviewees. Participants' names as well as the name of the centre are disguised through pseudonyms.

Because of the limited number of participants, my study offers limited generalizability, but an in-depth view into perspectives and experiences of educators during the event of transitioning children to care. The researcher in an inductive inquiry is considered the primary data collection instrument (Creswell 2009). As such, it was necessary for me to identify and interrogate my personal values, assumptions, and biases. I am aware that the data I collected and the interpretations I make are influenced by my previous experiences, are greatly subjective (Stake 1995), and I acknowledge that multiple interpretations exist (Creswell 2012), such as those of readers and participants in the study. What I present is my interpretation and pursuit as a researcher to make sense of certain observations by watching as closely and thinking as deeply as possible.

Finding and discussion

Three main themes crystallized in inquiry meetings and educators interviews: professionalism, childcare structures, and relationships.

Professionalism is the most dominant theme as it influences social childcare structures (as educators choose to apply a concept of fairness to all staff and change their shifts, working hours, and responsibilities weekly), as well as relationships. Professional relationships for educators mean ones that are not too close. Educators try to avoid attachment relationships and argue against primary caregiving, but instead choose a more flexible model of care where educators can easily replace one another. Therefore, when transitioning children into the centre and building relationships educators make themselves available to children in a model that I called 'child-selected care', before gradually introducing the child to the care of others. This unique style of care is different from primary caregiving in that it lets children pick their preferred caregiver to build a relationship, before introducing the child to care by other educators.

In my discussion, I first present findings according to the most prominent themes before discussing educators' arguments against primary caregiving, as well as comparing and contrasting primary caregiving with their chosen model of child-selected care.

Professionalism

Acting professional and being acknowledged by parents as professionals is what educators are most concerned with. They want parents to respect, trust, and value them, and feel that this is not always the case:

> This has probably a lot to do with academic learning versus child minding. It's nothing that I care about. But sometimes, the way that we are spoken to by parents in regards to their child sometimes feels like they are kind of, staging us as: you are just watching my child. You have to take my kid because, you know, that's your job. (Emma, December 11, 2012)

Educators emphasize professionalism in relation to distinguishing their personal from their professional self, and relationships with children in childcare from relationships with their families. Manning-Morton (2006) in her study on personal and professional awareness of educators concluded it being a major professional challenge for early childhood practitioners to engage closely with young children, as it touches deeply held personal values and often deeply buried personal experiences. The level of emotional demand in responsive relationships can lead educators to take on a defensive position, often expressed through the view that getting too close to children is not professional (Manning-Morton 2006). This is exactly what educators in my study express when emphasizing their professionalism in relation to distinguishing their personal from their professional self. This identity in favour of professionalism was also found in other research studies. Harwood et al. (2013) reported findings where educators narrated stories that juxtaposed different versions of professional self versus personal self. These authors concluded that educators appreciated the plurality of roles as educators and individuals illustrated in these oscillating identities.

Interestingly, even though our inquiry meetings met the criteria for meaningful professional development in that they included (a) educators working on pedagogical frameworks built upon theory, (b) active involvement in the process of improving practice, (c) focussing on practice-based learning in dialogue with colleagues, and (d) mentoring to facilitate reflections (Vandenbroek et al. 2016), educators in this study did not consider them as professional development, nor did they mention any need for on-going professional development. Their professional understanding also influences their decisions and behaviour concerning childcare structures.

Structures

While educators talk about childcare philosophy, policies, and regulations as given elements, it soon became apparent that many of these structures are actually chosen by themselves (as a group), and in the interest of fairness to all staff. Taking turns orienting families to childcare, weekly changing shifts and working hours, and their adherence to ratio when asked about parent–child visits before the transition to childcare are examples of how they interpret structures however it fits their understanding, and more in a one-fits-all than a family-oriented approach to childcare. Individual interpretations promote their understanding of relationships too. Their weekly changing shifts and accompanying schedules (food, bathroom, nap duties), for example, make it hard for educators to make themselves available as attachment figures for children and contact person for parents.

Building relationships with families

Educators feel that building relationships with parents is easier with some and harder with others, and that certain educators are better able to build such relationships with parents than others. Throughout our discussions as well as in interviews educators kept on referring to their open-door policy, and how they are open and willing to discuss any problem families might have. When one mother however, took them by their word, educators were taken by surprise:

> … you know, we always say: call if you want or email if you want, but we never actually think that they are gonna do it (laughs) … so when she started doing that we were like: oh my god, why is she calling so much! He is fine! But I guess cause we offered it, so … I mean we have to take it, right? (Andrea, June 5, 2013)

Educators found the mother's calls and emails interrupted their workday and had to find a solution that worked for both sides. This educator's honest response underlines that there is some ambivalence about really being in a partnership with parents because of the demands the relationship places on educators' time, and educators stated that they see themselves as experts and not as partners of parents. Even though educators continuously highlighted their availability for parental requests and concerns, they also feel there is limited time to actually enter into such conversations.

Relationships with children

Surprisingly, educators' opinions about attachment with children as well as their professional roles and relationships vary a great deal from conventional understandings of attachment theory and relational approaches to teaching. Most interestingly, in their quest to be professionals educators are concerned that close attachment relationships with children (from children to them, as well as from themselves to children) are unhealthy, and that children could potentially be 'over-attached' to a caregiver, meaning they would be dependent on the care of one particular educator. Noddings's (1984) concept of mutuality upholds that caring teaching–learning relationships are reciprocal between educators and children. This mutuality, also a tenet of attachment theory (Bowlby 1951), would be an example of why educators feel they could potentially be over-attached to a child, even though they are resisting calling this relationship an attachment. Even so, they are convinced that over-attachment can happen if an educator starts to neglect the needs of other children in favour of one child. Even though they do not call their relationship towards children attachments, they call it instead 'over-attachment of educators' or 'favouritism', and consider these relationships 'unhealthy'. Elfer (2012) reported historical evidence that educators avoid warm and responsive relationships with children because of their anxiety that feelings of attachment result in painful emotions when inevitable separations occur; even in centres committed to primary caregiving. This could be the case for these educators, as they prefer a distributed approach to attachment relationships, with harmony across all members as opposed to one-on-one attachment relationships. Findings of Ahnert, Pinquart, and Lamb (2006) support harmony within the group, as they found group-related sensitivity to be an important predictor for educators who were secure attachment figures for children. This, however, stands in contrast to relational pedagogy promoting sensitive responsive one-on-one caregiving to optimize development by relying on attunement and intersubjectivity (Dalli 2014; Lally 2010, 2013). Other authors further emphasized frequent positive interactions (De Shipper, Tavecchio, and Van IJzendoorn 2008) with a stable caregiver (Barnas and Cummings 1994; Howes and Hamilton 1992a, 1992b) as necessary factors for secure caregiver–child relationships. In a distributed approach to attachment relationships where it is not clear who is in charge of the needs of whom, regular one-on-one interactions (Mahn 2003) and finely tuned guidance (Dalli 2014; Rogoff, Malkin, and Gilbride 1984) are not assured for all children. Another emerging aspect of professionalism in early childhood education is 'professional love' as discussed by Dalli (2006) and Page (2011). These authors see professional love as a pedagogical tool; something educators can consciously use as pedagogical strategy (Dalli 2006) and in no way diminishes children's love for parents (Goldschmied and Jackson 2004). The concept of professional love or primary caregiving, however, stands in contrast to what educators described as too close and therefore unprofessional relationships.

Arguments against primary caregiving

While discussing the care model these educators use and their attachment assumptions, we also discussed primary caregiving. However, as educators are concerned that close attachment relationships with children are unhealthy, primary caregiving is rejected and educators listed several factors as working against this model. They are instead in favour of child-selected care, in which attachments are first supported, but then care is distributed between educators.

On a structural level educators are concerned with frequent absences (i.e. overtime compensation, sickness, practicums, etc.), as well as with weekly rotation of shifts and schedules. Frequent absences make it hard to provide regular occasions of attention for each child, and they would need to have a second-choice attachment figure for each child (Dalli et al. 2009). Depending on the shift educators work, their schedules include food preparation, diapering, nap room duties, etc. If primary caregiving were to be implemented educators would need to do most of these tasks for the children in their care.

Educator absences are a reality and make it hard to assure regular one-on-one attention and intimate care, which would enable educators to read a child's cue. From an attachment perspective frequent absences confound the educator's ability to read infants' or toddlers' cues and respond accordingly (Lally 2010, 2013). In this case, Theilheimer (2006) argued for adopting a primary caregiving model with two preferred caregivers (primary and secondary) that might help to moderate some of the negative implications of frequent absences: a child's second-choice person would care for the child in the absence of the primary caregiver.

On a relational level educators are concerned with over-attachment of children, as well as favouritism on their part.

> At some points, sometimes I had the impression that the child is so attached for example to me, (inaudible) to myself, that it is almost like mother-son or mother-daughter relationship. It shouldn't be. So it's also important for the team members, like co-workers to point it out too. Because sometimes we do not know. (Jamie, November 13, 2012)

Educators feel that over-attachment can happen to educators, if they become too involved with a child and this begins to influence their professional judgment and subsequent relationships with other children and educators. First, educators used the term 'over-attachment of educators' and later changed it to 'favouritism'. What further indicated their fear of favouritism is that for these educators a primary caregiver only cares for the children in her group. In their research report, Dalli et al. (2009) explain a primary caregiving approach that requires sensitive responsiveness to colleagues and builds a respectful and supportive team structure, contradicting the prevailing assumption that primary caregivers work in isolation.

A further barrier to close attachment relationships is the fact that educators do not always feel strongly connected to children who become attached to them. This creates a difficulty in reciprocity between caregiver and child. Educators see it as their professional responsibility to make themselves available as attachment figures. When it does not happen naturally, educators approach relationships from a professional stance, take their time to work on their emotions and try to offer themselves as attachment figures even though it takes more conscious effort to do so.

I really dislike that feeling. I feel guilt and so when it happened a few times, in all the years, so I just ask my colleagues, like I need a little bit of a break from this child, to work on my feelings. Because it is not fair. Slowly, in small steps, I involve this child with little things. Not maybe jump over this child because he or she chose me. But for me I think like separate myself, calm down, it's so not fair, because they can read us. (Jamie, October 2, 2012)

Indeed Goosens and IJzendoorn (1990) mentioned that the same caregiver can have children in her care that are securely attached to her, as well as children insecurely attached to her. In general, attachment theory does not take up feelings on part of educators, as the focus is the child's attachment to the caregiver. Goldschmied and Jackson (2004) propose that structural as well as personal support should be given to caregivers in a situation like this to enhance relationships with children, or the primary caregiver might be changed for a child. However, as stated in the quote above the problem of missing reciprocity also arose in their child-selected care model.

Two further arguments against primary caregiving have to do with parents. The first obstacle is that the educator parents might choose to communicate with might not be the one working most closely with their child; many parents choose the lead educator as their contact person. This creates problems of communication and affects the educators' ability to enter and sustain a relationship with parents. It is true that parents might choose an educator to build a relationship with if they are not aware who the primary caregiver for their child is. It might be overcome if it is made clear from the beginning which educator the family is working with most closely.

Second, educators feel some parents do not appreciate close relationships between educators and children. They noted that some parents comment on educator–child relationships in ways that make educators feel parents are not welcoming of close relationships.

You can sense that, when parents come in, you know, the little sly comments about: 'Oh yeah, he was talking about you all weekend!' Or: 'I think maybe he should be your baby'. (Emma, October 2, 2012)

These educators are not alone with such feelings; Elfer (2012) also found that educators showed anxiety about the appropriateness of attachments in professional work with young children, as well as anxiety about parents' reactions to close relationships between educators and children. However, if parents show difficulties accepting attachment relationships between their child and his/her educators it might be helpful to explain to parents that it is beneficial for their child to have a special person to turn to during the long hours they spend in childcare (Goldschmied and Jackson 2004). Ebbeck and Yim (2009) argued that a primary caregiver enhances professionalism of the early childhood field, but they also highlighted that there is a need to further refine primary caregiving to better help children's first transition from home to childcare, as well as to encourage more centres to adopt a primary caregiving approach.

Child-selected care model versus primary caregiving

When comparing child-selected care and primary caregiving, in theory, the child-selected care model chosen by these educators might be considered more favourably, as the child can pick a caregiver to attach to, and does not need to attach to a caregiver based on availability in her group. However, if educators perceive this first attachment as too close or taking the form of 'over-attachment' the child is directed toward other caregivers. This is done to avoid an attachment between the caregiver and the child that is too dependent on care by one specific caregiver only, and might help educators to guard their emotions as separation will inevitably occur (Elfer 2012). Educators have to balance their attention between the new child and children attending for longer, and are in constant ambiguity between the needs of the individual and the needs of the group. If educators need to consider the perspective of the group interest over individual needs, distributing relationships seems to be in the interest of a harmonious approach across caregivers and children. On the other hand, parents do not know who is mainly responsible for their child when settling-in starts, educator-perceived unhealthy relationship (over-attachment) leads to handing-over the child to other educators (not when the child is ready, but in crisis mode), which is hard on educator and child.

Many researchers agree that primary caregiving is beneficial to foster relationships and a smooth transition to childcare (Brooker 2008; Daniel and Shapiro 1996; Ebbeck and Yim 2009; Goldschmied and Jackson 2004; Lally 2010, 2013). Primary caregiving assures regular occasions when a particular caregiver's attention is given to a particular child for a stable relationship to occur. These relationships enhance the child's sense of security, and enable the educator to read the child's cues and respond accordingly (Lally 2010, 2013). Primary caregivers are generally responsible for the intimate care of infants and toddlers, like feeding and changing routines, and offer regular individual attention to the children in their care (Goldschmied and Jackson 2004; Mahn 2003). Ebbeck and Yim (2009) found a positive influence of primary caregiving on children, parents, and educators, and in their study on the implementation of primary caregiving both parents and educators were in favour of the system. They agreed that this system enhances not only infants' and toddlers' well-being and their establishment of secure attachment with adults, but also strengthens parents' trust in educators.

Taken together, educator absences cannot be avoided in childcare. However, a relationship-based approach where educators and parents respect and value each other (McMullen and Dixon 2009) and the implementation of primary caregiving in this infant/toddler centre might lessen negative influences related to frequent educator absences for children. In a team of three full-time and one part-time educators each child will have his or her hierarchy of attachment figures (Bowlby 2005). If educators take a child-directed focus on care and show some flexibility, it should be possible that one of the two most favoured educators could be available for the child throughout the day. Educators would need to critically reflect their practice of managing interactions with children and families and to pay special attention to their emotions, as well as those of children (Elfer 2012), instead of referring to policies and regulations. For educators primary caregiving offers new possibilities to build relationships with parents, which might help those educators who feel left out by parents. Lastly, educators' perception of primary caregiving might change once they investigate its application to their everyday practice. Further, if educators would consider the concept of professional love this might change their perception on professionalism in relationships with children.

Conclusion

This research shed light on four educators' perspectives on their role as professionals, their attachment assumptions, and highlighted the complexity of relationships happening in their centre. Regarding professionalism, results of this study show that these educators wish to be respected, valued, and appreciated as professionals and continuously adapt their practice to fit their understanding. Educators clearly distinguish their professional from their personal self, a finding that is congruent with what Harwood et al. (2013) found: that educators had different versions of professional and personal selves. As educators' strive towards professionalism they seek harmony across the whole group and balance the tension between the needs of an individual and the needs of the group. To be professional in their relationships with children, these educators practice a child-selected care model, where relationships that are too individually focussed (i.e. between the educator and the child) are actively avoided or re-routed toward whole group involvement. Regarding relationships with parents, there seems to be ambivalence towards a true parent–educator partnership. Educators see themselves as experts and not partners of parents, and view themselves as possessing expertise, emphasizing the need to teach parents the appropriate way to interact with their children. Under such circumstances it is not surprising that some parents resist close relationships in childcare (Clark 2010). Taken together, I agree with Ebbeck and Yim (2009) that there needs to be more research into the practical application of how primary caregiving can change roles and relationships in childcare. It would be interesting to research these educators' emotional experiences in more detail, and to discuss concepts of professional love as well as a detailed account of primary caregiving with them, to investigate how a different view on professional relationships with families might change their perspectives regarding their role, as well as their transition practices in this centre. I agree with Elfer (2012) that there is a need for professional reflections in early childhood education including critical attention to the influence of personal emotion in professional practice. Educators need to acknowledge continuous professional development and reflective practice as an entitlement, as it is legitimate and necessary if change in professional practice should be facilitated and sustained (Elfer and Dearnley 2007). As this is a case study, I cannot draw conclusions to educators or practices in other centres. My findings, however, provide a basis for discussion about how educators can be professionals while working with a pedagogical approach that puts relationships first.

Acknowledgements

The author gratefully acknowledges the crucial contribution of Dr Margaret MacDonald in supervising this research, as well as the educators and families participating in this study.

Disclosure statement

No potential conflict of interest was reported by the authors.

References

Ahnert, L., M. Pinquart, and M. E. Lamb. 2006. "Security of Children's Relationships with Nonparental Care Providers: A Meta-Analysis." *Child Development* 74 (3): 664–679. doi:10.1111/j.1467-8624.2006.00896.x.
Barnas, M. V., and E. M. Cummings. 1994. "Caregiver Stability and Toddlers' Attachment-Related Behavior Towards Caregivers in Day Care." *Infant Behavior and Development,* 17 (2): 141–147. doi:10.1016/0163-6383(94)90049-3.

Bodrova, E., and D. L. Leong. 2007. *Tools of the Mind. The Vygotskian Approach to Early Childhood Education (2nd edition)*. Upper Saddle River. New Jersey: Pearson Merill/Prentice Hall.

Bowlby, J. 1951. *Maternal Care and Mental Health: A Report Prepared on Behalf of the World Health Organization as a Contribution to the United Nations Programme for the Welfare of Homeless Children*. Geneva: World Health Organization.

Bowlby, J. 1969. *Attachment and Loss*. New York: Basic Books.

Bowlby, J. 2005. *A Secure Base: Clinical Applications of Attachment Theory*. London: Routledge.

Brooker, L. 2008. *Supporting Transitions in the Early Years*. Berkshire, GB: Open University Press.

Clark, R. M. 2010. *Childhood in Society for Early Childhood Studies*. Exeter: Learning Matters.

Creswell, J. W. 2009. *Research Design: Qualitative, Quantitative, and Mixed Methods Approaches*. 3rd ed.Thousand Oaks, CA: Sage.

Creswell, J. W. 2012. *Educational Research. Planning, Conducting, and Evaluating Quantitative and Qualitative Research*. 4th ed.Boston, MA: Pearson Education.

Creswell, J. W. 2014. *Research Design: Qualitative, Quantitative, and Mixed Methods Approaches*. Thousand Oaks, CA: SAGE.

Dalli, C. 2006. "Re-visioning Love and Care in Early Childhood: Constructing the Future of our Profession." *The First Years New Zealand Journal of Infant and Toddler Education* 8 (1): 5–11.

Dalli, C. 2014. "Quality for Babies and Toddlers in Early Years Settings: Occasional Paper 4." *TACTYC, Association for the Professional Development of Early Years Educators*. http://tactyc.org.uk/wp-content/uploads/2014/04/Occ-Paper-4-Prof-Carmen-Dalli.pdf.

Dalli, C., N. Kibble, N. Cairns-Cowan, J. Corrigan, and B. McBride. 2009. "Reflecting on Primary Caregiving Through Action Research: The Centre of Innovation Experience at Childspace Ngaio Infants' and Toddlers' Centre." *The First Years* 11 (2): 38–45.

Daniel, J., and J. Shapiro. 1996. "Infant Transitions: Home to Center-Based Child Care." *Child and Youth Care Forum* 25 (2): 111–123.

De Shipper, J. C., L. W. C. Tavecchio, and M. H. Van IJzendoorn. 2008. "Children's Attachment Relationships with Day Care Providers: Associations with Positive Caregiving and the Child's Temperament." *Social Development* 17 (3): 454–470. doi:10.1111/j.1467-9507.2007.00448.x.

Early Childhood Educator Registry of British Columbia. 2015. http://www.mcf.gov.bc.ca/childcare/ece/.

Ebbeck, M., and H. Y. B. Yim. 2009. "Rethinking Attachment: Fostering Positive Relationships Between Infants, Toddlers, and Their Primary Caregivers." *Early Child Development and Care* 179 (7): 899–909. doi:10.1080/03004430701567934.

Elfer, P. 2012. "Emotion in Nursery Work: Work Discussion as a Model of Critical Professional Reflection." *Early Years* 32 (2): 129–141. doi:10.1080/09575146.2012.697877.

Elfer, P., and K. Dearnley. 2007. "Nurseries and Emotional Well-being: Evaluating an Emotionally Containing Model of Professional Development." *Early Years* 27 (3): 267–279. doi:10.1080/09575140701594418.

Goldschmied, E., and S. Jackson. 2004. *People Under Three. Young Children in Day Care*. 2nd ed. London, NY: Routledge.

Goosens, F. A., and M. H. IJzendoorn. 1990. "Quality of Infants' Attachment to Professional Caregivers: Relation to Infant-Parent Attachment and Day-Care Characteristics." *Child Development* 61: 832–837. doi:10.2307/1130967.

Harwood, D., A. Klopper, A. Osanyin, and M.-L. Vanderlee. 2013. "It's More Than Care: Early Childhood Educators' Concepts of Professionalism." *Early Years: An International Research Journal* 33 (1): 4–17. doi:10.1080/09575146.2012.667394.

Howes, C., and C. E. Hamilton. 1992a. "Children's Relationships with Caregivers: Mothers and Child-Care Teachers." *Child Development* 63 (4): 859–866. doi:10.1111/1467-8624.ep9301120075.

Howes, C., and C. E. Hamilton. 1992b. "Children's Relationships with Child Care Teachers: Stability and Concordance with Parental Attachments." *Child Development* 63 (4): 867–878. doi:10.1111/1467-8624.ep9301120082.

Lally, J. R. 2010. "School Readiness Begins in Infancy." *Phi Delta Kappan* 92 (3): 17–21.

Lally, J. R. 2013. *For our Babies: Ending the Invisible Neglect of America's Infants*. San Francisco, CA: WestEd.

Lieberman, A. F. 1993. *The Emotional Life of the Toddler*. New York: The Free Press.

Mahn, H. 2003. "Periods in Child Development: Vygotsky's Perspective." In *Vygotsky's Educational Theory in Cultural Context*, edited by A. Kozulin, 119–137. New York: Cambridge University Press.

Manning-Morton, J. 2006. "The Personal is Professional: Professionalism and the Birth to Threes Practitioner." *Contemporary Issues in Early Childhood* 7 (1): 42–52. doi:10.2304/ciec.2006.7.1.42.

Margetts, K., and A. Kienig. 2013. *International Perspectives on Transition to School: Reconceptualising Beliefs, Policy and Practice*. New York: Routledge.

McMullen, M., and S. Dixon. 2009. "In Support of a Relationship-Based Approach to Practice with Infants and Toddlers in the United States." In *Participatory Learning in the Early Years*, edited by D. Berthelsen, J. Brownlee, and E. Johansson, 109–128. London: Routledge.

Noddings, N. 1984. *Caring, a Feminine Approach to Ethics and Moral Education*. Berkeley: University of California Press.

Page, J. 2011. "Do Mothers Want Professional Carers to Love Their Babies?" *Journal of Early Childhood Research* 9 (3): 310–323. doi:10.1177/1476718X11407980.

Perry, B., S. Dockett, and A. Petriwskyi. 2014. *Transitions to School: International Research, Policy and Practice*. New York: Springer.

Radnor, H. 2002. *Researching Your Professional Practice. Doing Interpretive Practice*. Philadelphia, PA: Open University Press.

Rogoff, B., C. Malkin, and K. Gilbride. 1984. "Interactions with Babies as Guidance in Development." In *Children's Learning in the 'Zone of Proximal Development'*, edited by B. Rogoff and J. V. Wertsch, 31–44. San Francisco, CA: Jossey-Bass.

Saldaña, J. 2013. *The Coding Manual for Qualitative Researchers*. Los Angeles, CA: SAGE.

Stake, R. E. 1995. *The Art of Case Study Research*. Thousand Oaks, CA: Sage.

Theilheimer, P. 2006. "Moulding to the Children: Primary Caregiving and Continuity of Care." *Zero to Three* 26 (3): 50–54.

Vandenbroek, M., M. Urban, J. Peeters, and A. Lazzuri. 2016. "Introduction." In *Pathways to Professsionalism in Early Childhood Education and Care*, edited by M. Vandenbroek, M. Urban, and J. Peeters. London: Routledge.

Vanier Institute of the Family. 2013. *Mothers in Canada: By the Numbers*. http://www.childcarecanada.org/documents/research-policy-practice/13/07/mothers-canada.

Vygotsky, L. S. 1978. *Mind in Society: The Development of Higher Psychological Processes*. Cambridge: Harvard University Press.

8 Parental involvement in Finnish day care – what do early childhood educators say?

Sevcan Hakyemez-Paul, Paivi Pihlaja and Heikki Silvennoinen

ABSTRACT
Research conducted in recent decades shows that parental involvement (PI) plays a significant role in the academic achievement and the healthy development of children. Gaining a better understanding of early childhood educators' views and the reasons for insufficient practices is important for improving PI. This mixed-method research investigates the views on PI held by early childhood educators in Finland. A representative sample of 287 educators from Helsinki completed a questionnaire which provided quantitative data and qualitative material. The results show that Finnish early childhood educators have positive attitudes towards PI and its various types in general. Learning at home is the most popular type of PI. The participants state that difficulties in PI are often caused by poor parental motivation and a lack of time on the part of both educators and parents.

Introduction

Early childhood is recognised as a developmentally crucial period for the entire lifespan (Sommer, Pramling Samuelsson, and Hundeide 2013), and early childhood education (ECE) forms the foundation for children's future academic life. In particular, children's experiences in the early years shape their future academic attitudes (Alexander, Entwisle, and Dauber 1993; Hoover-Dempsey and Sandler 1997; Fan 2001; Rimm-Kaufman et al. 2003; Coleman and McNeese 2009; Galindo and Sheldon 2012; Martin, Ryan, and Brooks-Gunn 2013). The positive effects of ECE on future academic achievements have been recorded in the Finnish context (Karhula, Erola, and Kilpi-Jakonen 2016). In addition to this future impact, the significant adults surrounding children affect their present well-being, giving ECE great importance in the present. Investigating the factors affecting the success of ECE is crucial to improving it (Galindo and Sheldon 2012).

According to Bronfenbrenner (1994), children's behaviour is influenced by their interactions with the surrounding contexts and by the interactions between these contexts. Healthy relationships between these surroundings are as important as the relationship between the child and the surroundings (Bronfenbrenner 1994). Two important settings provide the contexts for young children's learning and affect their future socioemotional well-being and academic achievement: the home and the educational institution (Galindo and Sheldon 2012).

A healthy relationship between the home and the educational institution forms the core of parental involvement (PI). In the most general terms, PI is parents' involvement in their children's schooling (Grolnick and Slowiaczek 1994) or 'parent and teacher collaboration [in] children's learning' (Uludağ 2008, 809). However, it is hard to fully describe PI in one succinct statement as the views of parents and educators might differ (Rapp and Duncan 2012). For instance, parents may believe that keeping their children safe and bringing them to school constitutes involvement in their education, whereas educators might consider only parents' active presence in the school premises to be PI (Anderson and Minke 2007).

Due to the different views on collaboration and the changes in educational views over time, the terminology used in the literature varies: 'parental involvement', 'parental participation', 'parental partnership' and 'parental engagement' (Alasuutari 2010; Karlsen Bæck 2010a, 2010b; Share and Kerrins 2013; Cottle and Alexander 2014). Although often used interchangeably, these terms are not synonymous. For example, Evangelou et al. (2008) describe *parental involvement* as reactive and *parental engagement* as proactive. Goodall and Montgomery (2014) argue that *engagement* has a deeper, more personal meaning than *involvement*. Although a long-time advocate of *parental involvement*, Epstein (2015) has switched to *parental partnership* to emphasise the equal roles of school and family. In this research, the term *parental involvement* is preferred, and it is defined as multifaceted collaboration between parents and educational institutions in various activities.

Several models of PI have been proposed. Pomerantz, Moorman, and Litwack (2007) roughly divide PI into home- and school-based involvement. In contrast, Epstein (2015, 32) presents an in-depth classification of PI in the 'overlapping spheres of influence' model which includes six types of involvement: parenting, communication, volunteering, learning at home, decision-making and collaborating with the family (Epstein and Dauber 1991). The present study is based on Epstein's model as it is comprehensive and reflects the role of educators (Tekin 2011). Four types of PI (communication, learning at home, volunteering and decision-making) from Epstein's model are investigated as the present study focuses on educational activities and the educators' role in the process through educational institutions.

The underlying presumption of PI is that parents and educators have equal roles in children's early learning (OECD 2001). Goodall and Montgomery (2014) conceptualise this idea of equal roles as a continuum which starts with PI and moves to parental engagement as the parent–school relationship strengthens. This research focuses on the first phase of this continuum and investigates the views and the practices of early childhood educators. This approach enables investigating early childhood educators' perceptions of the current state of PI in day-care centres, which, according to Karila (2005), is needed as the views of educators shape the practices.

According to OECD (2001), involving parents in education provides access to parents' wide knowledge of their children and promotes their positive views of children's learning. PI is especially crucial for ECE as young children need more care than older children (Morrow and Malin 2004). In addition to children's development, educational institutions and parents also benefit from effective PI (Hill and Taylor 2004; Çakmak 2010). Home–school collaboration allows both parents and teachers to learn from each other, thus parents can be supported as educational programmes are improved.

Despite the well-recognised benefits of PI, differences still exist between what the research recommends and what educational institutions actually implement (Hornby and Lafaele 2011). In reality, educational institutions and families fail to collaborate, and the gap between rhetoric and practice leads to insufficient PI (Henderson and Berla 1994; Christenson and Sheridan 2001). This research is aimed at unravelling the reasons for this insufficiency as well as the general views of educators on PI.

Finnish context

According to the legislation, Finnish ECE focuses on care, education and children's emotional, social, cognitive and physical development and emphasises cooperation with families (Niikko and Ugaste 2012). In Finland, ECE is provided to children younger than the compulsory school age (7). After parental leave, all children younger than school age are entitled to places in either day-care centres or family day care. One year before starting compulsory school, children attend one year of preschool education.

According to Finnish legislation (Early Childhood Education Act, 19.1.1973/36, 8.5.2015/580), the purpose of ECE is to promote children's development and well-being. The legislation also emphasises the importance of educators working together with parents to support them in bringing up their children but according to Hirsto (2010) it does not specify how to implement this partnership.

In the past decade, Finnish day care has undergone significant changes, including a change in the governing ministry, the number of children in groups and the required competences for staff. The legislation is regulating only the basics. Since the 1990s, decentralisation and legislative changes have shifted power to municipalities. Day-care group sizes have grown as the number of employees and the ratio of qualified day-care teachers have decreased (Pihlaja and Junttila 2001; Pihlaja, Rantanen, and Sonne 2010). Due to the public budget cuts, Finnish ECE has suffered in several respects.

Much research in the Finnish context has addressed early childhood educators' views and practices of PI and the obstacles to those practices (Hirsto 2010; Niikko and Ugaste 2012; Ugaste and Niikko 2015). However, no in-depth research on insufficient PI practices and their causes has been conducted. Hirsto (2010) states that communication is the PI type most frequently used by Finnish early childhood educators, while volunteering and decision-making are the least. Finnish early childhood educators stress the importance of parental collaboration (Niikko and Ugaste 2012) but also the difficulties in building it (Ugaste and Niikko 2015).

A comparative study showed that teachers in Finland consider parents to be more passive than teachers in other countries (Hujala et al. 2009). The present study aims to deepen understanding of these views and to uncover Finnish educators' opinions about the sufficiency of PI practices and the reasons for insufficient practices in order to draw a more detailed picture of PI in Finnish ECE today.

Method

Participants

Data were collected through a survey administered to early childhood educators working in Helsinki, Finland, in two waves over approximately five months in 2015. The institutions surveyed employed approximately 1200 educators, and the final sample responses from 287 educators. An accurate response rate could not be calculated as how many educators actually received the questionnaire was unknown. Table 1 presents the respondents' demographic information.

Instrument

The study instrument was a questionnaire designed to measure general views on PI and attitudes towards types of PI based on Epstein's (2015) model. Webropol was used as the online data collection tool. The questionnaire and a brief explanation of the research were sent to the Helsinki ECE manager, seeking permission to conduct the research. The questionnaire included an informed consent form, and the responses were anonymous. After permission was granted, the ECE manager sent a link to the questionnaire to the ECE expert in Helsinki, who forwarded it to all the ECE institutions in Helsinki (approximately 300 at the time) with the request that the principals distribute the link to educators.

The quantitative data and the qualitative material were collected simultaneously with the same instrument. The questionnaire consisted of five parts. The first part, *general view* (9 items), explored the respondents' general attitudes towards PI and used a Likert scale (1 = *'totally disagree'* to 5 = *'totally agree'*). The other four parts focused on the PI types and the reasons for insufficient practices, if any. The second part, *communication* (7 items), measured the frequency of PI through communication; the third part, *volunteering* (5 items), the frequency of PI through volunteering; the fourth part, *learning at home* (6 items), the frequency of encouragement of parents to support educational activities at home; and the fifth part, *decision-making* (5 items), the frequency of PI in the decision-making process. These four parts used a Likert scale (1 = *never*; 5 = *always*) in all but four multiple-choice questions in total.

Table 1. Descriptive statistics of participants' background variables.

Variable	Number	Per cent
Gender		
Female	280	97.6
Male	7	2.4
Experience in the field		
0–5 years	92	32.3
6–10 years	33	11.2
11–20 years	57	20.0
21–40 year	104	36.5
Educational background		
Kindergarten teacher	203	70.7
Social pedagogue*	77	26.8
Other	7	2.4
Education level		
University of applied sciences	75	26.1
University	132	46.0
Old kindergarten teacher seminars	67	23.3
Master's degree	10	3.5
Age group of the children		
0–3	68	23.7
3–5/6	147	51.2
6–7	58	20.2
Mixed age	14	4.9

*Social pedagogy is a bachelor's degree of social services gained from universities of applied sciences in Finland.

A reliability test was run for all items in the questionnaire which found that they were all reliable (30 items; $\alpha = .79$). The test was repeated separately for each section, producing Cronbach's alpha for each section: general view: .6, communication: .45, volunteering: .77, learning at home: .66 and decision-making: .62. Some items in the general views section were excluded from the analysis due to low Cronbach's alpha values. The communication section had a low Cronbach's alpha, so its items were examined separately.

The last four parts also contained one multiple-choice item with an open-ended option. These items targeted the reasons underlying insufficient PI practices. The participants were asked to select any option only if they believed that existing practices were insufficient and were allowed to choose more than one option. The open-ended option allowing the participants to explain the reasons for insufficient practices in their own words enabled obtaining new, in-depth knowledge of PI (e.g. Lund 2012). The open-ended answers generated the qualitative material, providing insights into different aspects of PI practices, and supplemented the quantitative data (e.g. Erzberger and Kelle 2003, 473).

Analysis

A mixed-method design was used in this study, which is presented as a valid method to mitigate the limitations of single-method studies and to confirm the study (Greene and Caracelli 1997; Creswell et al. 2008). Mixed-method analysis allows a combination of measurements and interpretations through data-adequate ways (Biesta 2010, 101). The qualitative material was analysed to gain more detailed information on the reasons for insufficient PI practices. Regarding the open-ended options, the respondents made 84 statements in the communication section, 76 statements in the volunteering section, 41 statements in the learning at home section and 43 statements in the decision-making section. These statements provided new information about the participants' reasons for insufficient practices beyond the options listed in the questionnaire.

In the first step of the quantitative analysis, factor analysis was performed for each section, clustering the items into factors to assess whether they measured the desired factors. Next, frequency tests with multiple-choice items were conducted to identify the underlying reasons for insufficient practices of particular PI types. In addition, the frequency tests were repeated for the items in the communication section. Cross-tabulation analysis was performed to reveal the associations between the background variables and the insufficiency statements.

In the qualitative analysis, content analysis was performed by adapting grounded theory, where the analysis is based on the material (Strauss and Corbin 1996). This analysis added depth to the quantitative research results. All the sections of the questionnaire were included in this analysis.

The qualitative material was drawn from the open-ended answers to the questionnaire items investigating insufficient PI practices. All the responses to the open-ended option were analysed using coding procedures. The level of investigator triangulation was good (>90%). In open coding, the material was labelled for the reasons for problems given by the participants (e.g. time, skills, resources, cultural differences, interest, trust, stress, administration and motivation). The labels generated ($N = 18$) were grouped by similarities to create categories for axial coding. Five high-order categories were extracted from the axial coding. After creation of the categories, the distribution of the reasons by the PI type was assessed (e.g. Strauss and Corbin 1996; Böhm 2004).

Results

General views on PI and attitudes towards PI types

As the first step to understand how Finnish early childhood educators perceive PI, educators' general views (9 items) on this matter were investigated. The mean scores ($M = 3.65$, Table 2) show that Finnish early childhood educators view PI positively. The participants were also asked about their opinions on who has the responsibility to establish the home–institution relationship. The responses show that Finnish early childhood educators believe that this responsibility lies primarily with educators ($M_{3rd\ item} = 3.56$, $M_{4th\ item} = 2.95$, $M_{5th\ item} = 2.83$).

Descriptive statistics were calculated to determine the popularity of the PI types. The most common type is to involve parents in *learning at home* ($M = 3.43$), while the least popular is to involve parents as volunteers ($M = 2.39$) (Table 3).

The item-based analysis for the communication section shows that the most common means of communication in PI is face-to-face conversations. Additionally, written communication is used more frequently than telephone communication (Figure 1).

Reasons for insufficient practices by PI type

Each section targeting a particular PI type included a question with an open-ended option to allow the participants to explain why they might think the practices for that PI type are insufficient. In this design, unfilled multiple-choice questions were considered to indicate that the practices for the particular PI type were sufficient (the participants were instructed to skip the question if they thought that the particular PI type was adequately practised).

In the responses, 72% of the participants (Figure 2) think that communication is not practised sufficiently as a PI type. Involving parents as volunteers is regarded as more problematic, with 81% of participants reporting insufficient practice. Although the most common PI type, learning at home is also practised insufficiently (63% of the participants). As well, 66% of the participants claim that PI in decision-making is not practised sufficiently.

The associations between the background variables and the perceptions of insufficient PI practices were checked through a series of cross-tabulation tests. After repeating the test

Table 2. Means and standard deviations of general views of Finnish early childhood educators

	N	Percentages	Mean	Std. Deviation
General view	282	53.7	3.65	.56
Building a relationship between educational institution and parents is teachers' duty	286	56.1	3.56	1.09
Building a relationship between educational institution and parents is principals' duty	286	31.7	2.95	1.10
Building a relationship between educational institution and parents is parents' duty	284	25.8	2.83	1.04
Valid N (list wise)	282			

Table 3. Means and standard deviations of PI types.

	N	Minimum	Maximum	Mean	Std. Deviation
Volunteering	280	1.00	5.00	2.39	.66628
Learning at home	276	1.00	5.00	3.43	.57961
Decision-making	284	1.00	5.00	2.57	.61551
Valid N (list wise)	269				

for each background variable and each PI type, the results reveal a significant association between the participants' age and the frequency of perceived insufficient use of communication as a PI type ($p = .015$). Another correlation is found between the age groups of the children and perceived insufficiency in PI through volunteering ($p = .047$). However, no other associations were found.

To identify the reasons for the difficulties in practising specific PI types, frequency tests were run separately. The most common reason cited for insufficient practices across all PI types is that 'parents do not want to be involved'. The least common reason is that 'my education is not enough to practice this PI type' (Figure 2).

In-depth analysis of insufficient PI

The open-ended answers provide a deeper understanding of the reasons for insufficient PI. The most-oft chosen reason among the multiple choices is that 'parents do not want to be involved', and the responses to the open-ended options open a new dimension to this statement (Table 4). The cultural views on PI in ECE are quite homogenous. Most reasons are related to parents or the conditions of day-care centres, rarely to the teachers themselves or to their practices. The main categories for insufficient practices are time management, individual incompatibility, management and administration, unclear purpose of ECE and lack of trust and competence.

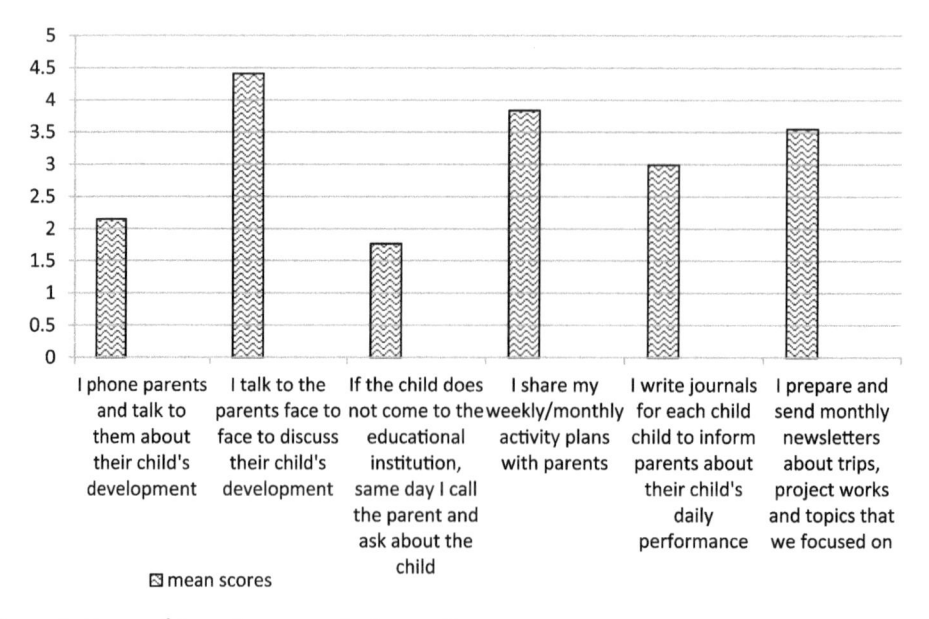

Figure 1. Means of items in communication section.

WORKING WITH PARENTS AND FAMILIES IN EARLY CHILDHOOD EDUCATION 109

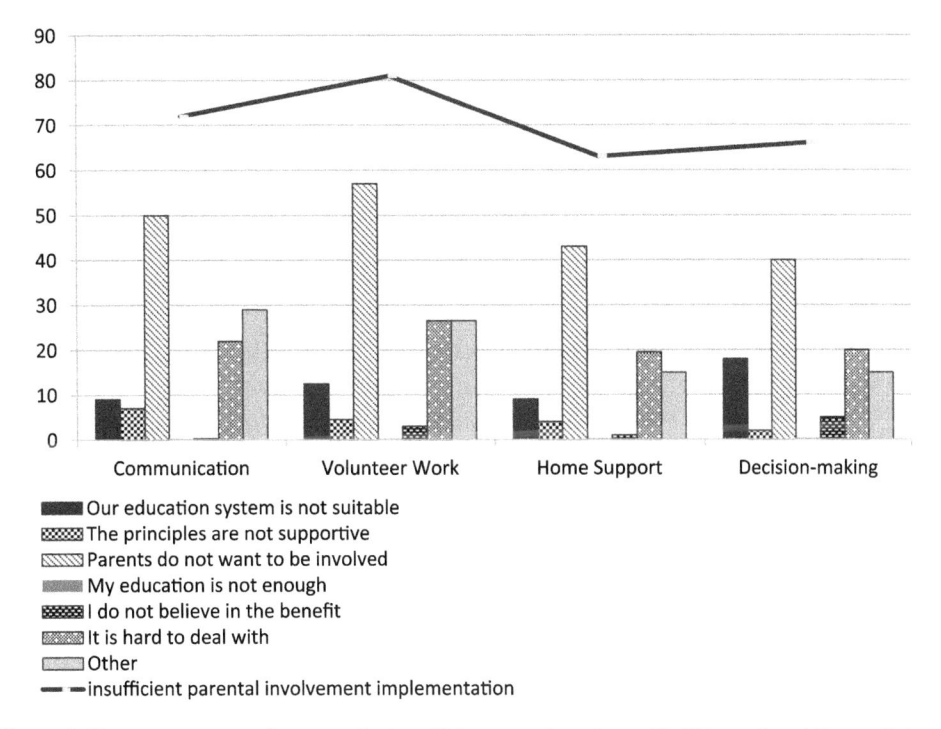

Figure 2. The percentages of reasons for insufficient practice of specific PI types* and the participants who states that the PI practices are insufficient. *Per cent of participants who stated that they cannot use the specific PI type sufficiently. Participants could mark more than one reason.

Time management is the most frequently reported reason for insufficient practice of PI (130 times) in the open-ended responses. This category includes all time-related references, such as after-work activities, parental duties due to family size and the workload and the everyday busyness of both parents and teachers. The statements mostly point to parents' lack of time, followed by more general statements related to educators' time management issues and workload.

In statements regarding insufficient communication practices as PI, the teachers primarily discuss their daily workload and lack of time to find feasible means of communication for PI. For example, a respondent states: 'time is limited. My main task is to interact with the children. I do not have much time for parents'. In the answers addressing learning

Table 4. Number of mentions of other reasons of insufficient practice of PI types.

	Communication	Volunteer works	Learning at home	Decision-making
Time management	48	**50**	24	8
Personal differences	**18**	7	5	5
Interest	**10**	6	3	1
Resources	9	3	3	2
Regulation	1	1	1	12
Unclear task of ECE	8	2	3	2
Need	2	4	7	1
Trust	0	**3**	3	0
Attitude	5	0	2	1
Competence	3	**4**	0	2

at home and involving parents as volunteers, though, the focus is more often on the parents' lack of time. For example, regarding learning at home, the participants mention the parents' lack of time and busy everyday life. Similarly, regarding volunteering, a respondent explains that 'parents work during the hours when the children are in day care, which is why they cannot participate in activities'. Another teacher supports this position, stating that 'the parents cannot come in the daytime, and we are not allowed to work outside working hours'.

Individual incompatibility (55 times) encompasses differences in language, culture and viewpoints. This reason is mentioned in connection to every PI type and is the most commonly given reason for not using communication in PI. Language barriers are mentioned most frequently. One participant states: 'with some parents, there is no fluent common language, and cooperation is very difficult for that reason'. Another writes, without mentioning any parties involved, 'the language barrier, cultural differences'. According to the participants, the parents and the professionals have different individual interests, and both may also lack interest, motivation and willingness. The statements regarding individual incompatibility are almost exclusively associated with the parents and are related to all PI types, although most concern communication and volunteering. Illustrating this point, one participant states that 'some parents are not interested', and another participant somewhat accusatorily describes 'a lack of motivation on the parents' part to participate in open cooperation'. The participants also mention 'attitude' (8 times), most often referring negative or passive parental attitudes towards PI: 'the lack of appreciation for preschool education becomes obvious in the parents' attitude'.

Management and administrative obstacles (32 times) are also among the reasons for insufficient practices. The participants explain that the lack of resources in ECE increases the pressure and workload; there are too many children in groups, an inadequate number of staff and facilities or both. A teacher notes that 'resources have been pressed to the limit'. Regulations also limit PI, especially when incorporating parents in decision-making: 'all [the] important decisions have already been made somewhere else!' Another teacher asks: 'why ask about a matter which they cannot (neither can we) have any influence on?!'

The respondents' understanding of ECE and collaboration with parents is worth mentioning. The unclear purpose of ECE (15 times) and the need for involvement (14 times) are reasons for insufficient practices of many PI types. Again, these two reasons are attributed to both parents and educators and mentioned for every PI type. Regarding the purpose of ECE and parents' role in it, one participant explains: 'parents do not always understand or realise the significance of pre-primary education. The children are "shuffled away", so parents have time and possibility to do their own business'. Supporting this statement, another respondent writes: 'some of parents think that it [children's education is a matter] belonging to the day-care and not to them. They pay for the service'. Another contradicts the importance of PI: 'why should parents participate in the first place? Parents work, which is why it is difficult to demand that they participate'. Similarly, another participant states: 'the staff does not want to bother the parents'. These quotations illustrate that PI is seen as a burden on parents, conflicting with the perceived need for PI. For instance, one participant states that '(parents) do not regard their own participation', whereas another argues against the need: 'I ask: why should they?'

A lack of trust and competence in the fields of education or child-rearing is also mentioned (18 times) as a reason for insufficient PI. Trust goes two ways: trust in oneself and trust in others. Based on the responses, the parents' trust in the educators' knowledge and management skills leads to insufficient PI. Participants also mention that the parents do not trust in themselves enough to facilitate their children' learning at home. Regarding parental support at home and PI through volunteering, a respondent states that 'parents trust in our professional competence and do not value their own participation'. Another teacher speculates that 'the parents do not necessarily trust themselves as implementers of pre-primary school activities'.

Lack of competence can be divided into lack of emotional competence (2 times) and lack of intellectual competence (7 times). The participants describe their own lack of experience and skill and the parents' lack of knowledge. For example, one participant describes her knowledge of professional culture and experience in pre-primary education as inadequate, while another believes that the parents' lack of competence and uncertainty differs from the 'correct way' to participate.

The teachers see the reasons for insufficient practices as external to themselves and mostly attribute failing practices to parents or management and administrative factors. The teachers do not reflect on their own practices. Differences between institutions might exist, as one respondent marvels: 'I cannot say why parents are not asked to participate in this day-care centre where I now work. In previous centres, the parents were always welcome.'

Discussion

The study findings show that Finnish early childhood educators have positive attitudes towards PI and agree on its importance. Deeper analysis, however, reveals that these positive attitudes are quite superficial. This tendency aligns with the findings of Hujala et al. (2009) that Finnish early childhood educators want to restrict education to institutions and regard parents as passive. The item-based analysis shows that the respondents believe that although parents, educators and principals together establish collaboration between the educational institution and the home, educators bear slightly greater responsibility in this area. These findings differ from those reported in research conducted in the United States, where kindergarten teachers are not convinced of their obligation to carry out PI (Swick and McKnight 1989).

Finnish early childhood educators agree that learning at home best meets their needs as this appears to be the most popular PI type. Previous research by Hindman et al. (2012) and Hakyemez (2015) found similar results indicating that the most common type of PI is, indeed, learning at home. This observation is also supported by Sabancı (2009), who reported that teachers favour learning at home while principals view communication, volunteering and decision-making more positively than teachers. This difference might result from educators' busy schedules as parental support of student learning at home reduces educators' professional burden. In contrast, involving parents as volunteers is not common as parents also usually have a busy work-life. Furthermore, considering that educators themselves do not have much power in decision-making processes, PI in decision-making is understandably difficult.

Finnish early childhood educators prefer face-to-face and written communication over telephone communication. Hirsto (2010) also reported that Finnish early childhood educators frequently use face-to-face and written communication to inform and involve parents. These face-to-face conversations often take place in unofficial encounters during pick-up and drop-off (Venninen and Purola 2013), especially to address problems (Sormunen, Tossavainen, and Turunen 2011).

The most important contribution of this research is to clarify the reasons for insufficient PI practices. Most commonly, the participants stated that they do not believe that the parents want to be involved (Figure 2). This result corresponds with the Greek case, where teachers consider the parental participation rate to be insufficient (Koutrouba et al. 2009). The least frequent reason given by the participants is that they do not view their own education as adequate to practice a particular PI type. These results indicate high professional self-esteem among early childhood educators.

Räty, Kasanen, and Laine (2009) explain that Finnish parents see child-rearing as their duty and teaching as the responsibility of educational institutions. This belief might explain why early childhood educators think that parents are unwilling to be involved. In the second and third most commonly given reasons, some educators find it difficult to conduct PI and believe that the Finnish ECE system does not provide sufficient opportunities to do so. Thus, despite high professional self-esteem, Finnish early childhood educators might benefit from further support in involving parents, and changes in attitudes towards PI also merit discussion.

Another notable finding is the unclear purpose of ECE in Finland, which reflects an underlying dilemma in ECE services. Finnish society established day care as a social service to facilitate employment (Välimäki 1998), not as an educational context for children (Hujala et al. 2009). This understanding can be seen in the participants' answers describing ECE institutions as a place for children only while their parents work (Onnismaa 2001). This misconception can also be seen in other European Union countries. For instance, Greek families regard ECE professionals as mere babysitters, dismissing ECE as the beginning of formal education (Rentzou 2011). Onnismaa (2001) found that day care emphasises the privacy of the home and the privacy of the day care as two unrelated contexts in children's lives. This privacy concern explains why early childhood educators believe that PI activities bother parents.

Although learning at home is the most common PI type in this study, 63% of the Finnish early childhood educators admit that they do not exploit it sufficiently (Figure 2). A lack of time and heavy work load are the primary barriers, as in other EU countries (Koutrouba et al. 2009). In recent years, educators' workload has increased as resources have decreased (Rintakorpi 2015; Karila 2016). Work-life places also heavy demands on parents, so they may see any day-care activities with their children as extra burdens.

In addition to long working hours, cultural and language differences exert a negative influence. Parents who lack cultural and language competences prefer not to be involved in education-related subjects. Families' demographic characteristics also play an important role in the quality of PI (Baker and Stevenson 1986). Parents with poor educational backgrounds and low incomes tend to avoid school-related activities, while well-educated parents with high educational and socioeconomic levels support their children's education through involvement (Hilado, Kallemeyn, and Phillips 2013). Mahmood (2013), however, reported that early childhood educators state that upper-middle class parents tend to focus more on their careers and to dedicate less time to their children's education.

In the present findings, volunteering is the most-problematic and least-used PI type (Figure 2). Finnish traditions may constitute one reason. Day-care services were originally established in the 1970s to support the national economy and to encourage women to enter the labour market. Day care enabled both parents to have full-time employment (Välimäki 1998). At the same time, volunteering is considered to be the most time-consuming PI type, but its popularity is also challenged by language and cultural differences, as well as time management issues. These obstacles might stem from teachers' inability to cope with cultural differences and the difficulties families of foreign origin encounter while adapting to the Finnish system. Cultural differences are recognised as an obstacle to involvement in many countries. Mahmood (2013) reported that first-year educators often find that their college education does not sufficiently prepare them to cope with cultural differences. Providing in-service education on multiculturalism and resolving the obstacles caused by cultural differences could help educators involve parents from different ethnic and cultural background.

Regarding communication as a PI type, 72% of the participants state that they cannot adequately use communication methods, pointing to an important disconnection between day care and home. According to the participants, the primary causes of inadequate communication are cultural differences and the lack of time and a common language. This disconnection urgently needs to be addressed.

Two-thirds of the participants do not think that they sufficiently involve parents in decision-making, while two-fifths believe that parents do not want to be involved. The qualitative material from this study identifies municipal regulations as one cause of insufficient PI in decision-making. Although the law does not forbid parental participation in decision-making, it does not allow much room for parents to speak up (Rabusicová and Emmerová 2002). According to the participants in this study, the regulations do not leave room for educators to involve parents in decision-making. Nevertheless, educational institutions are well able to maintain effective PI programmes as long as administrators acknowledge the importance of well-structured institution–home collaboration and allow teachers' autonomy to work with parents in decision-making (Berger 2008). However, educators do not unanimously embrace involving parents in the decision-making process. Many early childhood educators believe that these tasks should be done by professionals with specific pedagogical skills and education in the field (Venninen and Purola 2013).

The survey respondents also state that parents trust professionals and do not feel the need to be involved. This finding supports findings of previous research on PI in Finland, in which parents indicate satisfaction, trust and commitment to their children's day care, although 80% of the parents state that they are committed to being involved, but only 40% are actually willing to participate in children's group activities (Pihlaja, Kinos, and Mäntymäki 2010).

Limitations and further research

It was not possible to establish the response rate to the survey used in this study as regulations required the involvement of many third parties in data collection. Nevertheless, the number of participants is substantial, supporting the validity of the results. This study focuses on educators' views and attitudes towards PI and its types. Further research could address parental views and attitudes. A bridge between these parties could provide a better understanding of how to improve PI in ECE.

The findings also identify issues at the administrative and the legislative levels. The participants frequently point to restrictive regulations and a lack of administrative support as reasons for insufficient PI. Examining the application of new Finnish ECE legislation to these institutions, therefore, could yield valuable insights into the current and the future state of these institutions and their collaboration with parents.

Finally, cultural differences, an oft-cited reason for insufficient PI in ECE, provide a platform to analyse migrant families and their position in the Finnish educational system. With increasing mobility and multiculturalism, the integration of individuals into society has gained increasing importance.

Acknowledgements

This research was conducted while the authors were employed at the University of Turku.

Disclosure statement

No potential conflict of interest was reported by the authors.

References

Alasuutari, M. 2010. "Striving at Partnership: Parent–Practitioner Relationships in Finnish Early Educators' Talk." *European Early Childhood Education Research Journal* 18 (2): 149–161.
Alexander, K. L., D. R. Entwisle, and S. L. Dauber. 1993. "First-grade Classroom Behavior: It's Short and Long Term Consequences for School Performance." *Child Development* 64 (3): 801–814.
Anderson, K. J., and K. M. Minke. 2007. "Parent Involvement in Education: Toward an Understanding of Parents' Decision Making." *Journal of Educational Research* 100 (5): 311–323.
Baker, D. P., and D. L. Stevenson. 1986. "Mothers' Strategies for Children's School Achievement: Managing the Transition to High School." *Sociology of Education* 59 (3): 156–166.
Berger, E. H. 2008. *Parents as Partners in Education: Families and Schools Working Together*. 7th ed. Upper Saddle River, NJ: Merrill/Prentice Hall.
Biesta, G. 2010. "Pragmatism and the Philosophical Foundations of Mixed Methods Research." In *Mixed Methods in Social & Behavioral Research*, edited by A. Tashakkori and C. Teddlie, 95–117. Thousand Oaks, CA: Sage.
Böhm, A. 2004. "Theoretical Coding: Text Analysis in Grounded Theory." In *A Companion to Qualitative Research*, edited by U. Flick, E. von Kardorff, and I. Steinke, 270–275. London, UK: Sage.
Bronfenbrenner, U. 1994. "Ecological Models of Human Development." In *International Encyclopedia of Education*. 2nd ed., edited by T. Husen and T. N. Postlethwaite, 37–42. Oxford: Elsevier. Vol. 3, Reprinted in: Gauvain, M., ed., Readings on the Development of Children, 2nd. ed., 37–42. New York: Freeman.
Çakmak, ÖÇ. 2010. "Okul öncesi eğitim kurumlarında aile katılımı" [Parental Involvement in Early Childhood Education Institutions]. *Abant İzzet Baysal University Journal of Social Sciences* 2010-1 (20): 1–17.
Christenson, S. L., and S. M. Sheridan. 2001. *Schools and Families: Creating Essential Connections for Learning*. New York: Guilford Press.

Coleman, B., and M. N. McNeese. 2009. "From Home to School: The Relationship among Parental Involvement, Student Motivation, and Academic Achievement." *International Journal of Learning* 16 (7): 459–470.

Cottle, M., and E. Alexander. 2014. "Parent Partnership and 'Quality' Early Years Services: Practitioners' Perspectives." *European Early Childhood Education Research Journal* 22 (5): 637–659.

Creswell, J., V. Clark, M. Gutman, and W. Hanson. 2008. "Advanced Mixed Methods. Research Design." In *The Mixed Methods Reader*, edited by V. Clark and J. Creswell, 209–240. Los Angeles, CA: Sage.

Early Childhood Education Act, 19.1.1973/36, 8.5.2015/580. Accessed November 30, 2016. http://www.finlex.fi/fi/laki/ajantasa/1973/19730036?search%5Btype%5D = pika&search%5Bpika%5D = varhaiskasvatuslaki.

Epstein, J. L. 2015. *School, Family and Community Partnerships: Preparing Educators and Improving Schools. Student Economy Edition*. 2nd ed. Boulder, CO: Westview.

Epstein, J. L., and S. L. Dauber. 1991. "School Programs and Teacher Practices of Parent Involvement in Inner-city Elementary and Middle Schools." *Elementary School Journal* 91 (3): 289–305.

Erzberger, C., and U. Kelle. 2003. "Making Inferences in Mixed Methods: The Rules of Integration." In *Handbook of Mixed Methods in Social & Behavioral Research*, edited by A. Tashakkori and C. Teddie, 457–490. Thousand Oaks, CA: Sage.

Evangelou, M., K. Sylva, A. Edwards, and T. Smith. 2008. *Supporting Parents in Promoting Early Learning: The Evaluation of the Early Learning Partnership Project (Research Report DCSF-RR039)*. London, UK: Department for Children, Schools and Families.

Fan, X. 2001. "Parental Involvement and Students' Academic Achievement: A Growth Modeling Analysis." *Journal of Experimental Education* 70 (1): 27–61.

Galindo, C., and S. B. Sheldon. 2012. "School and Home Connections and Children's Kindergarten Achievement Gains: The Mediating Role of Family Involvement." *Early Childhood Research Quarterly* 27 (1): 90–103.

Goodall, J., and C. Montgomery. 2014. "Parental Involvement to Parental Engagement: A Continuum." *Educational Review* 66 (4): 399–410.

Greene, J. C., and V. J. Caracelli, eds. 1997. *Advances in Mixed Method Evaluation: The Challenges and Benefits of Integration Diverse Paradigms*. San Francisco, CA: Jossey-Bass.

Grolnick, W. S., and M. L. Slowiaczek. 1994. "Parents' Involvement in Children's Schooling: A Multidimensional Conceptualization and Motivational Model." *Child Development* 64 (1): 237–252.

Hakyemez, S. 2015. "Turkish Early Childhood Educators on Parental Involvement." *European Educational Research Journal* 14 (1): 100–112.

Henderson, A., and N. Berla. 1994. *A New Generation of Evidence: The Family Is Critical to Student Achievement*. Washington, DC: Centre for Law and Education.

Hilado, A. V., Kallemeyn, L., and L. Phillips. 2013. "Examining Understandings of Parent Involvement in Early Childhood Programs." *Early Childhood Research & Practice* 15 (2).

Hill, N. E., and L. C. Taylor. 2004. "Parental School Involvement and Children's Academic Achievement: Pragmatics and Issues." *Current Directions in Psychological Science* 13 (4): 161–164.

Hindman, A. H., A. L. Miller, L. C. Froyen, and L. E. Skibbe. 2012. "A Portrait of Family Involvement During Head Start: Nature, Extent, and Predictors." *Early Childhood Research Quarterly* 27 (4): 654–667.

Hirsto, L. 2010. "Strategies in Home and School Collaboration among Early Education Teachers." *Scandinavian Journal of Educational Research* 54 (2): 99–108.

Hoover-Dempsey, K. V., and H. M. Sandler. 1997. "Why do Parents Become Involved in Their Children's Education?" *Review of Educational Research* 67 (1): 3–42.

Hornby, G., and R. Lafaele. 2011. "Barriers to Parental Involvement in Education: An Explanatory Model." *Educational Review* 63 (1): 37–52.

Hujala, E., L. Turja, M. F. Gaspar, M. Veisson, and M. Waniganyake. 2009. "Perspectives of Early Childhood Teachers on Parent-Teacher Partnerships in Five European Countries." *European Early Childhood Education Research Journal* 17 (1): 57–76.

Karhula, A., J. Erola, and E. Kilpi-Jakonen. 2016. *Home Sweet Home? Long-term Educational Outcomes of Childcare Arrangements in Finland*. Working Papers on Social and Economic Issues. Turku Center for Welfare Research.

Karila, K. 2005. "Vanhempien ja päivähoidon henkilöstönkeskustelut kasvatuskumppanuuden areenoina" [The Discussion of Parents and Professionals in the Arena of Educational Partnership]. *Kasvatus* 36 (2): 285–298.

Karila, K. 2016. *Vaikuttava Varhaiskasvatus [Effective Early Childhood Education]*. Helsinki: Board of Education.

Karlsen Bæck, U.-D. 2010a. "Parental Involvement Practices in Formalized Home–School Cooperation." *Scandinavian Journal of Educational Research* 54 (6): 549–563.

Karlsen Bæck, U.-D. 2010b. "'We Are the Professionals': A Study of Teachers' Views on Parental Involvement in School." *British Journal of Sociology of Education* 31 (3): 323–335.

Koutrouba, K., E. Antonopoulou, G. Tsitsas, and E. Zenakou. 2009. "An Investigation of Greek Teachers' Views on Parental Involvement in Education." *School Psychology International* 30 (3): 311–328.

Lund, T. 2012. "Combining Qualitative and Quantitative Approaches: Some Arguments for Mixed Methods Research." *Scandinavian Journal of Educational Research* 56 (2): 155–165.

Mahmood, S. 2013. "First-year Preschool and Kindergarten Teachers: Challenges of Working with Parents." *School Community Journal* 23 (2): 55–85.

Martin, A., R. M. Ryan, and J. Brooks-Gunn. 2013. "Longitudinal Associations among Interest, Persistence, Supportive Parenting, and Achievement in Early Childhood." *Early Childhood Research Quarterly* 28 (4): 658–667.

Morrow, G., and N. Malin. 2004. "Parents and Professionals Working Together: Turning the Rhetoric Into Reality." *Early Years* 24 (2): 163–177.

Niikko, A., and A. Ugaste. 2012. "Conceptions of Finnish and Estonian Pre-school Teachers' Goals in Their Pedagogical Work." *Scandinavian Journal of Educational Research* 56 (4): 481–495.

OECD (Organisation of Economic Cooperation and Development). 2001. *Starting Strong: Early Childhood Education and Care*. Paris: Organisation of Economic Cooperation and Development.

Onnismaa, E.-L. 2001. "Varhaiskasvatus ja – lapsuus lainsäädäntödiskurssissa" [Early Education and Early Childhood in Legislative Discourses]. *Kasvatus* 32 (4): 355–365.

Pihlaja, P., and N. Junttila. 2001. *Julkishallinnon hajauttaminen – miltä päiväkodin lapsiryhmät näyttävät muutosten jälkeen [Decentralisation of Public Administration – How Do Child Groups Look Like After the Reforms?]*. Helsinki: Association of Kindergarten Teachers 1/2001.

Pihlaja, P., J. Kinos, and M. Mäntymäki. 2010. "Päivähoitosuhteen laadun komponentit. Vanhempien kokemukset päivähoitosuhteesta" [Perceived Relationships Quality. Parents Experiences of Day Care Relationship]. In *Pienet Oppimassa. Kasvatuksellisia Näkökulmia Varhaiskasvatukseen ja Esiopetukseen* [The Little Ones Learning], edited by R. Korhonen, M.-L. Rönkkö, and J. Aerila, 189–201. Turku: Turun opettajankoulutuslaitos.

Pihlaja, P., M.-L. Rantanen, and V. Sonne. 2010. *Varhaiserityiskasvatus Varsinais-Suomessa. Vastauksia monitahoarvioinnilla* [Early Childhood Special Education in South-Western Finland]. Turku: Varsinais-Suomen sosiaalialan osaamiskeskus.

Pomerantz, E. M., E. A. Moorman, and S. D. Litwack. 2007. "The How, Whom, and Why of Parents' Involvement in Children's Schooling: More Is Not Necessarily Better." *Review of Educational Research* 77 (3): 373–410.

Rabusicová, M., and K. Emmerová. 2002. "The Role of Parents as Educational and Social Partners of Schools in the Czech Republic: Legislation and Media Analysis." *European Educational Research Journal* 1 (3): 480–496.

Rapp, N., and H. Duncan. 2012. "Multi-dimensional Parental Involvement in Schools: A Principal's Guide." *International Journal of Educational Leadership Preparation* 7 (1): 1–14.

Räty, H., K. Kasanen, and N. Laine. 2009. "Parents' Participation in Their Child's Schooling." *Scandinavian Journal of Educational Research* 53 (3): 277–293.

Rentzou, K. 2011. "Parent-caregiver Relationship Dyad in Greek Day Care Centres." *International Journal of Early Years Education* 19 (2): 163–177.

Rimm-Kaufman, S. E., R. C. Pianta, M. J. Cox, and R. H. Bradley. 2003. "Teacher-rated Family Involvement and Children's Social and Academic Outcomes in Kindergarten." *Early Education and Development* 14 (2): 179–198.

Rintakorpi, K. 2015. "Dokumentointi varhaiskasvatuksen kehittämisen menetelmänä" [Documentation: A Method to Develop ECE]. *Kasvatuss* 46 (3): 269–275.

Sabancı, A. 2009. "Views of Primary School Administrators, Teachers and Parents on Parental Involvement in Turkey." *Eurasian Journal of Educational Research* 36: 245–262.

Share, M., and L. Kerrins. 2013. "Supporting Parental Involvement in Children's Early Learning: Lessons From Community Childcare Centres in Dublin's Docklands." *Child Care in Practice* 19 (4): 355–374.

Sommer, D., I. Pramling Samuelsson, and K. Hundeide. 2013. "Early Childhood Care and Education: A Child Perspective Paradigm." *European Early Childhood Education Research Journal* 21 (4): 459–475.

Sormunen, M., K. Tossavainen, and H. Turunen. 2011. "Home-school Collaboration in the View of Fourth Grade Pupils, Parents, Teachers and Principals in the Finnish Education System." *School Community Journal* 21 (2): 185–212.

Strauss, A., and J. Corbin. 1996. *Basics of Qualitative Research Techniques and Procedures for Developing Grounded Theory*. Thousand Oaks, CA: Sage.

Swick, K. J., and S. McKnight. 1989. "Characteristics of Kindergarten Teachers who Promote Parent Involvement." *Early Childhood Research Quarterly* 4 (1): 19–29.

Tekin, A. K. 2011. "Parent Involvement Revisited: Background, Theories, and Models." *International Journal of Applied Educational Studies* 11 (1): 1–13.

Ugaste, A., and A. Niikko. 2015. "Identifying the Problems That Finnish and Estonian Teachers Encounter in Preschool." *European Early Childhood Education Research Journal* 23 (4): 423–433.

Uludağ, A. 2008. "Elementary Preservice Teachers' Opinions About Parental Involvement in Elementary Children's Education." *Teaching and Teacher Education* 24 (3): 807–817.

Välimäki, A.-L. 1998. *Päivittäin: lasten (päivä)hoitojärjestelyn muotoutuminen varhaiskasvun ympäristönä suomalaisessa yhteiskunnassa 1800 ja, 1900 luvulla* [Every Day: The Evolution of the Children's (Day)-Care System as an Environment for Early Growth in Finnish Society in the, 19th and, 20th Centuries]. Oulu: University of Oulu.

Venninen, T., and K. Purola. 2013. "Educators' Views on Parents' Participation on Three Different Identified Levels." *Journal of Early Childhood Education Research* 2 (1): 48–62.

9 How do early childhood practitioners define professionalism in their interactions with parents?

Ute Ward

ABSTRACT

This study deepens the understanding of the interactions between early childhood practitioners and the parents of young children in English day care settings, nurseries and pre-schools. Using a phenomenological approach and semi-structured interviews with 17 experienced practitioners the study highlights practitioners' lived experiences and their conceptualisation of relationships with parents. A shared definition of professionalism in these interactions does not emerge. However, a model is developed which includes three dimensions practitioners use to describe their professionalism in their relationships with parents. It becomes apparent that practitioners' attitudes and approaches to their work with parents are varied and highly individual with an indication that they change with experience. This leads to the recommendation of support for all pre-service and in-service practitioners to reflect on the practitioner–parent relationship alongside the consideration of each child's development and learning.

Introduction

In England statutory guidance and research highlight how important partnership between the adults in the nursery and in the home is for the well-being and education of young children (Sylva et al. 2004; Early Education 2012; Cottle and Alexander, 2014; DfE 2014). As a lecturer, I hear many students agree that partnership working is beneficial and part of their professional role. Nonetheless many also shrink away from engaging with parents or even take a dismissive view of them. To prepare students effectively for their future work with parents and to develop a vision of themselves as professionals who interact with parents confidently and competently it seems necessary to understand how practitioners experience their interactions with parents and how they define their professionalism in these relationships. Although this is explored mainly with reference to the English context, practitioners and academics in many other countries will be familiar with issues like marketisation, accountability and performativity in their early childhood sectors. The focus on practitioners' experience and on their own explanations led to a phenomenological approach in this research which used semi-structured interviews to elicit participants' narratives about their daily work with parents. The findings are presented with a discussion of salient points, and the final section makes recommendations for practice and for further research.

Literature review

In the last 25 years, the early childhood sector in England has experienced dramatic changes driven by a desire to improve children's life chances, to reduce child poverty and to enable mothers to return to work (DfE 2013; Moss 2014). The expansion of the number of education and child care places for children under the age of five years has been accompanied by Government initiatives to develop a more highly skilled early childhood workforce. Attempts are being made to simplify the range of different qualifications by introducing standardised criteria for early years educators (NCTL 2013a) and by developing a post-graduate early years teacher award (NCTL 2013b). However, these changes have so far not addressed the underlying tension between a traditional view of care being the dominant element in the early childhood sector and the more recent emphasis on education for the youngest children. Divisions remain between those practitioners who enter the workforce with no or low qualifications to care for and nurture young children and those practitioners who are highly qualified and emphasise their role as teachers (Colley 2006; Kaga, Bennett, and Moss 2010). Although the Government's increased attention to children's early childhood education has generally been welcomed in the sector, the neo-liberal accountability and performativity-based ethos incorporating strict funding guidelines, regular inspections and a national early childhood curriculum are seen as a top-down approach which gives little or no voice to the practitioners themselves (Lea 2014). Their changing professional identity is in the main expressed through government prescribed standards. However, in recent years several papers have addressed the concept of early childhood professionalism (Taggart 2011; Murray 2013), and many are trying to give voice to the practitioners' own views of their professionalism (Osgood 2010; Brock 2013).

Early childhood professionalism is widely described as a social construct, and researchers adopt differing approaches, for example, a post-structural or a feminist perspective (Urban 2010 and Osgood 2010, respectively). They share the stance that it is necessary to look beyond neo-liberal thinking with its emphasis on accountability and male values. The Government-driven development of qualifications (NCTL 2013b) match the desire in the early childhood workforce for status and recognition as a profession rather than an occupation. The latter can be practised with fewer and lesser qualifications and appears to suit the more traditional view of the early childhood workforce as being dominated by care and maternal aspects (McGillivray 2008). The higher status, education-focused view of early childhood professionalism which is advocated in government guidelines and regulations (DfE 2013) is based on values which are perceived as more male orientated including the emphasis on accountability and performativity (Manning-Morton 2006). However, Manning-Morton (2006) argues that such a dichotomous, mutually exclusive way of thinking is not beneficial. The emotional demands and the emotional labour associated with the work with young children and their families are acknowledged as part of early childhood professionalism (Osgood 2010; Taggart 2011). Manning-Morton (2006) in particular stresses that the emotional challenges do not just arise from the interactions with children but also from potentially strained and challenging relationships with parents as well as from practitioners' own responses to events and experiences. The acknowledgement of emotional factors in early childhood education and care leads to an understanding of early childhood professionalism which includes uncertainty (Stronach et al. 2002) and which embraces ambiguity (Osgood 2010). Osgood (2010) advocates a new identity of a critically reflective emotional professional which practitioners define for themselves (professionalism from within) paying attention to personality, lived experience and emotionality. Based on her research with a small sample of nursery workers, Osgood (2010) identifies a number of traits for these new professionals, the most important one being caring, loving and compassionate, followed by being non-judgemental and being fair.

The focus for much of the writing regarding early childhood professionalism is on the work with children. In addition, there is a broad range of literature advising practitioners on relationship-building with parents (e.g. Hughes and Read 2012) and exploring factors influencing the work with parents either in the context of schools or in early childhood settings (Bakker and Denessen 2007). However, there is little insight into how practitioners understand their professionalism specifically in their interactions with parents. English curriculum guidance clearly states that practitioners should work in partnership with parents (DfE 2014) but the nature of this partnership is not explored. At the same time, the Government is casting the parent in the role of consumer and arguing for more choice and greater affordability in the early childhood sector (DfE 2013) leading to the increased marketisation of the sector (Penn 2014).

In Finland Venninen and Purola (2013) explored how practitioners envisage and conceptualise their interactions with parents. Based on a sample of 5262 practitioners, three different approaches or standpoints were identified. The Customer Standpoint lets the practitioners understand themselves as service providers and the parent as a customer whose wishes need to be accommodated whenever possible. Practitioners who assume the Professional Standpoint see themselves as the experts and perceive the parent as less knowledgeable and less competent to care for and educate children. Only in the Partnership Standpoint are practitioners and parents seen as equal, both bringing different but valuable expertise and knowledge to the shared efforts to support children (Venninen and Purola 2013). In Finland, only approximately 20% of early childhood practitioners supported the partnership approach. This was similar to the numbers adopting the Professional Standpoint, while the Customer Standpoint was evident in 45% of the participants (Venninen and Purola 2013). As these standpoints appear to reflect some of the tensions in the English early childhood sector this research study aimed to explore whether English practitioners conceptualise their professionalism in interactions with parents in similar ways. To extend the understanding of early childhood professionalism in relation to parents further, this study also enquired into which personal and professional attributes practitioners deem important when working with parents.

Methodology

Building on the interest in the practitioners' perspective and their lived experience, and on the belief that the barriers to effective engagement with parents can be highly personal this research took an existential-phenomenological approach (Cohen, Manion, and Morrison

2001; Denscombe 2014) gathering data through narratives. This approach allows for the exploration of practitioners' authentic accounts of their experience of working with parents while also reflecting the inherent complexity of practitioners' understanding of and approaches to parents (Denscombe 2014). Riessman (2000) argued that interviewees use narratives to position themselves and others, and that in telling their stories interviewees reflected their preferred or desired identities. Especially when relating events from the past, memory, experience and current influences may shape the narratives. It is this understanding of the social construction of practitioners' professionalism that is acknowledged through existential phenomenology.

The narratives and all qualitative data were collected through semi-structured interviews giving the participants the scope to narrate events and stories that were relevant to them and to make sense of their own experiences (Riessman 2000; Kvale 2007). The interview schedule contained both questions to gain practitioners' descriptions of professionalism and prompts to elicit narratives of actual events. The semi-structured nature of the interviews allowed for some comparisons between participants and between different sub-groups in relation to years of experience and levels of qualifications. In total 17 interviews were undertaken each lasting between 25 and 45 minutes. The ethics considerations underpinning the research activity were grounded in the British Education Research Association Ethical Guidelines (BERA, 2011) and approval for the study was gained from the Ethics Committee at King's College, London. To maintain confidentiality and anonymity pseudonyms were used for all participants as well as for all colleagues, children and parents who are mentioned in the narratives. As participants were sharing very personal insights and at times related events they experienced as uncomfortable or challenging, participants were asked at the end of each interview to reaffirm their consent and to indicate any parts of their narratives which should not be included in the research.

To address the perceived lack of rigour and trustworthiness of phenomenological studies (Denscombe 2014), two types of space triangulation were used in the selection of the participants. The 17 participants worked in 8 settings in three different counties in a variety of rural, urban and metropolitan contexts. This avoided the dominance of local practices and enhanced the variety of data contexts. Rigour and trustworthiness were further enhanced through piloting the interview schedule and by the interviewer adopting a neutral stance during rapport-building and interviewing (Miller and Glassner, 2004).

All participants were female; their levels of qualifications ranged from basic post-16 qualifications to post-graduate and teacher training qualifications. Eight worked in supervised roles, while nine were supervisors or professional leaders in their settings. To meet the eligibility criteria for participation in this study, participants had to have at least weekly contact with parents and had to have a minimum of five years' early childhood experience. The mean period of experience was 16 years (minimum 6 years, maximum 43 years). All interview transcripts were read, coded, re-read and re-coded several times. The emerging themes were compared to the standpoints identified by Venninen and Purola (2013). Sub-groups were then examined to establish their correlation to years of experience and levels of qualifications. In addition, the data were searched for traits and attributes which participants used to describe their professionalism in their interactions with parents. These were then compared to the traits Osgood (2010) identified in her research on early childhood professionalism.

Findings and discussion

The interviews provided rich, varied data and many insights into the participants' professional experiences. Some commonalities emerged across the different narratives, namely regarding personal and professional attributes, standpoints, different dimensions in the conceptualisation of professionalism and the impact of experience and qualifications.

Practitioners' attributes

Participants identified the following attributes as pre-requisites for effective interactions with parents: non-judgmental approach; acceptance of divergent parental views; honesty, openness and truthfulness; warmth; empathy; trustworthiness; friendliness; accessibility and approachability. The practitioner's communication skills were also emphasised:

> being able to read the parent and adjusting the way you talk to the parent;
>
> knowing how to share information with parents;
>
> being able to pick the right time to talk to them.

A strong knowledge-base was stressed which included knowledge of the child, her family and the curriculum as well as a sound understanding of the practitioner's role and the parent's role in a child's life.

There is some overlap with Osgood's (2010) professional attributes. For example, both lists include being non-judgemental and being an effective communicator. However, many of the attributes included in Osgood's list were not mentioned by practitioners in this study. This may be due to the fact that rather than asking broadly about professional skills, this research focused on interactions and relationships with parents and therefore knowledge and knowledge-acquisition were not mentioned. More strongly reflected in this study are the emotional values suggested by Taggart (2011) such as empathy and honesty. References to caring and loving are absent in the current list of attributes. It may be that practitioners feel more comfortable applying these terms to their relationships with children rather than to their interactions with adults for fear of being misunderstood.

In interviews, participants are likely to describe desired or preferred identities (Riessman 2000), which appears to be evident from the list of attributes based on practitioners' descriptions of their professionalism. In their narratives about actual events and experiences, practitioners were still likely to portray desired identities, however, these appeared to diverge from the attributes mentioned in their descriptions of professionalism. The concept of espoused theory expresses this divergence more effectively than Riessman's (2000) suggestion of desired or preferred identities. When asked about their values in the work with parents, practitioners expressed their espoused theory (Argyris and Schoen, 1974). However, in their recollections of actual events, practitioners replaced the espoused theories of interactions with parents with divergent theories in action (Argyris and Schoen, 1974), which pointed to considerable complexity and at times to conflicted attitudes in the work with parents. For example, several participants mentioned the professional hierarchies within their early childhood settings, which they felt were reinforced by parents choosing to talk to the teacher rather than the nursery nurse. This led to some practitioners feeling disempowered in their interactions with parents.

Furthermore, conflicted attitudes to parents were evident for those practitioners who lived in the community adjacent to their early childhood settings. This meant they encountered their neighbours, friends and occasionally family members in a professional capacity. Constant role adjustment was required, and it was difficult for some practitioners to balance their desire to be empathetic and warm with the levels of professional detachment they deemed appropriate. Osgood's (2010) participants mentioned the need to separate the private and the professional self for practitioners. The findings here suggest that this becomes more difficult when the professional context overlaps with private relationships. Practitioners consistently endeavoured to meet the needs of children and their families but these were highly individual and often dynamic, which meant that professional boundaries required frequent adjustment, as Anne pointed out:

> A boundary isn't straight, clear-cut; it is different for everybody and you have to use your professional judgment to know when and where to draw that boundary.

Practitioner's standpoints in their work with parents

The complexity and variable nature of the relationships with parents were also reflected in the different standpoints that participants shared in their narratives. As with Venninen and Purola (2013), three different standpoints could be identified. Many practitioners were very aware of the commercial aspects in the early childhood setting and parent relationship:

> Parents have a different expectation of you as well because they are paying for the service and it is very much MY child. It is almost as if you are only there for their child. (Vera)

Such expectations left some practitioners feeling powerless and at the mercy of parents' demands. Although they were aware of the potential negative impact of this, few of them felt able to challenge this or to work proactively to improve the situation, as Zara did:

> I took the role he [the father] was giving me for that session but in the next consultation I was more assertive. I didn't go in in a submissive way because that is not my role. I want to work with someone but I don't want to be told what to do. He needed to see me more as an equal. It should be working together.

The more forceful expression of the customer standpoint in England compared to the Finnish definitions may be based in the prevailing political discourse about parents as consumers and in the greater commercialisation of the English early childhood sector (Penn 2014).

Both the professional and the partnership standpoints were evident in the practitioners' narratives. The small size of the sample does not allow for a statistical analysis of distribution. However, some patterns emerged where several practitioners from the same setting were interviewed. In one setting practitioners predominantly presented the professional standpoint; in another staff members consistently presented the partnership standpoint. In a third setting, practitioners did not appear to have a collective approach but presented aspects of different standpoints. These tentative correlations between individual practitioners' standpoints and a team's overall ethos may warrant further investigation to avoid parents receiving mixed messages from different staff members.

As with the Finnish study, English practitioners stressed that standpoints are not fixed and permanent but may be dependent on the parent in the interaction and the nature of the situation. However, they are a good expression of underlying views and attitudes. Three of the English practitioners also appeared to imply an additional basic standpoint, which places the practitioner's own role and experience as a parent in the foreground. This was evident, for example, when practitioners spoke about situations when unwell children were dropped off at the nursery. Ruth could empathise as she had been in a similar situation:

> I was going 'What am I going to do with my child? I've got to go to work', you know, ... and then I can understand why parents sometimes get a bit uppity. And it is not necessarily acceptable and it is not necessary but it is what we do! Because sometimes we just do that!

Ruth started the narration talking from the practitioner's perspective, then spoke about her own experience (at the start of the quote) and ended with a strong identification as a parent (using the pronoun 'we'). Equally, she sometimes assumed to know what a parent wanted or needed based on her experience and without consulting with the parent. This standpoint was also identified by some managers who saw practitioners putting aside setting guidance and knowledge gained in training in favour of personal experience as a parent. Based on the initial insights from this study, a new standpoint, namely the parent standpoint, can be defined:

> In the parent standpoint the parental feelings and experience of the practitioner shape communication and interactions with parents. The practitioner is predominantly motivated by a desire to nurture, care and be empathetic and may act on assumed parental needs without consultation.

The issues arising from the tensions between a practitioner's parental identity and professional identity are at present not well-researched and warrant further investigation, potentially contributing to the discussion of professionalism from within (Osgood 2010) and of emotional labour in early childhood practice (Taggart 2011).

Dimensions of professionalism in the work with parents

Practitioners narrated a wide range of different events in the interviews while simultaneously reflecting on their experiences and reactions (Riessman 2000). In their sense-making it became evident that, in spite of taking different standpoints, interviewees were referring to similar aspects to help them conceptualise their professionalism in the work with parents. These aspects can be summarised in a model with three dimensions (Figure 1). These dimensions help to explain why conceptualisations of professionalism vary greatly and are highly subjective. Each dimension should be understood as a continuum, and practitioners position themselves at different points according to context, basic beliefs and setting values. This model builds on and expresses standpoints but offers a more unified approach to explaining individual differences. When practitioners show a preference for the professional standpoint, they invariably understand themselves as more detached from the parents than a practitioner who is very empathetic towards parents. Although the majority of practitioners stress the centrality of the child in their interactions with parents, it is evident that practitioners taking the parent standpoint shift their focus towards the parent. This can also be seen in practitioners who see the parent predominantly as a customer whose demands must be met. Practitioners taking a passive stance often cite guidance and regulation as factors that limit their ability to

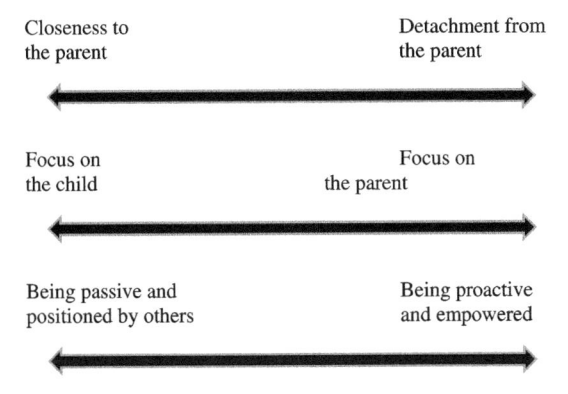

```
Closeness to                    Detachment from
the parent                      the parent
       <----------------------------->

Focus on                        Focus on
the child                       the parent
       <----------------------------->

Being passive and               Being proactive
positioned by others            and empowered
       <----------------------------->
```

Figure 1. Dimensions of professionalism in the work with parents.

shape their professional roles. Parents are at times seen as defining practitioners' scope to act on their professional expertise (as Vera's example showed). Interestingly, qualifications appear to have some influence on where practitioners may position themselves on these dimensions, for example, more highly-qualified practitioners describe themselves as feeling empowered to shape their interactions with parents (as Zara demonstrated). In addition to visualising the differences in approaches to the work with parents, this set of dimensions may provide the basis for reflection on practice either individually, in staff teams supporting continuous professional development or in critical incidence analysis.

The impact of experience and qualifications

As all participants had at least five years' experience they were able to reflect on the development over time of their approaches to working with parents, and although the sample was small, some trends in the relevance of experience and qualifications in the work with parents emerged. All participants felt that through experience and practice their confidence in working with parents had increased, for example:

> I used to be scared stiff of meeting with parents .... When I was very inexperienced it used to be quite stressful. I remember when I was a newly qualified teacher and parents evening, I found it extremely stressful 'cos what they might ask me and would I know the answer. It took a few years before you could talk really confidently about children. (Jenny)

Early in their careers, practitioners often avoided parents, they may belittle their concerns or believe that parents are always right. There was some evidence that the customer standpoint was more prevalent amongst younger or less-experienced staff members. Only after several years in practice did practitioners become more understanding of parental concerns and took a more child-centred approach in their interactions with parents. Overall the narratives supported Rodd's comments that younger staff members find it difficult to establish effective working relationships with parents (Rodd, 20122012). Older practitioners (40 years and older) described the interactions with parents as less stressful, and amongst them the professional standpoint appeared more prevalent. However, there appears to be one contrasting theme. Regardless of age or years of experience the practitioners qualified at post-graduate level felt more confident and empowered to build partnership relationships with parents. This would support the strong drive for a more highly qualified workforce, which is currently prevalent in England (Nutbrown 2012; NCTL 2013b). However, more large-scale research is required to investigate these initial findings further.

Implications

The aim of this research was to gain a deeper understanding of the practitioners' perceptions of their professionalism in their interactions with parents. The findings provided numerous insights, in particular regarding the complex nature of relationships between practitioner and parent. To enable effective interactions practitioners need to be aware of their own attitudes and approaches both in their espoused theory and in their theory in action (Argyris and Schoen, 1974), regarding their standpoints and their overlapping professional and personal identities. An initial awareness of these issues should form part of pre-service training. As any tensions or conflict are more likely to manifest themselves during the lived experience, it seems crucial that any period in placement involves direct engagement with parents and offers trainees and students opportunities to reflect on their experiences. The model presented here may provide a framework for these reflections and for discussions with mentors and supervisors.

In-service practitioners may also benefit from regular reflections on their attitudes and approaches to parents. It is already common practice in most settings to discuss individual children's needs, learning journeys and achievements. As each child is unique, so is each parent and each practitioner. Based in the knowledge that parental engagement in their children's learning and effective relationships between parents and practitioners have considerable influence on a child's development and learning (Cottle and Alexander 2014; Sylva et al. 2004), practitioner–parent relationships should be discussed regularly. Practitioners should be supported to reflect on, adapt and enhance their interactions with parents. This places great responsibility not just on individual practitioners but also on supervisors and managers. Strong leadership that is grounded in a commitment to parental engagement appears paramount (NCSL 2010), and middle managers may need additional training in order to be able to support their teams. In light of the different standpoints in teams, leaders and managers need to support their staff teams to develop a detailed whole setting vision for their work with parents. The model of dimensions developed in this study may provide an effective tool to help practitioners to discuss and understand their individual conceptualisations of professionalism in the interactions with parents.

Although this research extends the understanding of practitioners' views of their own professionalism in their work with parents, some additional questions present themselves. Firstly, this research provides an initial attempt to raise awareness of the potential impact of parenthood on the professional identity of early childhood practitioners. Although described in negative terms by managers, such potential impact was seen to be positive by practitioners. This already suggests complex and varied perspectives, and a deeper understanding of the experiences of 'parent–practitioners' seems needed.

Secondly, this research focused on practitioners' views and perspectives. It now seems paramount to consider the parents' point of view. This should include an exploration of the professional and personal attributes, parents value in practitioners and of the type of relationship that parents want to form with practitioners. Parents' responses to the different standpoints practitioners may also warrant further research. Only by listening to and understanding both parties in the parent–practitioner relationship will we be able to work towards effective partnership.

Disclosure statement

No potential conflict of interest was reported by the authors.

References

Argyris, C, and DA. Schoen. 1974. *Theory in Practice: Increasing Effectiveness*, Jossey-Bass. San Francisco: Jossey-Bass.
Bakker, J., and E. Denessen. 2007. "The Concept of Parent Involvement: Some Theoretical and Empirical Considerations." *International Journal About Parents in Education* 1 (0): 188–199.
British Educational Research Association. 2011. Ethical Guidelines for Educational Research. Accessed 10 August 2016. Available from https://www.bera.ac.uk/researchers-resources/publications/ethical-guidelines-for-educational-research-2011
Brock, A. 2013. "Building a Model of Early Years Professionalism from practitioners' Perspectives." *Journal of Early Childhood Research* 11 (1): 27–44.
Cohen, L., L. Manion, and K. Morrison. 2001. *Research Methods in Education*. 5th ed. London: RoutledgeFalmer.
Colley, H. 2006. "Learning to Labour with Feeling: Class, Gender and Emotion in Childcare, Education and Training." *Contemporary Issues in Early Childhood* 7 (1): 15–29.
Cottle, M., and E. Alexander. 2014. "Parent Partnership and "Quality" Early Years Services: Practitioners' Perspectives." *European Early Childhood Education Research Journal* 22 (5): 637–659.
Denscombe, M. 2014. *The Good Research Guide*. 5th ed. Maidenhead: Open University Press.
Department for Education (DfE). 2013. *More Great Childcare*. Accessed 13 November 2013. www.education.gov.uk/publications.
Department of Education (DfE). 2014. *Statutory Framework for the Early Years Foundation Stage*. Accessed 16 May 2014. https://www.gov.uk/government/uploads/system/uploads/attachment_data/file/335504/EYFS_framework_from_1_September_2014__with_clarification_note.pdf.
Early Education. 2012. *Development Matters in the Early Years Foundation Stage*. London: Early Education.
Hughes, A., and V. Read. 2012. *Building Positive Relationships with Parents of Young Children*. Abingdon: Routledge.
Kaga, Y., J. Bennett, and P. Moss. 2010. *Caring and Learning Together. A Cross-National Study on the Integration on Early Childhood Care and Education within Education*. Paris: UNESCO.
Kvale, S. 2007. *Doing Interviews*. London: SAGE.
Lea, S. 2014. "Early Years Work, Professionalism and the Translation of Policy into Practice." In *Early Years Policy: The Impact on Practice*, edited by Z. Kingdon and J. Gourd, 13–32. Abingdon: Routledge.
Manning-Morton, J. 2006. "The Personal is Professional: Professionalism and the Birth to Threes Practitioners." *Contemporary Issues in Early Childhood* 7 (1): 42–52.
McGillivray, G. 2008. "Nannies, Nursery Nurses and Early Years Professionals: Constructions of Professional Identity in the Early Years Workforce in England." *European Early Childhood Education Research Journal* 16 (2): 242–254.
Miller, J, and B. Glassner. 2004. "'The "inside" and the "outside": Finding realities in interviews'." In *Qualitative Research: Theory, Method and Practice*, edited by D Silverman, 125–139. London: SAGE Publications.

Moss, P. 2014. "Early Childhood Policy in England 1997-2013: Anatomy of a Missed Opportunity." *International Journal of Early Years Education* 22 (4): 346–358.

Murray, J. 2013. "Becoming an Early Years Professional: Developing a new Professional Identity." *European Early Childhood Education Research Journal* 21 (4): 527–540.

National College for School Leadership (NCSL). 2010. *Leadership for Parental Engagement*. Nottingham: National College for School Leadership.

National College for Teaching & Leadership (NCTL). 2013a. *Early Years Educator (Level 3) Qualifications Criteria*. Accessed 16 May 2015. https://www.gov.uk/government/uploads/system/uploads/attachment_data/file/211644/Early_Years_Educator_Criteria.pdf.

National College for Teaching & Leadership (NCTL). 2013b. *Teachers' Standards (Early Years)*. Accessed 1 January 2014. https://www.gov.uk/government/publications/early-years-teachers-standards.

Nutbrown, C. 2012. *Foundations for Quality*. Accessed 10 July 2012. http://media.education.gov.uk/MediaFiles/A/0/9/%257BA098ADE7-BA9A-4E18-8802-D8D4B060858D%257DNUTBROWN%20FINAL%20REPORT%20-%20final.pdf.

Osgood, J. 2010. "Reconstructing Professionalism in ECEC: The Case for the 'Critically Reflective Emotional Professional." *Early Years: An International Research Journal* 30 (2): 119–133.

Penn, H. 2014. "The Business of Childcare in Europe." *European Early Childhood Education Research Journal* 22 (4): 432–456.

Riessman, C. 2000. "Analysis of Personal Narratives." In *Handbook of Interviewing*, edited by J. Gubrium and J. Holstein, 331–346. London: SAGE.

Rood, J. 2012. *Leadership in Early Years*. Maidenhead: Open University Press.

Stronach, I., B. Corbin, O. McNamara, S. Stark, and T. Warne. 2002. "Towards an Uncertain Politics of Professionalism: Teacher and Nurse Identities in Flux." *Journal of Education Policy* 17 (1): 109–138. doi:10.1080/02680930110100081.

Sylva, K., E. Melhuish, P. Sammons, I. Siraj-Blatchford, and B. Taggart. 2004. *The Effective Provision of Pre-School Education [EPPE] Project: Technical Paper 12*. London: Institute of Education.

Taggart, G. 2011. "Don't We Care?: the Ethics and Emotional Labour of Early Years Professionalism." *Early Years: An International Research Journal* 31 (1): 85–95.

Urban, M. 2010. "Rethinking Professionalism in Early Childhood: Untested Feasibilities and Critical Ecologies." *Contemporary Issues in Early Childhood* 11 (1): 1–7.

Venninen, T., and K. Purola. 2013. "Educators' Views on Parents' Participation on Three Different Identified Levels." *Journal of Early Childhood Education Research* 2 (1): 48–62.

10 Written communication with families during the transition from childcare to school

How documents construct and position children, professionals, and parents

Joanne S. Lehrer

ABSTRACT

This article explores how documents play a role in shaping perceptions of children, professionals, and parents during the transition from childcare to kindergarten in Québec. Positioning analysis was used to explore governmentality, documentality, and interobjectivity in the communication agendas and child assessment documents of seven children. Results revealed that communication agendas constructed different images of the ideal child, professional, and parent in childcare and in school. Assessment documents in both settings categorise children as either 'doing well' or 'at-risk', position professionals as experts, and parents as playing a supportive and often passive role with regard to their children's education.

Introduction

This article explores how documents play a role in shaping perceptions of children, professionals, and parents during the transition from childcare to kindergarten. Drawing upon Foucault's (1991) concept of governmentality, Ferraris' (2013) documentality, and Latour's (1996) interobjectivity, communication documents – between childcare centres and families; schools and families; and childcare centres and schools – were analysed in order to draw attention to the ways in which they construct and position children, early childhood educators, kindergarten teachers, and parents during the transition from one educational context and culture to another, and how these constructions differ across the two settings.

Theoretical framework

Governmentality suggests that, in order to govern its subjects, the modern state creates and uses specific forms of knowledge which lead to self-governing individuals who police themselves by internalising the interests of the state (Foucault 1991; Rutland and Aylett 2008). Specifically, control is exercised through the act of 'caring for'. This 'care' includes the government caring for its people, institutions caring for their members, parents caring for their children, and so forth (Foucault 1981). Furthermore, knowledge 'defines its object in ways that facilitate certain courses of action and not others' (Rutland and Aylett 2008, 631), and techniques for inscribing knowledge allow for 'evaluation, calculation, and intervention' (Miller and Rose 1990, 7), governing and 'policing' children, families, and educational institutions, as they 'construct identity, conduct, and the way in which reality is experienced' (Bloch et al. 2003, 7). Ferraris (2013) takes this notion of inscription further, positing that documents form the foundation for governmentality, where our reliance on social objects to document and inscribe acts constructs institutional reality and directs human actions (Ferraris 2013). Documentality posits that there are three types of objects: natural, social, and ideal. Natural objects exist independently of subjects; social objects exist in space and time and depend on subjects; and ideal objects exist outside space and time and are independent of subjects (Ferraris 2013).

Actor-network theory (Latour 2005) provides another way to consider the agency of documents that have been inscribed within early childhood educational institutions, suggesting that human actors and non-human (or more than human) actants make up transient material-semiotic (conceptual) networks (Latour 2005). In other words, humans and objects enter into an entangled web of relations that is constantly being made and remade. Within this framework, the concept of interobjectivity (Brandt and Clinton 2002; Latour 1996) posits that human interactions are framed by objects, including documents, that stabilise reality. While humans, individually and collectively, mediate interactions, objects are also mediators, imbuing, resisting, and re-crafting interactions. Applying these theoretical concepts to institutions of early childhood education and care (ECEC), I support Karila and Alasuutari's (2012) assertion that ECEC institutions function as a technique of governance, producing 'discourses that regulate the lives of children, parents, and families' (23).

With regard to communication documents in ECEC, the documents themselves, as well as the humans who create, complete, share, and receive them (and the computers, pens, children's cubbies or backpacks in which the documents are placed, the tables, chairs and classrooms where the adults meet, the childcare centre or kindergarten classroom where the children are observed, etc.) make up an actor-network that continually negotiates the subject positioning of all the actors, and, beyond specific situations, adds to a general cultural or societal understanding of who children are, what early education is for, and how parents and educators are expected to behave in order to create certain ideal objects, such as the good childcare child, the good kindergarten student, the good parent, the good educator, and so forth.

Documentation practices in ECEC

Positioning of children, professionals, and parents within ECEC institutions through the use of written documents is the subject of a growing body of research. These studies have explored letters sent home regularly to all the parents in the group (Forsberg 2007; Löfdahl 2014); pedagogical documentation (Liljestrand and Hammarberg 2017; Rintakorpi, Lipponen, and Reunamo 2014); portfolios (Knauf 2016); individual educational plans used to support parent–educator conferences (Alasuutari, Markström, and Vallberg-Roth 2014; Karila and Alasuutari 2012); and yearly reports on childcare quality (Löfdahl 2014). Documents have been shown to produce normative understandings of children, educators, teachers, and parents; to govern behaviour and actions, to categorise children as 'abnormal', 'insecure', or 'at-risk'; and to position parents as subordinate to educators (Alasuutari, Markström, and Vallberg-Roth 2014; Forsberg 2007; Karila and Alasuutari 2012; Liljestrand and Hammarberg 2017). They also mediate relationships between educators and parents (Forsberg 2007; Karila and Alasuutari 2012; Rintakorpi, Lipponen, and Reunamo 2014). Through joint interaction with these documents, educators and parents construct and perform identities, and negotiate, renegotiate, and contest discourses (Alasuutari, Markström, and Vallberg-Roth 2014; Rintakorpi, Lipponen, and Reunamo 2014).

Although research does not appear to have explored 'home–school books' 'communication agendas' or 'daily notebooks' (e.g. Gonzalez-Mena 2014; Whalley 2007; Whalley, Arnold, and Orr 2013), as research data, Garrity's (2014) exploration of parent–educator engagement found that the use of these documents is a common communication strategy in Irish early childhood settings. These books are used to communicate 'functional information' related to sleep, meals, and routines, as well as information about the activities children participate in each day. They travel between the home and the childcare centre, and are occasionally used in a bidirectional manner. Educators, parents, and childcare administrators in Garrity's (2014) study reported mixed assessments of the usefulness of these documents. Some parents appreciated them, others found oral communication more useful. One director said she felt the books were a barrier to building interpersonal relationships, and others worried that if educators spent too much time writing in the books they would neglect the children. Educators also noted that parents would read the books less frequently as their child got older or became accustomed to the centre (Garrity 2014).

Documentation practices during the transition from childcare to school

The transition from childcare to school, and relationships with families during this time, is the subject of a vast body of international research (e.g. Dockett and Perry 2004; Fabian and Dunlop 2006; Magretts and Keinig 2013). Changes in identity, daily routine, and relationships characterise this period, as children adapt to a larger group, and a relationship with the adult based on learning and formal outcomes rather than care (Rimm-Kaufman and Pianta 2000). Parents also experience changes, as they adjust to a stricter schedule and increased responsibilities such as preparing lunches (Griebel and Niesel 2013; Petrakos and Lehrer 2011), and as daily informal oral communication is replaced by infrequent written communication (Pianta and Cox 1999; Rimm-Kaufman and Pianta 2000).

With regard to written communication over the course of this transition, research has explored the use of portfolios transferred from the childcare centre to the school (Backhaus, Bogatz, and Hanke 2013; Jones 2006; Peters et al. 2009). While parents appear to be satisfied with their decision to transfer these documents, some parents were worried they would lead to teacher bias with regard to their child (Backhaus, Bogatz, and Hanke 2013).

Other studies have examined child observation checklists or 'preschool report cards' that are transferred between the two settings (Besnard et al. 2014; Cotnoir 2015; O'Kane and Hayes 2013; Rogers, Hopps-Wallis, and Perry 2016; Rous et al. 2010).

While most of these studies present an unproblematised view of these documents, Rogers and colleagues (2016) found a number of challenges involved, such as redundancy of preschool assessments when children are evaluated by schools, avoidance of negative reports because the educators knew the parents would have access to them, and a desire to sit down and discuss with the future teacher instead of transferring the document. It should be noted that these studies are based on interviews with practitioners and parents, but do not include analyses of the documents themselves.

Research context

In Québec (Canada), the majority of children begin attending school at the end of August when they are five-year old, or will turn five before the end of the month of September (MELS 2012). This non-obligatory year, characterised as a year of transition, is called kindergarten, and is located in the primary (elementary) school building, and taught by university-trained preschool and primary teachers (MELS 2012) who follow the *Preschool Educational Programme*, promoting play-based pedagogy and holistic development (MELS 2006). The teacher–child ratio within this context is 1:20 (Gouvernement du Québec 2017a). During the year prior to kindergarten, those children fortunate enough to have a place in a government-funded and regulated childcare centre attend a group composed of 10 children and 1 educator, who is a college-educated (typically a three-year program in a pre-university post-secondary institution) qualified professional (Gouvernement du Québec 2017b) who follows the *Educational Program for Childcare*, also based on play and holistic development (MFA 2007).

Within these childcare centres, communication agendas are standard practice, though their use is not legislated and is not universal. In additional, 'transition tools' (child development checklists) are increasingly common (Horizon 0-5 2014; MELS 2010). In fact, a recent report on childcare services in the province suggests that this type of tool should be standardised and universally implemented (Institut du nouveau monde 2017). When children start kindergarten, there is usually some form of communication agenda that goes home with the child each day, as well as the four report cards mandated by the government (Gouvernement du Québec 2017a): the first one is titled 'first communication' and is designed by the school or school board. The second three are standardised across the province (MELS 2011). The aim of this study was to explore how these documents construct and position children, professionals, and parents and how these constructions differ across the two settings.

Methodology

Study design

Based on the concepts of governmentality (Foucault 1981, 1991), documentality (Ferraris 2013), and interobjectivity (Latour 1996), I analysed both communication documents and child assessment documents used by early childhood educators and kindergarten teachers during the transition from childcare to school (during the final year of childcare and during the first four months of kindergarten).

Analysis strategy

In order to operationalise the conceptual framework, I used Bamberg's (1997) positioning analysis. Positioning analysis (Bamberg 1997) was originally intended to analyse narrative accounts of human experience, focusing on how and for what purpose narratives are performed. Bamberg (1997) explains that people position themselves and others in roles while telling stories, and '"produce" one another [...] situationally as "social beings"' (336). I chose this method because I was seeking to understand how the documents create 'resonances between the interests of the state and the interests of individual subjects' (Rutland and Aylett 2008, 631), as well how discourses are produced and inscribed within a particular network (Latour 2005; Rutland and Aylett 2008). Positioning analysis is a three-stage process. I conducted close readings of the documents, asking adapted versions of Bamberg's questions.[1] First, the question *How are the characters positioned in relation to one another?* was posed. Then, the question *How does the document position the characters to the audience?* was asked. The final questions, *What is the document attempting to tell?* and *What does the document say about me?* attempt to bridge an analysis of the content and the structure of the document in order to tentatively put forth an understanding of how these documents serve to construct the social reality of the children's and parents' transitions from childcare to school. The results section presents a summary of the three-stage analysis for each document.

Procedure

Documents pertaining to seven children (two girls and five boys), attending four different childcare centres in one area of the city of Montréal (two French-language, one English-language, and one bilingual English-French), and then six different kindergarten classes in six different schools (and four different school boards[2]) were collected as part of the author's doctoral research project between March 2013 and January 2014. All standard permissions and ethical considerations were obtained as part of the larger project. In particular, parents accepted that the educators and teachers share the documents with the researcher, although some took the initiative of making me copies on their own. In addition, confidentiality and anonymity were ensured, and all names of people and institutions used in this text are pseudonyms.

These documents included communication agendas from childcare centres and schools; *Moving on to School* (CASIOPE 2017), a 'transition tool' completed by the child's educator and shared with the school (or not) by the parent; the child's preliminary report card issued after a month and a half of school (October); and the first official report card issued in November. As described below, while there was some variation within the childcare centre communication agendas, these were quite similar. The school communication agendas and the preliminary report cards varied more widely. The *Moving on to School* document and the official report card were standardised regardless of language, although some schools added an annex to the official report card. As the intention of the project was to explore how the different documents construct and position various early childhood actors, this variety (both in language of instruction and documents employed) was reflective of various possibilities for children transitioning from childcare to school in one area of the city. It allowed for conclusions that highlight both similarities and differences in how the documents position children, professionals, and parents.

Results

The analyses focused on the document itself, including both the pre-printed document and how the professionals and parents conformed or resisted its invitations and constraints through their inscriptions. In order to answer the research questions, the results of the three-level positioning analysis will be presented for each type of document. First, communication agendas in childcare centres will be compared with communication agendas in kindergarten classes, and then child assessment documents in childcare will be compared with child assessment documents in schools. The documents will be presented briefly, accompanied by images, before the analysis of each type of document, focusing on how it constructs and positions children, professionals, and parents.

Communication agendas

Childcare centres

Description. Without exception, these documents are commercial booklets that educators (and sometimes parents) write in daily. They include both closed-ended items for selection (typically attitude, behaviour, appetite, and nap), as well as open-ended sections where the educator (and sometimes the parent) is invited to write (see Figures 1–4). The open-ended sections contain three types of information: general information about the activities the group participated in that day (e.g. circle time, songs, stories, free play, outdoor play,

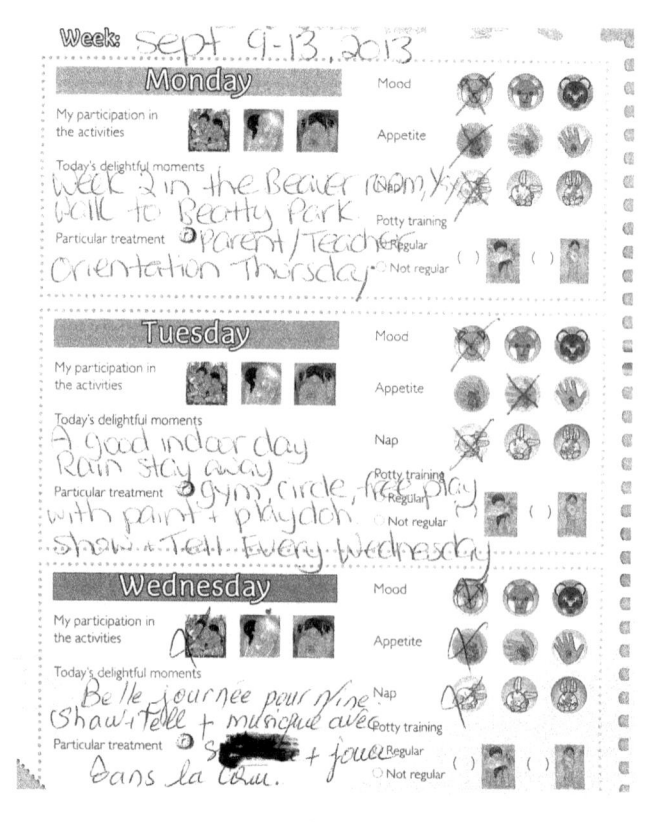

Figure 1. Childcare centre communication agenda, example one.

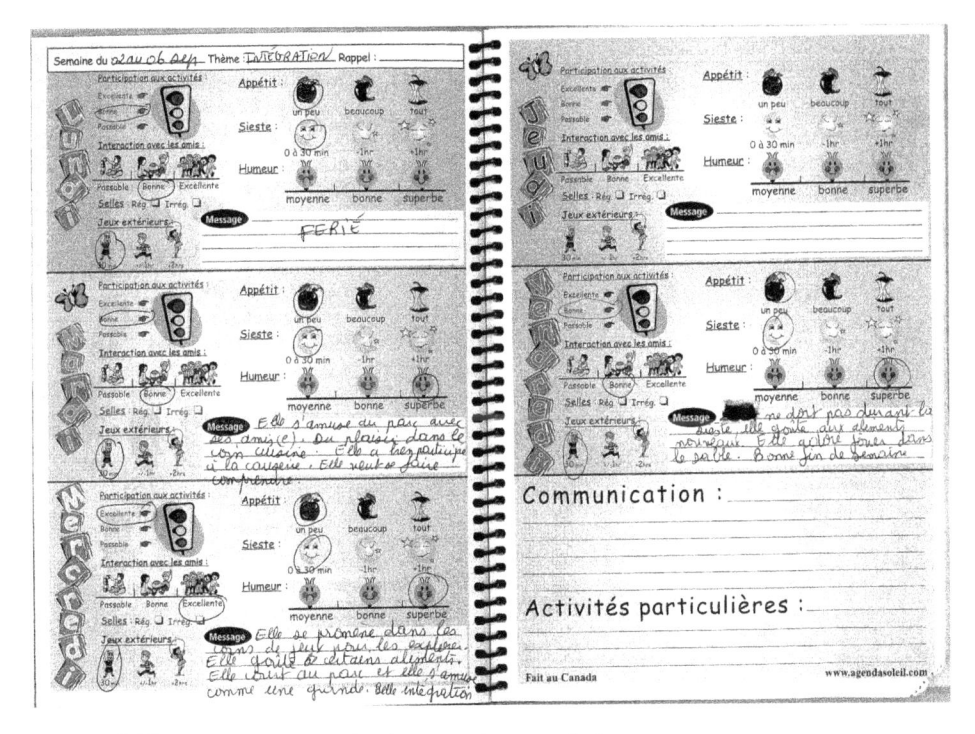

Figure 2. Childcare centre communication agenda, example two.

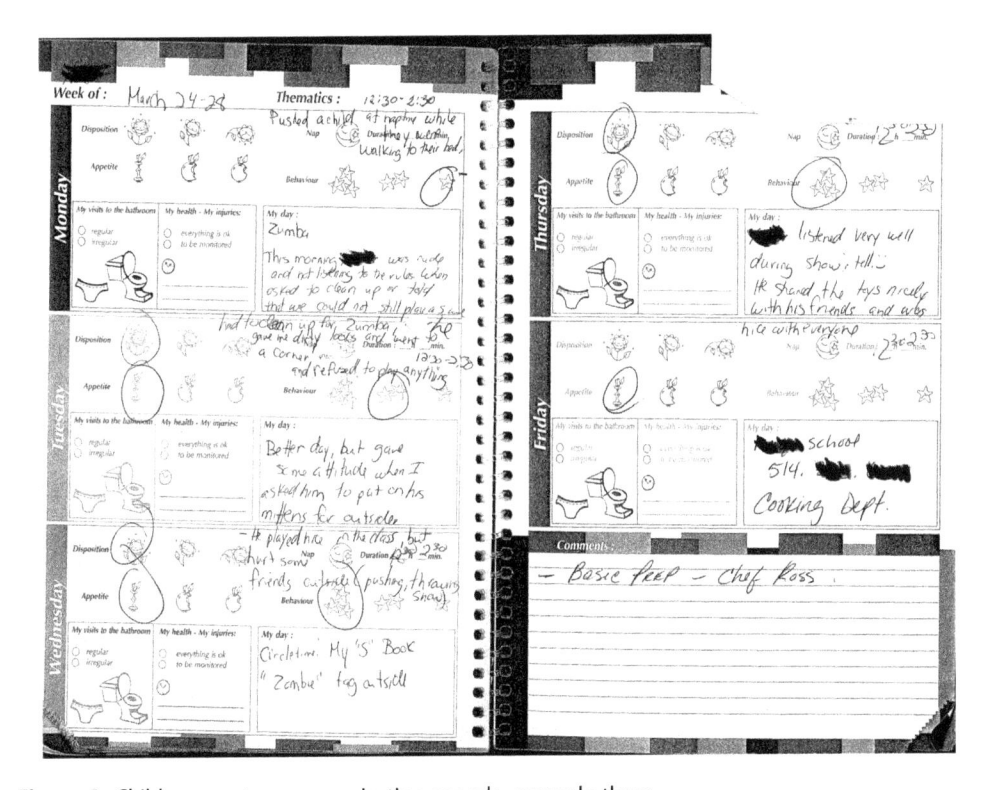

Figure 3. Childcare centre communication agenda, example three.

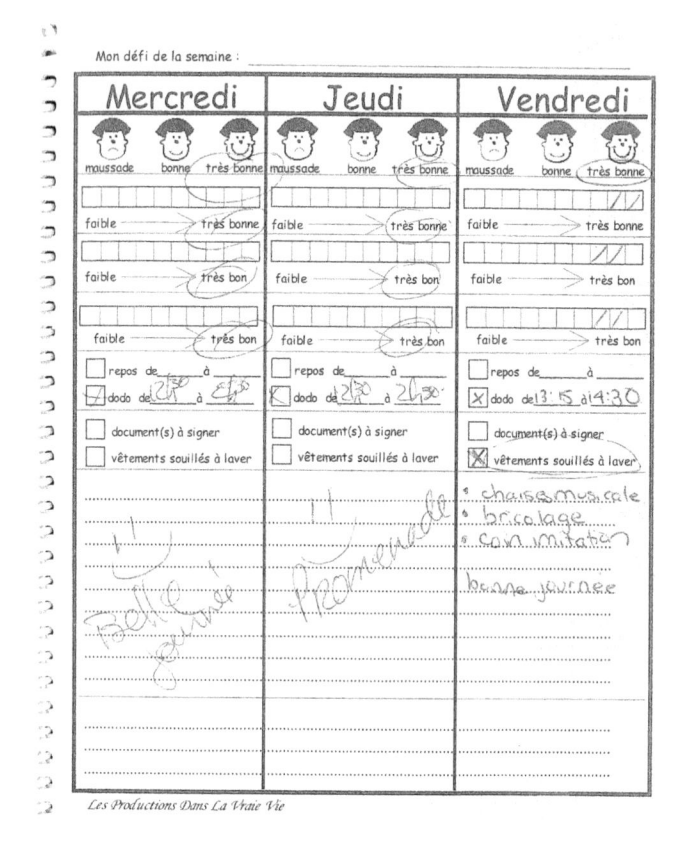

Figure 4. Childcare centre communication agenda, example four.

arts and crafts activities, field trips, etc.); individual information about the child's activities or behaviour (e.g. 'Nicholas coughed a little during naptime' and 'Emma enjoys playing with (names of friends). She played with Lego today and participated well during dance class!'); and general messages to parents ('great day', 'Happy Valentine's day!', 'Don't forget the centre is closed next Monday').

Construction and positioning of the child. These daily reports construct an image of the 'good childcare child' as one who is happy and conforms to adult behaviour expectations, participates in a multitude of activities, both free play and structured games and events, eats 'a lot', and sleeps at naptime. The 'good childcare child' enjoys childcare, has friends, and reacts well to adult interventions with regard to behaviour or learning. For example, 'Nicholas calmed down moments after mom left' and 'Youpi! Emma slept nicely, I changed her place!' One educator occasionally writes messages in the child's voice. For example, 'Today I played in the gym and I prepared a wonderful surprise for you daddy!' This seems to reinforce the identity of the happy child enjoying his day in childcare.

Construction and positioning of the educator. While the educators' additions and the agendas themselves seem to construct the child in a similar way, their use of the documents differs in relation to how they construct themselves. The format of the communication agendas construct the educators as being observant of the children and diligent in informing the parents of the details of their child's day. The information they provide regarding the daily activities, children's health and challenges, as well as concern expressed for the parents' emotions ('Nicholas calmed down moments after mom left') position the educators as providing a stimulating and varied educational programme, being concerned about the child's well-being, caring about the parent, and attempting to collaborate with parents when their careful observations identify issues of concern. These concerns were most often related to meeting behaviour expectations or not eating enough, although they sometimes involved 'challenges' from a developmental psychology perspective (particularly with regard to learning another language or language difficulties). For example, 'Daniel had difficulty listening to the rules today' or 'He ate well, super!' These entries often take the form of a series of comments over the course of a week or so, alternating difficult days with improvements, constructing the child as constantly progressing towards the ideal childcare child.

Sometimes, these documents give the impression that educators have a 'schoolified' (Clausen 2015; OECD 2006) understanding of ECEC. Particularly in the two English-language centres, the educators refer to themselves as 'teachers', use the word 'classroom' instead of 'group' and mention learning letters or doing worksheets and activity books, in contrast to the two French-language centres where the word 'educator' and 'group' are used and 'preschool' type activities are not mentioned in the agendas. Some educators (from all the centres) added stickers to the agenda, either occasionally or on a regular basis.

Construction and positioning of the parents. The communication agendas construct the parent as a passive consumer of information about their child, although the educators' entries regarding the children's problem behaviour seem to position them as potential partners in correcting these behaviours. While the documents themselves sometimes have a space for parents to sign, and sometimes explicitly invite 'messages from parents', these invitations are rarely taken up. Those parents that do accept these invitations seem to position themselves as involved parents who are interested in communicating and collaborating with the educators. For example, 'Thanks a lot Anna [volunteering on the field trip] was really fun!' or 'Gabriel will be in at 9:30 due to an appointment'.

Kindergarten classes

Description. There was also some sort of communication agenda in all but one of the kindergarten classes.[3] However, these took various forms. One resembled the childcare agenda (see Figure 5), others took the form of alternating a page with the monthly calendar and a page for notes (see Figures 6 and 7), and one was a simple lined notebook, repurposed as a communication agenda (see Figure 8). As the format and space allotted was varied, these agendas did not all serve to position the children, teachers, and parents in the same way.

Construction and positioning of the child. The first example included pictograms of activities that the child selected on a daily basis, representing what she had done that day, as well as a monthly calendar on which she had drawn the 'weather' (clouds or a sun) daily. The only other agenda to include traces of the child's participation was the repurposed notebook, in which the child occasionally added his own 'messages' at the bottom of some pages. The first agenda positions the child as an active participant in the home–school communication process, performing her role as a student in accordance with expectations. However, there is no evidence that she made any of her own decisions

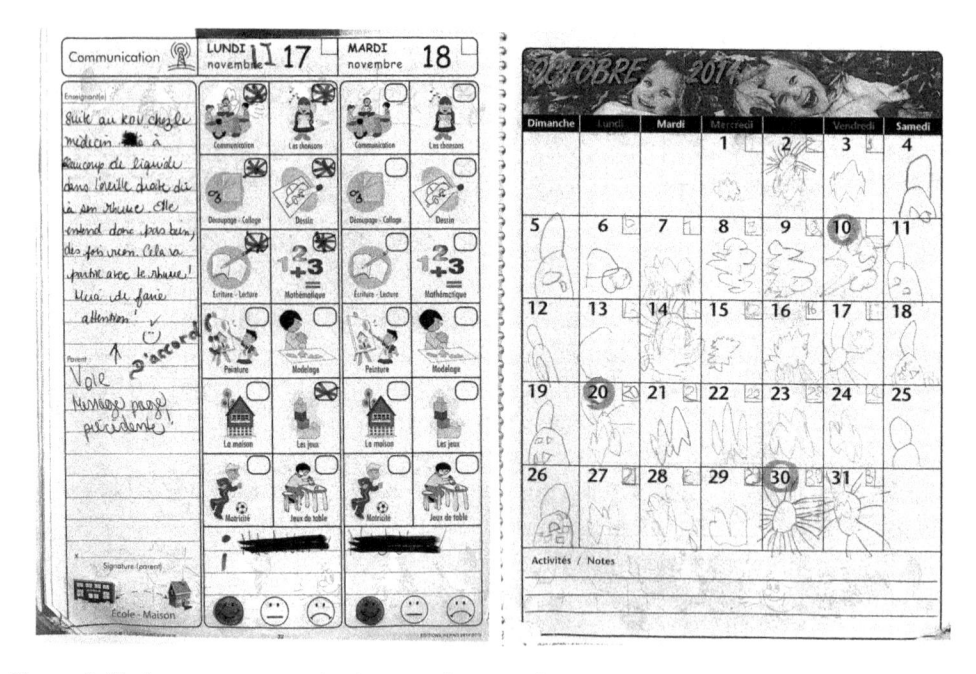

Figure 5. Kindergarten communication agenda, example one.

regarding what to communicate, how, or to whom. On the other hand, the child who scribbles at the bottom of the notebook seems to have taken his own initiative in attempting to involve himself in the communication process, positioning himself as asserting his

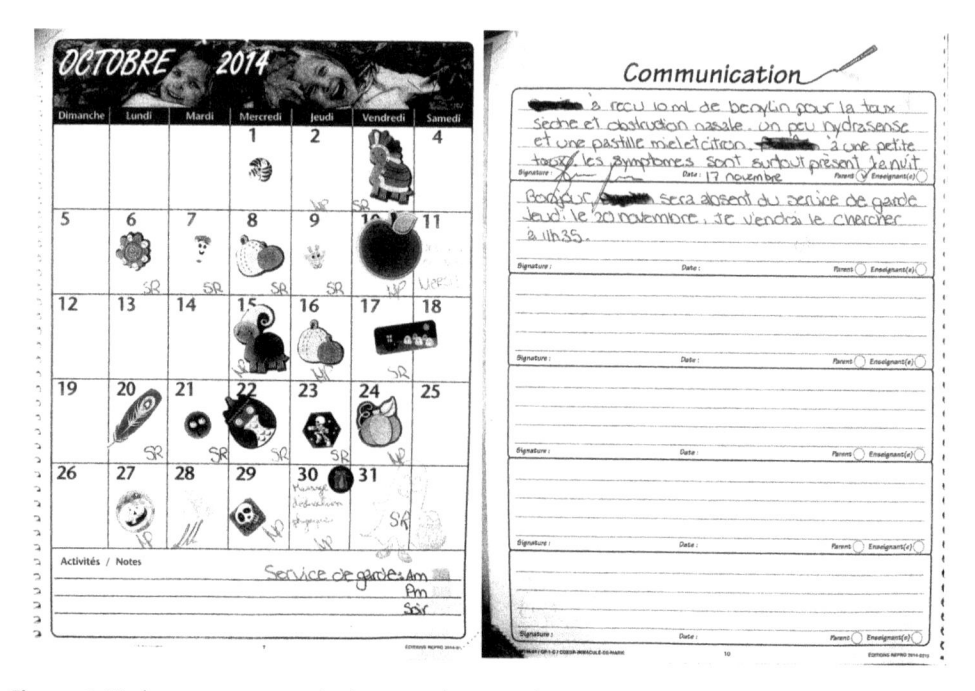

Figure 6. Kindergarten communication agenda, example two.

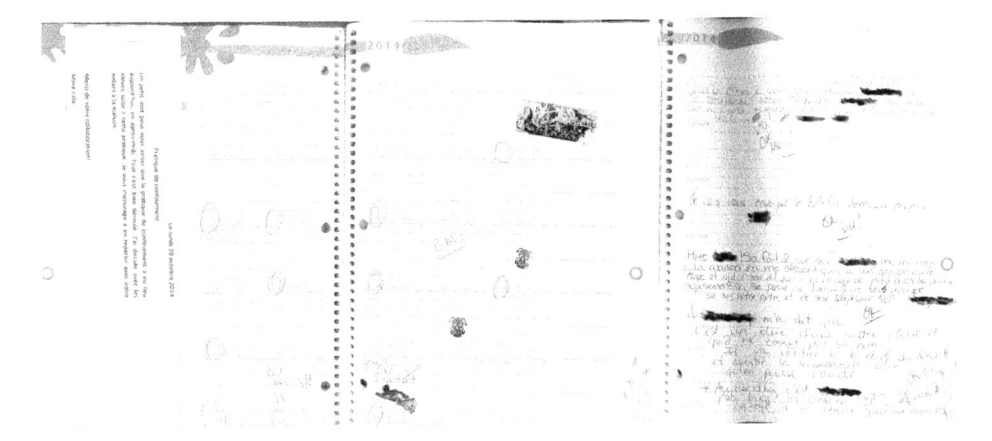

Figure 7. Kindergarten communication agenda, example three.

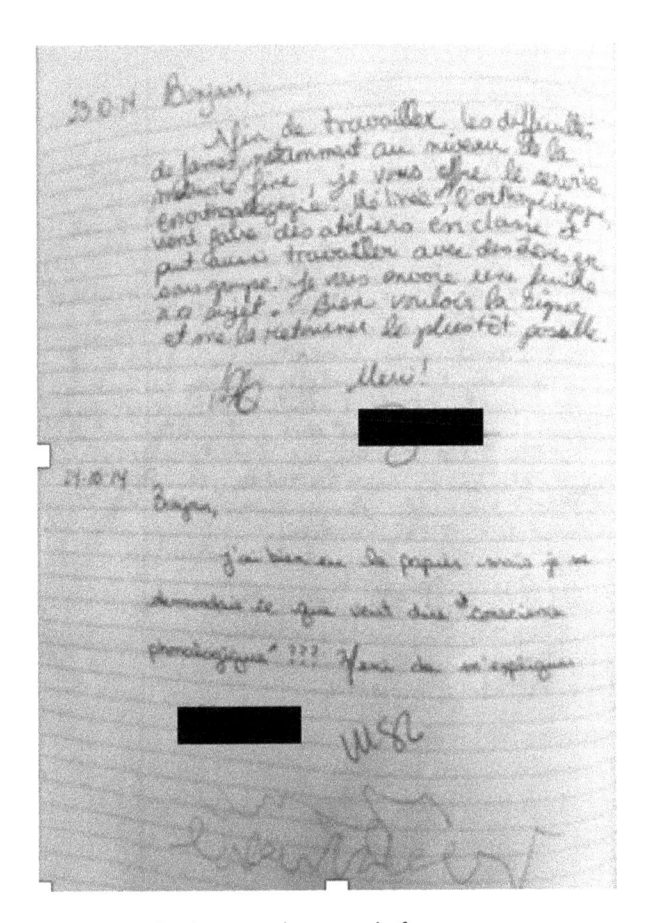

Figure 8. Kindergarten communication agenda, example four.

own identity through writing, though it is possible he may have been encouraged to do so. It seems as if the adults have allowed him access to the document, though there are no responses to, or translations of, his additions.

All of the agendas, with the exception of the notebook, include a set of three faces (smiling, neutral, frowning) or a colour coded system (green-yellow-red, or sticker-yellow-red) to keep track of the child's behaviour each day. Two of these documents have this system integrated within the printed agenda itself, while the other two are added in by the teacher.

Construction and positioning of the teacher. In contrast to the childcare agendas which seemed to value educator's observation skills, these documents position teachers as evaluating and posing judgements on children, who are positioned as objects to be evaluated and reported on, specifically with respect to following school rules.

Individual messages written by teachers to parents include requests to return items to school or sign forms, information about health or accidents at school, and responses to parent questions or requests. These messages position teachers as responding to parent concerns, informing parents of any incidents involving their child, and soliciting parent 'collaboration'.

Construction and positioning of the parents. Some agendas require parents to sign daily. This positions them as both 'policed' or under surveillance by the teachers who require their conformity to school expectations of 'collaboration' as well as subjugated to teacher's constructions of their children (parents are not invited to share their opinion).

These documents, in contrast to the childcare agendas, include more conversations initiated by parents. In fact, the majority of written communication is initiated by mothers, with teachers often responding 'seen' or 'OK'. These entries inform the teacher about absences and health issues, request information about school procedures, homework, help finding a lost object, or request that the teacher phone the parent. They also include holiday greetings and assertions that the parent will follow-up at home regarding problem behaviour. For example,

> Dear Mrs. M, Gabriel and I discussed his responsibilities at school (listening, cleaning up, relaxing). He understands that there will be consequences at home if he gets a yellow or a red at school. It should go better. Have a nice day, (mother's name)

Parent use of these documents constructs them as active agents, informing and asking questions of the teacher. They also seem to accept the teacher's requests, signing the document and responding positively to teacher demands. One of the mothers also wrote messages to her son, for example, 'I'm so proud of you sweetie, great first week' or 'Happy Halloween Ironman', written in both English and French (the family spoke English but the child attended school in French). This parent seems to consider the document as a keepsake for her son as he gets older, addressing her comments to him when he cannot yet read. Another possibility is that she is performing her close relationship with her son for the teacher (which might explain the bilingual messages), presenting herself as a 'good mother' who loves and supports her son.

One parents' entry at the beginning of the year seems to testify to her difficulty transitioning from the childcare agenda to a blank notebook,

> Please, I would like to know how Thomas' week was? The activities you did? His behaviour with you and the other children? Did he ask to go to the washroom? I'd like to know please because I haven't heard anything and I'd like to know what's going on with my son. Thanks!!!

WORKING WITH PARENTS AND FAMILIES IN EARLY CHILDHOOD EDUCATION 141

Child assessment documents

Moving on to school child observation checklist

Description. The document itself is 10 pages long. The cover page contains demographic information about the child (name, home language), the educator and childcare centre, and the name of the child's future school. There is also a space for the child to draw a self-portrait, and two lines for the educator to list the child's interests (see Figure 9). The six documents collected for this study vary with regard to the extent that this page is completed. Often, the home language, self-portrait, child's interests, and contact information for the childcare centre are missing.

Five pages are dedicated to a checklist that is divided by developmental domain (see Figure 10). There is a legend ('it is easy for me'; 'I progress with support'; 'despite support it is difficult'; 'not observed'), as well as pictograms illustrating the different items that educators are to assess. Without exception, every single of the 57 items is completed for every child. The majority of the items are marked 'easy for me', though some are 'progress with support' and tying shoes is often 'not observed'. The final page is divided into two sections, one authorising the school to communicate with the childcare centre (usually left blank), and another informing the school of 'special support services' received while the child was in childcare. Even when the parent and educator informed me during

Figure 9. Moving on to school cover page.

Figure 10. Example of moving on the school checklist.

the interviews (for the larger project) that the child received such services,[4] this section is always left blank.

Construction and positioning of the child. This document constructs the child as either 'very ready' or 'almost ready' for school, relying on a developmental psychology 'regime of truth' (Foucault 1975). The child's self-portrait appears to be a decoration, and his/her interests seem secondary to the checklist.

Construction and positioning of the educator. The ability of the document to facilitate communication between the two settings seems less prioritised by the educators and the parents than the child evaluation. This document positions the educator as an 'early childhood professional' carefully observing children according to a predetermined framework, and assessing whether or not they meet some universal standard of 'readiness'.

Construction and positioning of the parents. The parents are positioned by the document as consumers of information, and as having the power to authorise, or not, communication between the childcare centre and the school.

Preliminary report card

Description. The government's basic school regulation mandates that the school send home a preliminary report informing parents of the student's learning and behaviour 'no later than 15 October' (Governement du Québec 2017a, article 29). Each school had its own version of this document, although they all involved some form of checklist and usually a narrative comment by the teacher (see Figures 11–12). These documents are between one and four pages long and sometimes include a shorter checklist and/or a comment section for the parent to complete, as well as a space for the child to draw. Some of these reports are loosely organised around the *Preschool Educational Programme* (the official curriculum document), while others are not.

These documents are completed by teachers, either by hand or using a computer. When they are completed by hand, teachers occasionally add a comment next to checklist items. For example, one teacher added 'chatty' next to 'respects classroom rules', while another explained 'needs multiple reminders' next to a similar statement. Some examples of their comments at the end of the document include,

> Mathéo works hard and is always in a good mood. He has easily adapted to the class routines and participates actively in proposed activities. Sometimes reminders for silence are necessary (lining up, in class). In general, he seems to have adapted well to his new environment. Teaching him is a pleasure.

> Gabriel is learning that he's not the only one in the class and I can't respond to all his needs instantly. Each one gets a turn! There is already an improvement. He has learned the class routine. He should be proud of himself!! J

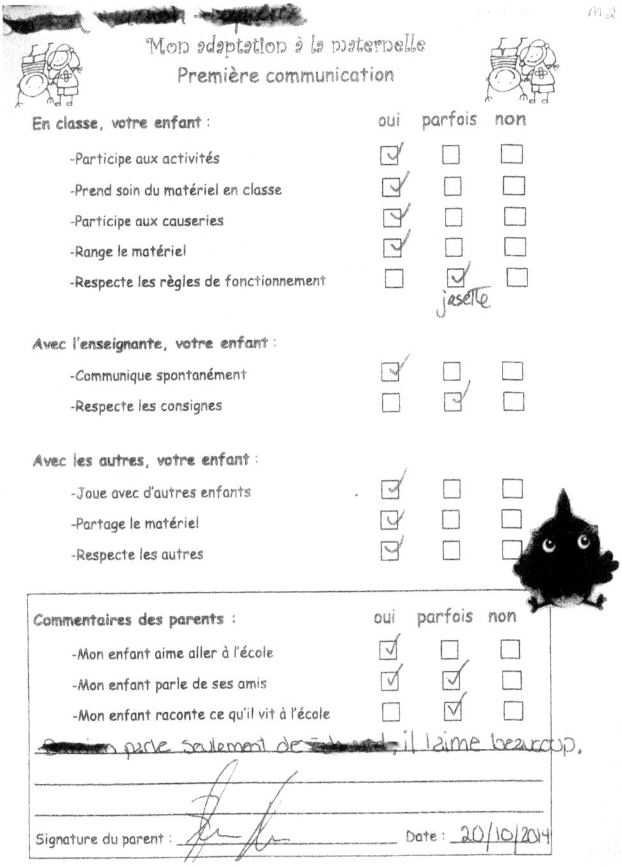

Figure 11. Preliminary report card, example one.

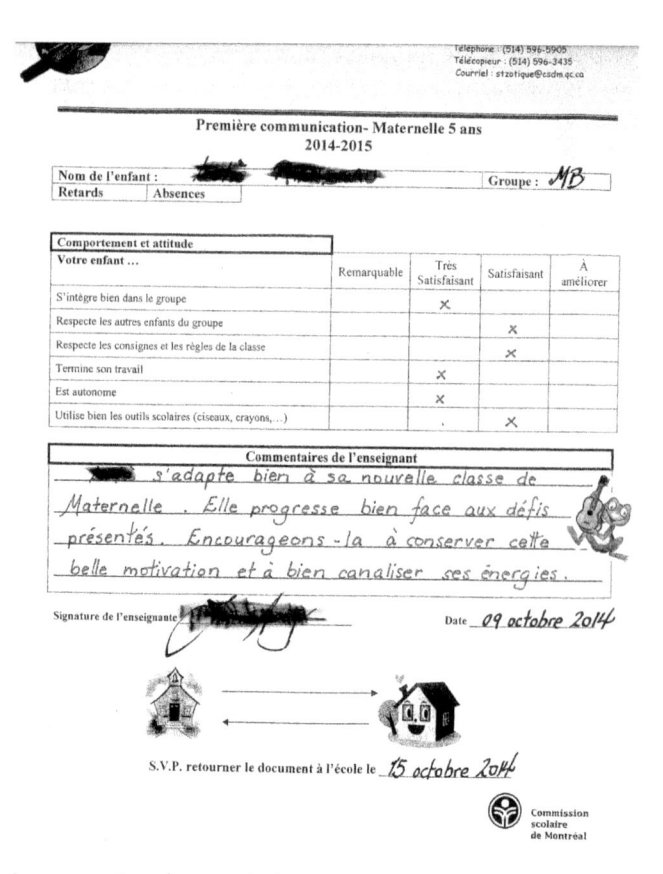

Figure 12. Preliminary report card, example two.

Parent comments pertain to children's friendships, the fact that the child does (or does not) want to go to school in the mornings, the fact that the child likes the teacher, and the fact that the mother is proud of the child. Some parents address their comments to the teacher while others address them to the child.

Construction and positioning of the child. These documents seem to position children as either meeting the classroom expectations, or as struggling to adapt to the routines and expectations of kindergarten.

Construction and positioning of the teacher. Teachers are positioned as observant and knowledgeable about the children, transmitting information to parents about whether or not there is reason to be concerned about their child's progress.

Construction and positioning of the parents. The preliminary report cards position parents as collaborating by signing and returning the forms, writing comments if invited to, asking children questions about their experiences in school, and practicing skills identified by teachers as being difficult for their children to learn in order to support their children's school success.

Official report card
Description. The official report card (see Figure 13) is closely aligned to Quebec's *Preschool Educational Programme* (MEQ 2006), organised according to six 'competencies':

2. RÉSULTATS

	Étape 1	Étape 2	Étape 3
Se développer sur le plan sensoriel et moteur	C		
Développer sa personnalité	B		
Entrer en relation avec les autres	B		
Communiquer oralement	C		
Se familiariser avec son environnement			
Mener à terme des projets et des activités			
Commentaires : Votre enfant manifeste régulièrement sa participation aux activités de communication orale (lève la main, hoche la tête, risque un mot). À la maison comme à l'école, encourageons votre enfant à expérimenter différentes activités de motricité fine (déchirer, découper, coller, lacer, modeler, tracer, dessiner, boutonner, manipuler de petits objets, enfiler).			

Figure 13. Official kindergarten report card.

(1) develops sensorimotor skills; (2) develops his/her personality; (3) relates well with others; (4) communicates orally; (5) becomes familiar with his/her environment; and (6) completes projects or activities. These report cards assign children letter grades from A to D for each of the evaluated competencies (A = very good progress; B = satisfactory progress; C = making progress with some difficulties; and D = serious difficulties). There are also two sections for teacher comments, one for comments 'regarding the student's strengths, challenges and progress' and another for 'various comments such as regarding other learning that has taken place during class or school projects'. Teacher comments did not seem to respect the two different sections. Most teachers added one general comment in one of the two sections. These were often addressed to the parents, and ended with an encouraging message to the child. Children's work habits, attitude, and behaviour in class; favourite play activities; and challenges are described. For example,

> Daniel is at ease in the class. He participates well in activities and applies himself enormously in what he does. He likes to talk with his friends and make them laugh. However, he must pay attention to chattiness, that sometimes overtakes him and slows him down when he is working. He likes to draw and is very creative. Bravo Daniel for the wonderful work and continue!

One teacher mentioned the opportunity to discuss the report card during the parent–teacher interview in her written comment, and another provided the parent with tasks to do at home,

> At home, like at school, encourage him to try different fine motor activities (ripping, cutting, gluing, lacing, modelling, tracing, drawing, buttoning, manipulating small objects, beading) […] Encourage him to pronounce his words clearly.

Parents are invited to sign the document. All the schools used this report card, and two of them supplemented it with a more elaborate checklist.

Construction and positioning of the children. The grades appear to categorise children. Children received either all As; all Bs; a combination of Bs and Cs; or a combination of Bs, Cs, and Ds. These documents assign a judgement to the child and set out expectations about their future careers as students. The messages addressed to the children (there was no equivalent section in the childcare assessment) position children as responsible for their learning and as requiring praise and motivation to succeed.

Construction and positioning of the teachers. The report card positions the teacher as holding expert knowledge and having the power to emit judgements about the children's learning and overall school performance. One assumes that methods are used in order to observe or evaluate the children, but the report card does not provide this information.

Construction and positioning of the parents. The report card positions the parents as passive consumers of teacher expertise and evaluation of their child. The comments position them as interested and collaborative.

Report card annexes

Description. The two report card 'annexes' were checklists created by the schools that expanded upon each competency (see Figures 14 and 15). It is important to note that the behaviours or skills observed in the report card annex do not correspond to the definition of the competency in the educational programme, often positioning the preschool programme as more academic than it is officially supposed to be (MEQ 2006). One of these documents used the same legend as the report card, while the other allowed teachers to choose 'satisfactory', 'a strength', or 'needs work'. One of the teachers wrote in additional details by hand, such as 'sometimes forgets letters when writing his name'.

One annexe also included an invitation for the parents to comment. This parent used the opportunity to affirm her commitment to helping her child,

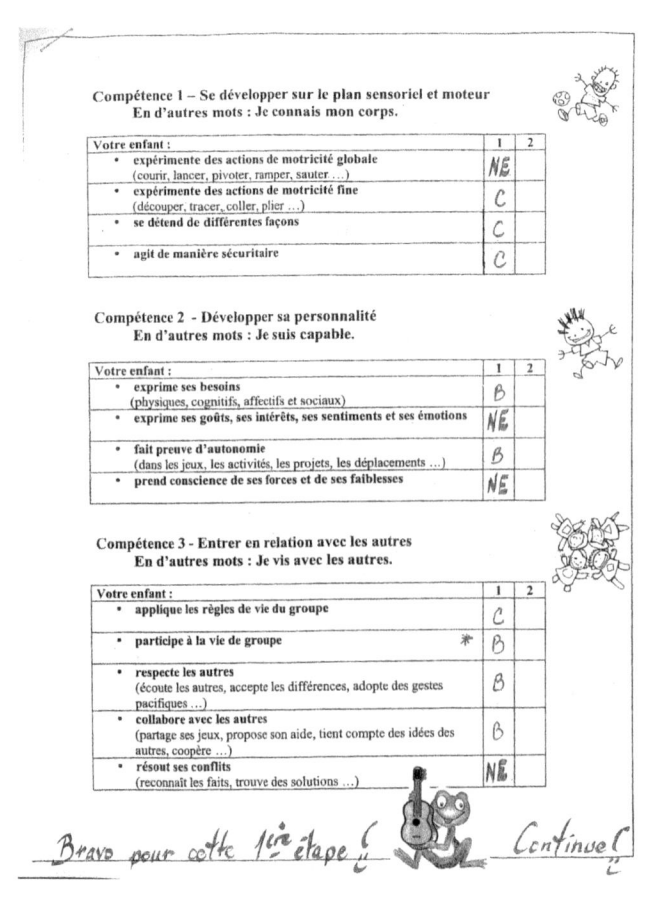

Figure 14. Report card annex, example one.

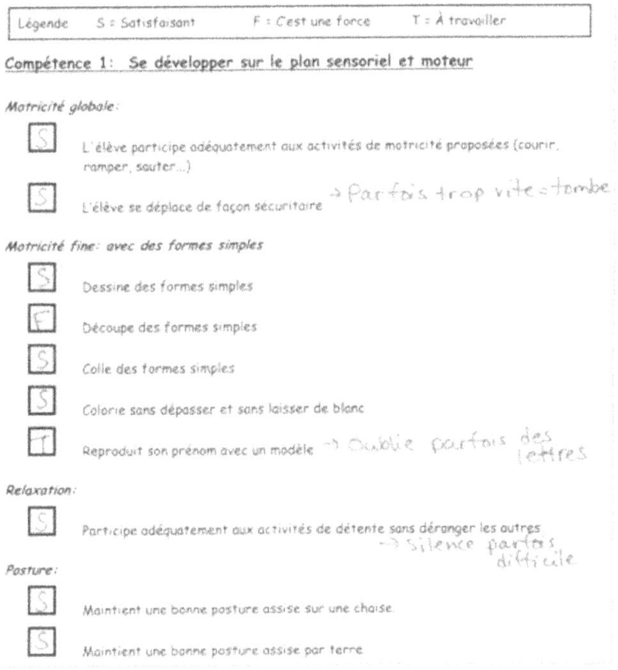
Légende S = Satisfaisant F : C'est une force T = À travailler

Compétence 1: Se développer sur le plan sensoriel et moteur

Motricité globale:

S L'élève participe adéquatement aux activités de motricité proposées (courir, ramper, sauter...)

S L'élève se déplace de façon sécuritaire → Parfois trop vite = tombe

Motricité fine: avec des formes simples

S Dessine des formes simples

F Découpe des formes simples

S Colle des formes simples

S Colorie sans dépasser et sans laisser de blanc

T Reproduit son prénom avec un modèle → Oublie parfois des lettres

Relaxation:

S Participe adéquatement aux activités de détente sans déranger les autres → Silence parfois difficile

Posture:

S Maintient une bonne posture assise sur une chaise

S Maintient une bonne posture assise par terre

Figure 15. Report card annex, example two.

> I help my daughter improve. We will practice patterns, tracing, and yoga to improve her concentration. We will work on her self-esteem and getting her to assert herself and not get discouraged.

Construction and positioning of the child. These documents seem to resist the official curriculum, emphasising children's learning of disciplinary subject matter (reading, writing, counting, etc.) and perhaps more clearly illustrating the teachers' images of an 'ideal kindergarten child'.

Construction and positioning of the teacher. These annexes seem to reinforce the positioning of the teacher as an expert whose main role is to evaluate children.

Construction and positioning of the parents. The parent comment positioned her as embracing her pedagogicalised (Popkewitz 2003) role in her child's education, putting activities in place in order to improve her daughter's grades in the future.

Conclusion

The aim of this study was to explore how documents construct and position children, professionals, and parents during the transition to school, and how these constructions differ across the two settings, relying on the concepts of governmentality, documentality, and interobjectivity. Similar to studies of other types of documents in ECEC, this study also found that the documents produce normative understandings of children, professionals, and parents (Alasuutari, Markström, and Vallberg-Roth 2014; Forsberg 2007; Karila and Alasuutari 2012; Liljestrand and Hammarberg 2017). Different types of documents appear to construct different images of children.

While Liljestrand and Hammarberg's (2017) pedagogical documentation panels constructed children as competent with regard to friendship, communication, and autonomy, and Knauf's (2016) portfolios positioned children as 'learning and developing subjects' (10), this study found that assessment documents in both the early childhood and kindergarten settings offer a dichotomous categorisation of the child as either 'doing well' or 'having difficulty'. However, the image of the ideal child constructed by the communication agenda in childcare, that of a happy child who eats a lot, responds to educator interventions, and participates, is replaced by a child who follows school rules, exceeds curricular expectations, and who escapes notice in kindergarten, as communication often focuses on problems. Our study also found that the documents revealed an absence of or a lack of value placed on the child's voice or perspective, similar to Karila and Alasuutari's (2012) analysis of parent–educator interview documents.

The construction of the professional by the documents is also different in the two contexts. While the early childhood educator is positioned as carefully observing the child, similar to the educators in Knauf's (2016) study, the teacher is constructed by the documents as evaluating and passing judgement on the child, similar to the educators in Karila and Alasuutari's (2012) study. Forsberg's (2007) study found that educators in Swedish preschools positioned themselves as experts 'able to prescribe how parents are supposed to be involved in children's education' (373). We found this to be the case in both settings.

Previous research has found that documents mediate relationships between parents and professionals (Alasuutari, Markström, and Vallberg-Roth 2014; Forsberg 2007; Karila and Alasuutari 2012; Rintakorpi, Lipponen, and Reunamo 2014). Karila and Alasuutari's (2012) analysis of parent–educator interview documents revealed that the form of the documents reproduced an asymmetric relationship between parents and professionals, as parents were positioned as 'objects of evaluation and education' (20) and, particularly, as requiring assistance to achieve 'proper parenthood' (20), thus limiting parents' role in the educational 'partnership'. Parents were constructed as 'responsible for monitoring, evaluating, and developing their child and child raising practices under the guidance of 'experts' (23). They also found that the forms draw heavily on developmental psychology concepts.

The documents analysed in this study also reproduce asymmetric relationships. When their children are in childcare, the documents construct parents as consumers of information about their children. When the children start school, parents appear to take on a somewhat more active role, initiating communication through the agenda and being solicited more often to 'collaborate' by signing the agenda or by working with their children to remedy the deficiencies identified by the documents and the teachers. However, they remain in a subordinate position to teachers' expertise.

I argue that these documents rely on the discourses of developmental psychology, readiness for school, and a vision of parent involvement where parents are subjugated to the institution's agenda. Through the positioning of the institutions, professionals, and parents as 'caring-for' children, the professionals and parents internalise the importance of 'school success' and prioritise it over other goals for the children once the children start school. Thus, the documents act as a technique of governmentality (Foucault 1991) and documentality (Ferraris 2013), limiting possible positions for all of the human actors, and therefore limiting possibilities for action, and creating asymmetrical intersubjective relations within the actor-networks (Latour 1996, 2005) that come together to produce the social reality of ECEC. The fact that these documents are often commercially produced or imposed by the government suggests that they may be used without critical reflection. However, the results of this study suggest that reconceptulising the documents used in both childcare and kindergarten in Québec, and critical reflection on how the documents are used, are necessary. In order to transmit an asset-oriented and active view of children and families, and a more complex vision of professionals, the communication agendas need to be redesigned, and the assessment documents need to be abandoned or transformed, perhaps inspired by different types of documents used elsewhere, such as pedagogical documentation (e.g. Bowne et al. 2012; Buldu 2010; Dahlberg, Moss, and Pence 2007; Wien 2013) and learning stories (Carr 2001; Carr and Lee 2012).

Notes

1. I adapted Bamberg's (1997) questions to apply the strategy to the analysis of documents.
2. All of the children attended kindergarten in French, although one child attended a French-immersion programme in an English-language school board.
3. In this class, messages were transferred in a plastic sleeve placed in a binder that went back and forth each day.
4. See Lehrer, Bigras, and Laurin (2017).

Acknowledgements

The authors would like to acknowledge the members of EECERA's special interest group on working with families who helped with the literature review.

Disclosure statement

No potential conflict of interest was reported by the author.

Funding

The authors would like to acknowledge the financial support of the Fonds société et culture Québec and the Social Sciences and Humanities Research Council of Canada.

ORCID

Joanne S. Lehrer http://orcid.org/0000-0002-3290-8027

References

Alasuutari, Maarit, Anne-Marie Markström, and Ann-Christine Vallberg-Roth. 2014. *Assessment and Documentation in Early Childhood Education.* London: Routledge.
Backhaus, Johanna, Andrea Bogatz, and Petra Hanke. 2013. "Collaboration Between Early Childhood Centres and Primary Schools in the Transition From Early Childhood Education to Primary School – the Parental Perspective." Poster presented at the Annual Meeting of the European Early Childhood Educational Research Association, Tallin, Estonia, August 28–31.

Bamberg, Michael G.W. 1997. "Positioning Between Structure and Performance." *Journal of Narrative and Life History* 1–4 (7): 335–342.

Besnard, Thérèse, Marie-Josée Cotnoir, Marie-Josée Letarte, and Jean-Pascal Lemelin. 2014. *L'Outil Mon Portrait de Magog, un outil de communication entre les milieux préscolaire et scolaire pour faciliter la transition des enfants*. Magog: Centre de santé et des services sociaux de Memphrémagog.

Bloch, Marianne, Kerstin Holmlund, Ingeborg Moqvist, and Thomas Popkewitz. 2003. "Global and Local Patterns of Governing the Child, Family, Their Care, and Education: An Introduction." In *Governing Children, Families, and Education: Restructuring the Welfare State*, edited by Marianne Bloch, Kerstin Holmlund, Ingeborg Moqvist, and Thomas Popkewitz, 3–34. New York: Palmgrave Macmillan.

Bowne, Mary, Kay Cutler, Debra DeBates, Deanna Gilkerson, and Andrew Stremmel. 2012. "Pedagogical Documentation and Collaborative Dialogue as Tolls of Inquiry for pre-Service Teachers in Early Childhood Education: An Exploratory Narrative." *Journal of the Scholarship of Teaching and Learning* 10 (2): 48–59.

Brandt, Deborah, and Katie Clinton. 2002. "Limits of the Local: Expanding Perspectives on Literacy as a Social Practice." *Journal of Literacy Research* 34 (3): 337–356. doi:10.1207/s15548430jlr3403_4.

Buldu, Mehmet. 2010. "Making Learning Visible in Kindergarten Classrooms: Pedagogical Documentation as a Formative Assessment Technique." *Teaching and Teacher Education* 26 (7): 1439–1449. doi:10.1016/j.tate.2010.05.003.

Carr, Margaret. 2001. *Assessment in Early Childhood Settings: Learning Stories*. Los Angeles, CA: Sage.

Carr, Margaret, and Wendy Lee. 2012. *Learning Stories: Constructing Learner Identities in Early Education*. Los Angeles, CA: Sage.

CASIOPE. 2017. *Moving on to School*. http://casiope.org/services-view/passage-a-lecole/.

Clausen, Sigrid Brogaard. 2015. "Schoolification or Early Years Democracy? A Cross-Curricular Perspective from Denmark and England." *Contemporary Issues in Early Childhood* 16 (4): 355–373. doi:10.1177/1463949115616327.

Cotnoir, Marie-Josée. 2015. "Évaluation d'une stratégie pour faciliter la transition scolaire des enfants à la maternelle: l'Outil Mon ortrait de Magog." *Master's thesis*, Université de Sherbrooke.

Dahlberg, Gunilla, Peter Moss, and Alan Pence. 2007. *Beyond Quality in Early Childhood Education and Care: Languages of Evaluation*. London: Routledge.

Dockett, Sue, and Bob Perry. 2004. "Starting School: Perspectives of Australian Children, Parents and Educators." *Journal of Early Childhood Research* 2 (2): 171–189. doi:10.1177/1476718X04042976.

Fabian, Hilary, and Aline-Wendy Dunlop. 2006. "Outcomes of Good Practice in Transition Processes for Children Entering Primary School." Background paper prepared for the Education for All Global Monitoring Report 2007 Strong Foundations: Early Childhood Care and Education, UNESCO. http://unesdoc.unesco.org/images/0014/001474/147463e.pdf.

Ferraris, Maurizio. 2013. *Documentality: Why It is Necessary to Leave Traces*. New York: Fordham University Press.

Forsberg, Lucas. 2007. "Involving Parents Through School Letters: Mothers, Fathers and Teachers Negotiating Children's Education and Rearing." *Ethnography and Education* 2 (3): 273–288. doi:10.1080/17457820701547252.

Foucault, Michel. 1975. *Discipline and Punish: The Birth of a Prison*. New York: Random House.

Foucault, Michel. 1981. "Omnes et Singulatim: Towards a Criticism of 'Political Reason.'" In *The Tanner Lectures on Human Values, Volume 2*, edited by Sterling M. McMurrin, 225–254. Salt Lake City: University of Utah Press.

Foucault, Michel. 1991. "Governmentality." In *The Foucault Effect: Studies in Governmentality*, edited by Graham Burchell, Colin Gordon, and Peter Miller, 87–104. Chicago: University of Chicago Press.

Garrity, S. 2014. *People think it's not the real world - but it's our world'. The significance of relationships found on the threshold between the private and the public: Exploring engagement between *mothers and early years practitioners in a changing Ireland*, it's. Galway: National University of Ireland.

Gonzalez-Mena, Janet. 2014. *50 Strategies for Communicating and Working with Diverse Families*. Boston, MA: Pearson.

Gouvernement du Québec. 2017a. *Basic School Regulation for Preschool, Elementary and Secondary Education*. Québec (Québec): Éditeur official du Québec.

Gouvernement du Québec. 2017b. *Educational Childcare act*. Québec: Éditeur official du Québec.

Griebel, Wilfried, and Renata Niesel. 2013. "The Development of Parents in Their First Child's Transition to Primary School." In *International Perspectives on Transition to School: Reconceptualising Beliefs, Policy and Practice*, edited by Kay Magretts, and Anna Kienig, 101–110. London: Routledge.

Horizon 0-5. 2014. *État sommaire : Démarches locales concertées montréalaises pour une transition harmonieuse vers l'école*. Montréal: Horizon 0-5. http://www.horizon05.com/actions-en-cours/passage-a-l-ecole.

Institut du nouveau monde. 2017. "Pour continuer à grandir », rapport de la *Commission sur l'éducation à la petite enfance*. Montrèal: Institut du nouveau monde.

Jones, Carolyn. 2006. "Continuity of Learning: Adding Funds of Knowledge From the Home Environment." *SET Research Information for Teachers* 2 (2006): 28–31.

Karila, Kirsti, and Maarit Alasuutari. 2012. "Drawing Partnership on Paper: How Do the Forms for Individual Education Plans Frame Parent– Teacher Relationship?" *International Journal About Parents in Education* 6 (1): 15–27.

Knauf, Helen. 2016. "Making an Impression: Portfolios as Instruments of Impression Management for Teachers in Early Childhood Education and Care Centres." *Early Childhood Education Journal*. doi:10.1007/s10643-016-0791-0.

Latour, Bruno. 1996. "On Interobjectivity." *Mind, Culture and Activity* 3 (4): 228–245. doi:10.1207/s15327884mca0304_2.

Latour, Bruno. 2005. *Reassembling the Social: An Introduction to Actor-Network Theory*. Oxford: Oxford University Press.

Lehrer, Joanne, Nathalie Bigras, and Isabelle Laurin. 2017. "Family-Early Childhood Educator Relationships as Children Prepare to Start School." In *Families and the Transition to School,*, edited by S. Dockett, P. Perry, and W. Griebel, 195–210. Singapore: Springer.

Liljestrand, Johan, and Annie Hammarberg. 2017. "The Social Construction of the Competent, Self-Governed Child in Documentation: Panels in the Swedish Preschool." *Contemporary Issues in Early Childhood*. doi:10.1177/1463949117692270.

Löfdahl, Annica. 2014. "Teacher–Parent Relations and Professional Strategies: A Case Study on Documentation and Talk About Documentation in a Swedish Preschool." *Australasian Journal of Early Childhood* 39 (3): 103–110.

Magretts, Kay, and Anna Keinig. 2013. *International Perspectives on Transition to School: Reconceptualising Beliefs, Policy and Practice*. London: Routledge.

MELS (Ministère de l'Éducation, du Loisir, et du Sport). 2006. *Programme de formation de l'école québecoise: Éducation préscolaire, enseignement primaire*. Québec: Ministère de l'Éducation.

MELS (Ministère de l'Éducation, du Loisir, et du Sport). 2010. *Guide Pour Soutenir une Première Transition Scolaire de Qualité*. Québec: Gouvernement du Québec.

MELS (Ministère de l'Éducation, du Loisir, et du Sport). 2011. *Les choix de notre école à l'heure du bulletin unique - Document de soutien à l'intention des équipes-écoles pour la révision des normes et modalités d'évaluation des apprentissages*. Québec: Gouvernement du Québec.

MELS (Ministère de l'Éducation, du Loisir, et du Sport). 2012. *Indicateurs de l'éducation – édition 2012*. Québec: Gouvernement du Québec.

MEQ (Ministère de l'Éducation du Québec). 2006. *Québec Education Program: Preschool and Elementary*. Québec: Gouvernement du Québec.

MFA (Ministère de la Famille et des Aînés). 2007. *Meeting Early Childhood Needs : Québec's Educational Program for Childcare Services, Update*. Montréal: Ministère de la Familles et des Aînés.

Miller, Peter, and Nikolas Rose. 1990. "Governing Economic Life." *Economy and Society* 19 (1): 1–31. doi:10.1080/03085149000000001.

OECD (Organisation for Economic Cooperation and Development). 2006. *Starting Strong II: Early Childhood Education and Care*. Paris: OECD.

O'Kane, Mary, and Nóirín Hayes. 2013. "The Child Snapshot' – A Tool for the Transfer of Information on Children from Preschool to Primary School." *International Journal of Transitions in Childhood* 6: 28–36.

Peters, Sally, Carol Hartley, Pat Rogers, Jemma Smith, and Margaret Carr. 2009. "Early Childhood Portfolios as a Tool for Enhancing Learning During the Transition to School." *International Journal of Transitions in Childhood* 3: 4–15.

Petrakos, Hariclia, and Joanne Lehrer. 2011. "Parents 'and Teachers' Perceptions of Transition Practices in Kindergarten." *Exceptionality Education International*, 21 (2): 62–73.

Pianta, Robert C., and Martha J. Cox, eds. 1999. *The Transition to Kindergarten*. Baltimore: Brookes.

Popkewitz, Thomas S. 2003. "Governing the Child and Pedagogicalization of the Parent: A Historical Excursis into the Present." In *Governing Children, Families, and Education: Restructuring the Welfare State*, edited by Marianne Bloch, Kirsten Holmlund, Inger Moqvist, and Thomas Popkewitz, 35–62. New York: Palgrave Macmillan.

Rimm-Kaufman, Sara, and Robert C Pianta. 2000. "An Ecological Perspective on the Transition to Kindergarten: A Theoretical Framework to Guide Empirical Research." *Journal of Applied Developmental Psychology* 21 (5): 491–511. doi:10.1016/S0193-3973(00)00051-4.

Rintakorpi, Kati, Lasse Lipponen, and Jyrki Reunamo. 2014. "Documenting with Parents and Toddlers: A Finnish Case Study." *Early Years: An International Journal of Research and Development* 34 (2): 188–197. doi:10.1080/09575146.2014.903233.

Rogers, Susanne, Katherine Hopps-Wallis, and Bob Perry. 2016. "Preschool-school Communication: The Challenges of Written Information Exchange." Paper presented at the Meeting of the European Early Childhood Educational Research Association, Dublin, Ireland, August 31–September 3.

Rous, Beth, Rena Hallam, Katherine McCormick, and Megan Cox. 2010. "Practices That Support the Transition to Public Preschool Programs: Results from a National Survey." *Early Childhood Research Quarterly* 25 (1): 17–32. doi:10.1016/j.ecresq.2009.09.001.

Rutland, Ted, and Alex Aylett. 2008. "The Work of Policy: Actor Networks, Governmentality, and Local Action on Climate Change in Portland, Oregon." *Environment and Planning D: Society and Space* 26: 627–646. doi:10.1068/d6907.

Whalley, Margy and the Pen Green Centre Team. 2007. *Involving Parents in Their Children's Learning, Second Edition*. London: Paul Chapman.

Whalley, Margy, Cath Arnold, and Robert Orr, eds. 2013. *Working with Families in Children's Centres and Early Years Settings*. London: Hodder Education.

Wien, Carol Anne. 2013. "Making Learning Visible Through Pedagogical Documentation." Ontario. Ministry of Education. Think, Feel, Act: Lessons from Research about Young Children.

Index

Note: **Bold** page numbers indicate tables, *italic* numbers indicate figures.

accountability 1, 3, 119
activity, care as 36–37
actor-network theory 130
administrative obstacles to parental involvement 110, 114
Ahnert, L. 95
Alasuutari, M. 130, 148
Altenburger, L. E. 64
anger in parent-teacher cocaring 64
attachment theory 91, 95
attention as symbolic meaning of care 37
Australia, transition to school in: bioecological theory 23; case studies 25–26; challenges and opportunities in 22; coding process 25; complex family circumstances 22; constructivist grounded theory approach 23–24, 25; continuity between home and school 22–23; data analysis 25–26; data collection 24–25; dialogue sought with schools 27; diverse cultural and language backgrounds 28; implications of research results 28–29; methodology for research 23–26; parental engagement with child's learning 26; parents/educators perspectives on 27–29; participants in research 23, 24; Person-Process-Context-Time (PPCT) model 23, 24–25; purpose of study 22–23; results of research 26–27, **27**; school experiences of parents 22; support from schools for parents 26–27; value of parents' participation 27; *see also* educators, role in transition to childcare; written communication during childcare/school transition

Bamberg, M. G. W. 133
Belgium *see* democratic deficit in parental involvement
bioecological theory 23
Bronfenbrenner, U. 23, 58, 102

Canada *see* educators, role in transition to childcare; written communication during childcare/school transition

care: child-selected model versus primary caregiving 97–98; in pre-school practices 36–38; primary caregiving, arguments against 96–97; Sweden, home and preschool collaboration in 52
Cheng, P.-W. D. 84
China, play beliefs in: authority, parental 16; changes in 5–6, 7; Chinese Parent Play Beliefs Scale (CPPBS) 16; confirmatory factor analysis 11–12; dichotomy in 7; 'eduplay' concept 7, 15; exploratory factor analysis 10–11, **11**; future research 17–18; home context 7–8; Home Play Activities Questionnaire (HPAQ) 10; implications of research results 16–17; measures 9–10; mediation models 12, **13**, *14*, **14**; methods of research 8–10, **9**; objectives of research 8; parental involvement in play 15–16; Parental Play Involvement Questionnaire (PPIQ) 9–10; participants in research 8, **9**; Play for Fun (PF) 10–11, **11**, 12, *14*, **14**, 15; Play for Learning (PL) 10, **11**, 12, *14*, **14**, 15; procedures for research 10; research into play 6; results from research 10–12, **11**, **13**, *14*, **14**; transferable lessons from research 17; *see also* learning at play, teachers' and parents conceptions of
choice of preschools 48
cocaring, parent-teacher, observational assessment of: aims of study 59; anger 64; benefits for children 57; Cocaring Behavior Coding Manual 59, 61–65, *62*, *63*, 66, 68; cocaring framework 56; coding of interactions 60–61; coldness 65–65; competition 65; composite variables for support and undermining 66; cooperation 62–63; coparenting research 57–58; correlation among scales 66, **67**, 68; data collection 60; displeasure 65; ecological systems theory (EST) 58; family systems theory (FST) 58; interactiveness 63; key features of cocaring 58–59; limitations of research 69–70; methods for research 59–61; need for observation 57;

observations 60; Observed Support 62–64, **63**; Observed Undermining 64–65; participants in research 59–60; pleasure 63–64; reliability of scales 65–66, 68; support 56–57, 62–64, **63**, 66, 68–69; systems approach 58; undermining 57, 64–65, 66, 69; warmth 64
coldness in parent-teacher cocaring 65–65
communication practices 109, 113; *see also* written communication during childcare/school transition
competition in parent-teacher cocaring 65
constructivist grounded theory approach 23–24, 25
cooperation in parent-teacher cocaring 62–63
coparenting research 57–58
Cowan, C. P. 64
Cowan, P. A. 64

Dahlstedt, M. 33
Dalli, C. 96
decision-making, parental involvement in 113
democratic deficit in parental involvement: care deficit 41; care in pre-school practices 36–38; context for research 33; defined 32; eagerness to know about pre-school activities 35–36, 41; equality of parents, assumption of 32; Flemish community of Belgium 33; focus groups sessions 34–35; further research 42; limitations of study 41; meaning-making about pre-school education 40–41; methods of research 33–35, **34**; non-participation as problem 33; participants in research **34**; policies and practices of schools 41–42; purpose of parental involvement 32–33; questions, raising with staff 38; reciprocal dialogue, creating 42; results from research 35–40; scripted practices, following 39; scripted practices, challenging 39–40; subordinate position, parents as adopting 38, 41; unequal power dynamics 41
discontinuity of care 37–38
displeasure in parent-teacher cocaring 65
Dockett, S. 27
documentality 130, 149–150
Doucet, F. 33

Ebbeck, M. 97, 98, 99
ecological systems theory (EST) 58
educators, role in transition to childcare: aim of research 90–91; attachment theory 91, 95, 96–97; child-selected model versus primary caregiving 97–98, 99; children, relationships with 95; coding of data 92; cultural-historical perspective 91; data collection and analysis 91–92; ethical issues in research 92; methodology for research 91–93; over-attachment 96; parents, relationships with 94–95, 99; primary caregiving, arguments against 96–97; professionalism 93–94, 95, 99; qualifications 90; relationships during transition 91; researcher 92; results of research 93–98; structures, interpretation of 94; *see also* England, professionalism of practitioners; Finland, educators' views on parental involvement
Eisenhart, M. A. 84
Elfer, P. 95, 97, 99
England, professionalism of practitioners: accountability 119; attributes for effective parental interaction 122–123; care/education tension 119–120; changes in sector 119; data collection 121; dimensions of professionalism 124–125, *125*; espoused theory 122; ethics in research 121; existential-phenomenological approach to research 120–121; experience of practitioners 125; Finland, interaction with parents in 120; future research 126–127; implications of research 126–127; and interaction with parents 120; literature review 119–120; methodology for research 120–121; overlap with private relationships 123; participants in research 121; performativity 119; pre-service training 126; qualifications of practitioners 125–126; reflection on attitudes and approaches 126; results of research 122–126, *125*; social construction of professionalism 121; standpoints in work with parents 123–124
Epstein, J. L. 32, 103
equaliser, pre-school education as 31–32
equality of parents, assumption of 32
espoused theory 122
Evangelou, M. 103
existential-phenomenological approach to research 120–121

family systems theory (FST) 58
Feinberg, M. E. 57
Ferrais, M. 130
Finland, educators' views on parental involvement: aims of research 104; benefits of parental involvement 103; communication practices 109, 113; context for research 104; data analysis 106–107; data collection 105–106; decision-making, involvement in 113; definitions of parental involvement 103; equal roles, presumption of 103; future research 114; general views 107, **107**; importance of early childhood education 102; individual incompatibility 110; insufficient involvement, reasons for 108–111, *109*, **109**, 112–113; limitations of research 113–114; management and administrative obstacles 110, 114; methods for research 104–107, **105**; mixed method analysis 106; models of parental involvement 103; participants in research 104–105, **105**; preferred types 111–112; purpose of early childhood education 112; standpoints on 120; superficiality of positive

attitudes 111; time management 109–110; trust and competence, lack of 111; types of parental involvement 107–108, *108*, **108**; understanding of parental involvement 110, 112; volunteering 113; *see also* educators, role in transition to childcare
Flemish community of Belgium *see* democratic deficit in parental involvement
Flitner, A. 74

Garrity, S. 131
Germany *see* learning at play, teachers' and parents conceptions of
Gillies, V. 46, 53
Goldschmied, E. 97
Göncü, A. 74
Goodall, J. 103
Goosens, F.A. 97
Gopnik, A. 46
governmentality 129–130, 149–150
Green, B. L. 22

Hakyemez, S. 111
Halgunseth, L. C. 57
Hamington, M. 41
Hammarberg, A. 148
Harkness, S. 7, 16, 74, 99
Harwood, D. 94
Higgins, S. 41
Hindman, A. H. 111
Hirch-Pasek, K. 16
Hirsto, L. 112
Home Play Activities Questionnaire (HPAQ) 10
Hughes, P. 41
Hujala, E. 111

IJzendoorn, M. H. 97
interactiveness in parent-teacher cocaring 63
interobjectivity 130
Ireland, home-school books in 131

Jackson, S. 97

Karila, K. 130, 148
Kasanen, K. 112
Knauf, H. 148
Kothari, B. H. 22
Koutrouba, K. 112

Laine, N. 112
Lamb, M. E. 95
Lang, S. N. 58, 68
Lareau, A. 32, 41
learning at play, teachers' and parents conceptions of: background of study 75; China, play in 73–74, 75; collectivism-individualism dichotomy 82–83; data collection and analysis 77–78; feasibility of German/Chinese transfer of play episodes 82; Germany, play in 74, 75; identifying learning at play 79–80; images of learning at play 80–82; implications of 74–75; importance of play 73; language, difficulties due to 78; limitations of research 84–85; methods of research 76–77; participants in research 75–76; questions for research 75; results of research 78–82; similarities between Germany/China 83–84; teachers/parents comparison 83–84; video clips descriptions 88–89
Li, H. 7, 15
Lightfoot, D. 46
Liljestrand, J. 148
Lin, Y. C. 7
Litwack, S. D. 103
Löfdahl, A. 46, 52

MacNaughton, G. 41
Mahmood, S. 112–113
Malsch, A. M. 22
management obstacles to parental involvement 110, 114
Manning-Morton, J. 93, 119–120
mental disposition, care as 36–37
Merleau-Ponty, M. 74
Mistry, J. 74
Montgomery, C. 103
Moorman, E. A. 103
Mosier, C. 74

Noddings, N. 95

observational assessment of parent-teacher cocaring: aims of study 59; anger 64; Cocaring Behavior Coding Manual 59, 61–65, *62*, **63**, 66, 68; cocaring framework 56; coding of interactions 60–61; coldness 65–65; competition 65; composite variables for support and undermining 66; cooperation 62–63; coparenting research 57–58; correlation among scales 66, **67**, 68; data collection 60; displeasure 65; ecological systems theory (EST) 58; family systems theory (FST) 58; interactiveness 63; key features of cocaring 58–59; limitations of research 69–70; methods for research 59–61; need for observation 57; observations 60; Observed Support 62–64, **63**; Observed Undermining 64–65; pleasure 63–64; reliability of scales 65–66, 68; support 62–64, **63**, 66, 68–69; systems approach 58; undermining 57, 64–65, 66, 69; warmth 64
Onnismaa, E.-L. 112
Osgood, J. 120, 122, 123
Overlapping Spheres of Influence model 32

Parental Play Involvement Questionnaire (PPIQ) 9–10
parenting as diverse and changing role 46
Parmar, P. 7, 16, 74
Péres Prieto, H. 46, 52
performativity 1, 3, 119

Person-Process-Context-Time (PPCT) model 23, 24–25
phenomenon, care as 36–37
Pinquart, M. 95
play beliefs in China: authority, parental 16; changes in 5–6, 7; Chinese Parent Play Beliefs Scale (CPPBS) 9, 16; confirmatory factor analysis 11–12; dichotomy in 7; 'eduplay' concept 7, 15; exploratory factor analysis 10–11, **11**; future research 17–18; home context 7–8; Home Play Activities Questionnaire (HPAQ) 10; implications of research results 16–17; measures 9–10; mediation models 12, **13**, *14*, **14**; methods of research 8–10, **9**; objectives of research 8; parental involvement in play 15–16; Parental Play Involvement Questionnaire (PPIQ) 9–10; participants in research 8, **9**; Play for Fun (PF) 10–11, **11**, 12, *14*, **14**, 15; Play for Learning (PL) 10, **11**, 12, *14*, **14**, 15; procedures for research 10; research into play 6; results from research 10–12, **11**, **13**, *14*, **14**; transferable lessons from research 17; *see also* learning at play, teachers' and parents conceptions of
pleasure in parent-teacher cocaring 63–64
Pomerantz, E. M. 103
positioning analysis 133
practitioners *see* educators, role in transition to childcare; England, professionalism of practitioners; Finland, educators views on parental involvement
pre-school education: benefits of parental involvement in 31–32; care in 36–38; as equaliser 31–32; equality of parents, assumption of 32; *see also* democratic deficit in parental involvement
presence, giving to somebody as symbolic meaning of care 37
primary caregiving: arguments against 96–97; child-selected model and 97–98
professionalism: educators' emphasis on 93–94; relationships with children and 95, 96, 97, 99; social construction of 121; *see also* England, professionalism of practitioners
Purola, K. 120

Québec *see* written communication during childcare/school transition

Radnor, H. 92
Rao, N. 7, 15
Räty, H. 112
Reissman, C. 121
remote parenting 48, 52, 53
Rentzou, K. 112

Sabanci, A. 111
scripted practices 39–40
Shumar, W. 41

social construction of professionalism 121
Stake, R. E. 92
subordinate position, parents as adopting 38
Super, C. M. 7, 16, 74
Sweden, home and preschool collaboration in: aim of research 47; appreciated features of preschools 49–50; care as concern 52; caring/education in preschool 46; change, working for 50–51; changing preschools 51–52; choosing a school 48; concerns, raising with the preschool 50–51; context 46–47; continuity in preschools 49–50; data gathering and analysis 48; demands on practitioners 45; enduring problems with preschool 51; ethics, research 48; implications of research 53; individualisation 48; indivisualisation 48; methodology of research 47–48; national curriculum 46; parent/practitioner relationships 50; Parental Code 46; parenting as diverse and changing role 46; parents' efforts to create 52–3; participants in research 47–48; remote parenting 48, 52, 53; research as difficult 45; results from research 48–52; stay or leave chosen preschool, choice of 49–52; system for preschool education 47
symbolic meanings of care 37
systems approach to parent-teacher cocaring 58

Taggart, G. 122
teachers *see* educators, role in transition to childcare; England, professionalism of practitioners; Finland, educators views on parental involvement
Theilheimer, P. 96
time management 109–110
Todd, E. S. 41
transition to school in Australia: bioecological theory 23; case studies 25–26; challenges and opportunities in 22; coding process 25; complex family circumstances 22; constructivist grounded theory approach 23–24, 25; continuity between home and school 22–23; data analysis 25–26; data collection 24–25; dialogue sought with schools 27; diverse cultural and language backgrounds 28; implications of research results 28–29; methodology for research 23–26; parental engagement with child's learning 26; parents/educators perspectives on 27–29; participants in research 23, 24; Person-Process-Context-Time (PPCT) model 23, 24–25; purpose of study 22–23; results of research 26–27, **27**; school experiences of parents 22; support from schools for parents 26–27; value of parents' participation 27; *see also* educators, role in transition to childcare; written communication during childcare/school transition

Tronto, J. C. 33, 41
trust and competence, lack of 111

Venninen, T. 120
volunteering 113

warmth in parent-teacher cocaring 64
written communication during childcare/school transition: actor-network theory 130; asymmetric parent/professional relationships 148; challenges involved 132; change in, need for 149; changes during transition 131; checklists/report cards 131–132; child assessment documents *141*, 141–147, *142*, *143*, *144*, *145*, *146*, *147*; child observation checklist *141*, 141–142, *142*; childcare centres *134*, 134–137, *135*, *136*; communication agendas *134*, 134–140, *135*, *136*, *138*, *139*; context for research 132; documentality 130, 149–150; documents analysed 133; ethics in research 133; governmentality 129–130, 149–150; home-school books in Ireland 131; interobjectivity 130; kindergarten classes 137–140, *138*, *139*; methodology for research 132–133; official report cards 144–146, *145*; portfolios 131; positioning analysis 133; positioning of children, professional and parents 130–131, 136–141, 142, 144, 145–146, 147–148; preliminary report cards 142–144, *143*, *144*; report card annexes *146*, 146–147, *147*; results from research *134*, 134–147, *135*, *136*, *138*, *139*, *141*, *142*, *143*, *144*, *145*, *146*, *147*; theoretical framework 129–130

Yawkey, T. 7
Yim, H. Y. B. 97, 98, 99

Milton Keynes UK
Ingram Content Group UK Ltd.
UKHW051425010923
427900UK00018B/466